Boats on Lough Leane, Killarney

Key to map pages

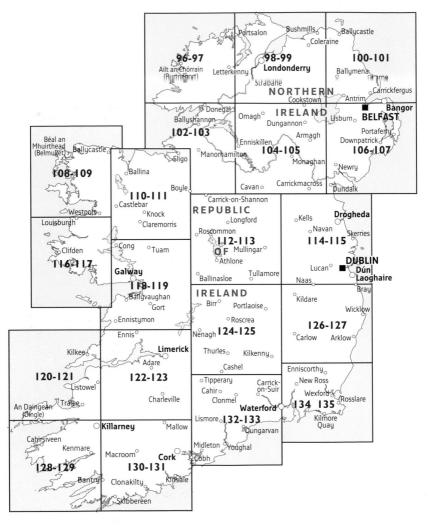

General information

Population of the Republic of Ireland is 4,234,925 (2006 Census), an 8% increase on the previous census held in 2002. The population of Northern Ireland is 1,685,000 (2001 Census)

Partition of Ireland took place in May 1921 creating Northern Ireland, which remained part of the United Kingdom, and the Irish Free State. At the time, the Free State kept the British monarch as head of state and did not become a Republic until 1949.

National Parliament. In the Republic of Ireland it is known as Oireachtas and consists of the President and two Houses: Dáil Éireann (the House of Representatives) and Seanad Éireann (the Senate). It sits at Leinster House in Dublin. The President of Ireland is elected by the people every seven years and has limited powers being more of a ceremonial role. The Northern Ireland Assembly was established as a result of the 1998 Belfast Agreement and meets at Parliament Buildings at Stormont.

An Garda Siochána (Guardians of the Peace) is the police force in the Republic of Ireland and was established in 1922. In Northern Ireland it is the Police Service of Northern Ireland.

Emigration. Historically, the Republic of Ireland has had the highest emigration rate of any European country due to various historical events – the interference in the Gaelic order, the devastation of the Famine years and the lack of economic growth. Around 40 million people in the USA and up to 30% of the Australian population are estimated to be of Irish descent. Canada was also a popular destination around the time of the Famine in the 1840s.

The National Day of Ireland is St. Patrick's Day on 17th March and is celebrated by Irish communities all over the world.

Discovering

Ireland

Atlas & Guide

Contents

Published by Collins
An imprint of HarperCollins Publishers
77-85 Fulham Palace Road, Hammersmith, London W6 8JB
www.collins.co.uk
e-mail: roadcheck@harpercollins.co.uk

Copyright © HarperCollins Publishers Ltd 2007

Collins® is a registered trademark of HarperCollins Publishers Limited

Mapping generated from Collins Bartholomew digital databases

Printed in China

ISBN-13   978 0 00 720421 2
ISBN-10   0 00 7204213   Imp 001   TC12212 / ADR

All photographs © HarperCollins Publishers Ltd unless stated otherwise

Northern Ireland town populations derived from the 2001 Census
  (Source: Northern Ireland Statistics and Research Agency www.nisra.gov.uk).

Republic of Ireland populations compiled from Census 2006 & 2002
  (Source: Central Statistical Office www.cso.ie)

Both are reproduced by permission.

The Provinces of Ireland

Although the four Provinces of Ulster, Leinster, Connaught and Munster have no administrative or legal status, they do have a large part to play in day-to-day Irish life, especially in the sporting arena - the four professional Irish rugby teams take these provincial names and there are annual Provincial GAA Hurling and Gaelic Football events where the champions of each province play off in Dublin to become All-Ireland Champions.

It is said in mythology that the four Provinces originated after the invasion of Ireland by five brothers of the Fir Bolgs who each governed a part of the kingdom which became the five Provinces. Of these, Meath was the smallest comprising the present day counties of Meath and Westmeath. After the Norman invasion it became part of Leinster to create the four Provinces we know today.

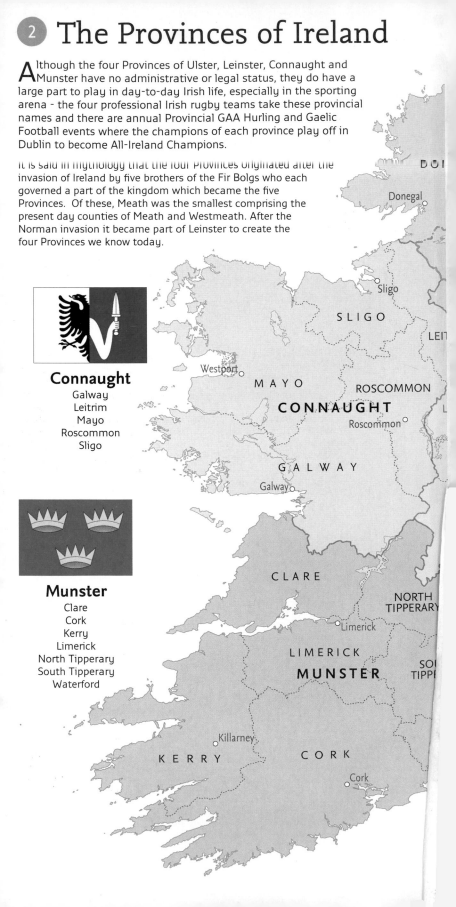

Connaught
Galway
Leitrim
Mayo
Roscommon
Sligo

Munster
Clare
Cork
Kerry
Limerick
North Tipperary
South Tipperary
Waterford

Ulster

Northern Ireland
Antrim
Armagh
Down
Fermanagh
Londonderry
Tyrone

Rep of Ireland
Cavan
Donegal
Monaghan

On this map the traditional six counties of Northern Ireland are shown. They do not have any administrative status but are still in wide usage so it has been considered worthwhile to show them here. Refer to the main mapping on pages 96 – 135 for the administrative districts for these areas.

Leinster
Carlow
Dublin City
Dún Laoghaire-Rathdown
Fingal
Kilkenny
Laois
Longford
Louth
Meath
Offaly
South Dublin
Westmeath
Wexford
Wicklow

4 Ulster

Ulster (population 1,952,000) is the most northerly province of Ireland. It comprises the whole of Northern Ireland and also Cavan, Donegal and Monaghan from the South. The earliest written sources about the history of Ulster date back to the 7th century.

The Troubles have had an effect on the number of tourists but, with the calm that has descended on the province in the years since the signing of the Good Friday Agreement in April 1998, the number of visitors has been increasing in recent years.

The scenic mountains, lakes and spectacular coastline, together with the famous Irish hospitality and 'craic' – the Irish for 'a good time' – means that Ulster has a huge amount to offer.

Live Traditional Music
Photo © Northern Ireland Tourist Board

Antrim coastline at Carrick-a-Rede
Photo © Northern Ireland Tourist Board

Belleek Pottery
Photo © Northern Ireland Tourist Board

The Southern Counties

The counties of Cavan, Monaghan and Fermanagh are characterised by rolling drumlin countryside and the abundance of inland waterways and lakes making it a haven for boating and angling. In fact, Fermanagh is known as 'Lakeland' because of the sprawling Upper and Lower Lough Erne. Cavan, 'The Lake County', includes the source of the Shannon which rises in the Cuilcagh Mountains in the west of the county.

Angling for all tastes is catered for; from the wide open spaces of the many loughs to the stretches of river which are abundant throughout the region. The area frequently hosts International events and Arvagh, Belturbet and Cootehill host annual angling festivals.

That is not to say that water activities are the only attraction. There are megalithic tombs, craft centres such as the famous Belleek pottery, Cavan and Fermanagh Crystal and the contrasting scenery of the forests of Lisnaskea, Mullaghfad, Belmore, Killikeen, Rossmore.

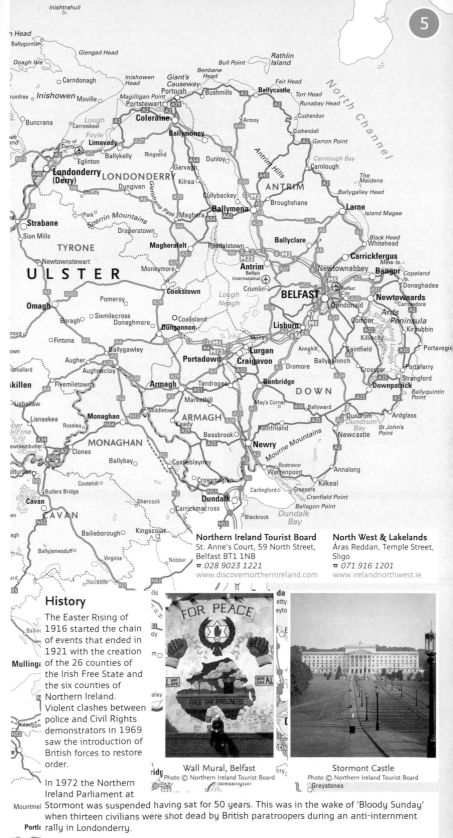

History

The Easter Rising of 1916 started the chain of events that ended in 1921 with the creation of the 26 counties of the Irish Free State and the six counties of Northern Ireland. Violent clashes between police and Civil Rights demonstrators in 1969 saw the introduction of British forces to restore order.

In 1972 the Northern Ireland Parliament at Stormont was suspended having sat for 50 years. This was in the wake of 'Bloody Sunday' when thirteen civilians were shot dead by British paratroopers during an anti-internment rally in Londonderry.

In 1994 an historic ceasefire by both IRA and Loyalists restored hope that, despite setbacks along the way including suspension of the Northern Ireland Assembly in 2002, a permanent and lasting peace will be created in Northern Ireland.

Northern Ireland Tourist Board
St. Anne's Court, 59 North Street,
Belfast BT1 1NB
☎ 028 9023 1221
www.discovernorthernireland.com

North West & Lakelands
Áras Reddan, Temple Street,
Sligo
☎ 071 916 1201
www.irelandnorthwest.ie

Wall Mural, Belfast
Photo © Northern Ireland Tourist Board

Stormont Castle
Photo © Northern Ireland Tourist Board

6 Ulster

Enniskillen is the county town of Fermanagh and stands on an island in the River Erne between the Upper and Lower Loughs. It is unfortunate that Enniskillen is probably most famous for the outrage on Remembrance Day in 1987 when 11 people were killed by a terrorist bomb blast, as the town has so much more to offer.

The Buttermarket was built in the 1830s for the export of, amongst other produce, butter which was the main produce exported from Fermanagh in the 19th century. It now houses the Enniskillen Craft and Design Centre.

Lough Erne   Photo © Northern Ireland Tourist Board

A climb of 108 steps to the top of Cole's Monument in Forthill Park is rewarded with a magnificent view of the town centre.

The Antrim Coast Road

Running from Larne to Limavady in Londonderry, the Antrim Coast Road gives a taste of everything and is one of the most scenic routes in Britain. In the east it

Fair Head

crosses the beautiful Glens of Antrim and is pinned between the Antrim Hills and the coast with its many bays, inlets and golden beaches. Passing Fair Head, it then runs westwards past the unique Carrick-a-Rede Rope Bridge, the Giant's Causeway World Heritage Site and ends at Magilligan which, at 10kms (6.2 miles), has one of the longest beaches in Ireland.

The South Down Coastline

The Mourne Mountains sweep down to the Irish Sea south of Newcastle. Slieve Donard, the highest peak in the range, rises straight out of the sea to a height of 852m (2795ft) and on a clear day the Isle of Man can be seen from the summit. The Silent Valley Reservoir west of Slieve Donard has a massive dry stone wall – the Mourne Wall - surrounding the catchment area which is over 35kms (22 miles) in length and took 18 years to build.

For those travelling between Dublin and Belfast with a little more time on their hands, a scenic alternative route from Newry is along the A2 coast road alongside Carlingford Lough, through Newcastle and then onto the A24 to Belfast.

Mountains of Mourne   Photo © Northern Ireland Tourist Board

Belfast

Situated on the River Lagan at the entrance to Belfast Lough, Belfast expanded during the industrial revolution when linen, rope making and ship building became the major industries of the area – the Titanic was built here and is home to the world's largest dry dock.

Belfast Dock Photo © Northern Ireland Tourist Board

There has been a period of major regeneration in recent years with the city's riverfront area being transformed with the construction of the Waterfront Hall, a major concert venue, and more recently an entertainment complex, the Odyssey. The 'Golden Mile', the area west of the City Hall, is a vibrant area of pubs, clubs and restaurants which has come to life even more since the peace process began.

The murals of West Belfast which adorn the gable ends of many houses, express the political viewpoints of the Protestant Shankill Road and the Catholic Falls Road and have become just as much a part of the tourist industry as the more traditional sites of the city.

Wall Mural, Belfast Photo © Northern Ireland Tourist Board

County Donegal

The peninsula west of Donegal town contains many places of interest. Amongst them Killybegs, the busiest fishing port in Ireland, Slieve League, at 601m (1972ft) are the highest sea cliffs in Europe and the megalithic remains around Glencolumbkille. This area is also part of the largest Gaeltacht (Irish speaking) area in Ireland.

Donegal Castle

The inland mountain ranges of the Derryveagh and Blue Stack Mountains run through the centre of Donegal and at 752m (2467ft) Errigal is the highest and most distinctive mountain in either range. The Glenveagh National Park contains a wider variety of landscape and also contains the largest herd of red deer in Ireland.

Adara is the focal point for weaving in Donegal including the famous Donegal Tweed. Demonstrations of the craft can be seen in some of the stores.

Inishmurray
Streedagh
Stags of Broad Haven
Downpatrick Head
Roskeeragh Point
Erris Head
Benwee Head
Béal Deirg (Belderg)
Lenadoon Point
Sligo Bay
Aughris Head
Broad Haven
Ballycastle
Killala Bay
Dromore West
Béal an Mhuirthead (Belmullet)
Bartragh
Killala
The Mullet
Bangor
N59
Slieve Gamph
Inishkea North
Inishkea South
Duvillaun Móre
N59
Mullany's Cross
SLIGO
Tobe
Blacksod Bay
Ballycroy
N26
Foxford
N26
Charlestov
Dooagh
Nephin Beg Range
Pontoon
Swinford
N5
Bohola
Knock
Achill Head
Achill Island
An Mhala Raithni
N17
N83
Gob an Choire (Achill Sound)
Corraun Peninsula
Newport
MAYO
Castlebar
Kiltimagh
Achillbeg Island
Clew Bay
N59
Knock
Ballyha
Clare Island
Westport
Murrisk
N5
N84
N60
Caher Island
Louisburgh
Murrisk
Claremorris
N60
Inishturk
Cregganbaun
Partry
Ballindine
Dunmo
Inishbofin
Partry Mts
Ballinrobe
Kilmaine
N17
N83
Inishark
Ballynakill Bay
Aasleagh
Lough Mask
CONNAUG
Clonbern
Omey Island
N59
Maumturk Mts
Joyce's Country
Cong
Tuam
Clifden
The Twelve Pins
Lough Corrib
N84
Mannin Bay
Connemara
Sraith Salach (Recess)
Headford
Oughterard
N63
Slyne Head
Cloch na Rón (Roundstone)
Iar Connaght
N59
N84
GAL
Baile Chláir (Claregalway)
Mo
Mweenish Island
N17 N18
Galway
Athenry
Gorumna Island
Galway
Oranmore
Golam Head
Connemara
An Spidéal (Spiddal)
Tawin Island
Kilcolgan
N18
North Sound
Inishmore
Eddy Island
N66
Inishmaan
Black Head
Kinvara
N67
Aran Islands
Murroogh
Burren
Ballyvaughan
Inisheer
Gort
South Sound
Lisdoonvarna
Doolin Point
Cliffs of Moher
Ennistymon

Ireland West Tourism
Aras Failte, Forster Street, Galway
☎ 091 537700
www.irelandwest.ie

North West & Lakelands
Áras Reddan, Temple Street, Sligo
☎ 071 916 1201
www.irelandnorthwest.ie

Connemara Photo © Ireland West

Connemara

West of Galway towards Clifden the landscape opens out into the majestic, varied landscape of Connemara. The mountain ranges of the Maamturks and Twelve Pins (or Bens) rise out of the largely flat bog which sweeps down to the coastline, dotted with tiny lakes and islands and numerous golden beaches. Even on the warmest summer days the area is seldom busy and the changing colours of the landscape that appear especially at sunrise and sunset is breathtaking.

Connemara is home to Raidió na Gaeltachta (RnaG) and Teilifís na Gaeilge (TG4), the national Irish language radio and television stations respectively.

Connemara

Connaught (population 503,083), also known as Connacht, is the most sparsely populated province in Ireland being one quarter of the area of Ireland with only 12% of the country's population.

It comprises counties Galway, Leitrim, Mayo, Roscommon and Sligo and is bounded on the west and north by the Atlantic and in the south and east by the River Shannon.

The Aran Islands, Connemara and North West Mayo are large Gaeltacht areas where Gaelic remains the first language.

Connaught has some of the most spectacular unspoilt scenery in Ireland – from the rugged Atlantic coastline of West Galway, North and West Mayo with its many bays and islands and the spectacular mountains of Connemara through the hills and lakes of Leitrim to the limestone central plain of Roscommon.

Achill Island   Photo © Mayo Naturally

Sea stack at Downpatrick Head
Photo © Mayo Naturally

Gaeltacht

The Gaeltacht are those areas of Ireland where Gaelic (Irish) is the main language and has a total population of around 86,000. They are mainly in the West – counties Donegal, Galway, Kerry and Mayo – though there are also areas in counties Cork, Meath and Waterford.

These areas are important in the future development of the language and link back to the 16th century when most of the population spoke Gaelic. British rule, together with the Great Famine of 1845 to 1849, took its toll on the traditional Irish culture which has seen Gaelic fall from its position in the middle of the 19th century as the dominant language. Currently 40% of the population are now Gaelic speakers, which is the highest percentage since then.

Today it is the responsibility of Údarás na Gaeltachta – the Regional Development Agency in Ireland – to develop the Gaeltacht regions economically, socially and culturally and to ensure that the Irish language not only survives but also thrives in the 21st century.

Connaught

The Aran Islands

The islands of Inishmore, Inishmaan and Inisheer comprise the Aran Islands which lie at the entrance to Galway Bay. The main industries are tourism, sheep raising (providing wool for the world renowned Aran sweaters) and fishing. Many of the fishermen still use the Currach – the traditional Aran boat. Inishmore (Inis Mór meaning Big Island) is the largest, most populated and most frequently visited

South East Coast, Inishmore

of the islands. The sandy beaches of Kilmurvey and Killeany contrast starkly with the sheer cliffs of the south of the island on which the ancient stone forts of Dún Aonghasa (Dún Aengus) and Dún Eoghanachta sit. The way of life on Inishmaan (Inis Meáin meaning Middle Island) is more traditional than almost anywhere else in Ireland and tourism is not of great importance. However, it is this tradition that gives the island it's individuality and the stone fort of Dún Chonchuir is as impressive as any on the islands.

Inisheer (Inis Óirr meaning East Island) is the smallest of the three islands and is closest to the mainland. The sandy beach on the north of the island is as beautiful as any on the west coast of Ireland and the ancient churches, holy wells and the 15th century O'Brien's Castle have archaeological interest.

W. B. Yeats (1865 – 1939)

Though born in Dublin in 1865, William Butler Yeats spent much of his childhood years in Sligo visiting his maternal grandparents. Tourist Board notices bring attention to those places which inspired his work and a museum and statue have been established in the town centre. He died in 1939 in Roquebrune, France and was buried there until 1948 when his remains were laid to rest as he requested "under bare Ben Bulben's head in Drumcliff churchyard"

Yeats Grave, Drumcliffe

Hooker on Galway Bay   Photo © Ireland West

Cruinniú na mBád, Kinvara

Before the introduction of gas and electricity, turf was the main source of fuel. Because of its scarcity around Kinvara it was transported across Galway Bay from Connemara in boats called Hookers. Cruinniú na mBád (Gathering of the Boats), a celebration of this tradition, was held for the first time in 1979 and has continued ever since, usually on the second weekend in August. Various boat races and traditional singing and dancing take place in a carnival atmosphere.

Sligo

Sitting in the shadow of the distinctive Benbulben mountain, Sligo is the largest town in North Connaught and is an ideal centre to explore North West Ireland. A relaxed atmosphere and traditional music can be enjoyed in its pubs and bars of a town that has changed little over the years. This is much in evidence if a visit is made to the County Museum which gives a good impression of old Sligo through its displays and photographs. There is also a section of the museum dedicated to W.B. Yeats.

Benbulben

There are a number of megalithic monuments within County Sligo – the largest and one of the oldest ancient cemeteries in Ireland is to be found at Carrowmore to the south west of Sligo town and at Carrowkeel, the remains of a prehistoric village are to be seen.

Keel Beach, Achill Island   Photo © Mayo Naturally

Achill Island

Ireland's largest island, Achill Island is permanently connected to the mainland by a road bridge except when raised for passing boats. At 672m (2205ft) Slieve More is the island's high point; the views from the summit are stunning in good weather. At its foot is what was once the largest settlement on the island but is now a deserted ruin. Stretching along the hillside for a distance of over 2kms (1.25 miles), the sheer size of the settlement is impressive though there is little definition remaining of the individual plots

Achill Seafood Festival in July offers delicious gourmet seafood and the Atlantic Drive gives splendid views particularly from the high point of the Minaun Heights.

Galway & the Claddagh

Galway is one of the fastest growing cities in Europe and has seen enormous change over the last few years. In spite of this it retains its intrinsic Irish character both physically, with the narrow winding streets of the city centre, and culturally, being on the edge of one of the largest Gaeltacht areas in Ireland.

The City is always lively and at no time more so than during one of the many festivals held each year – the Oyster Festival at the end of September, Galway Race Week usually at the beginning of August and the Arts Festival during the last two weeks of July.

The famous Claddagh Ring originated south of the River Corrib in the old fishing village of Claddagh whose origin predates that of Galway. The ring depicts a crowned heart clasped between two hands and can be worn in three different ways – worn on the right hand with the heart towards the fingertips means that the heart is free, towards the palm means that the heart is no longer available and worn on the left hand signifies that the wearer is married.

Galway Cathedral   Photo © Ireland West

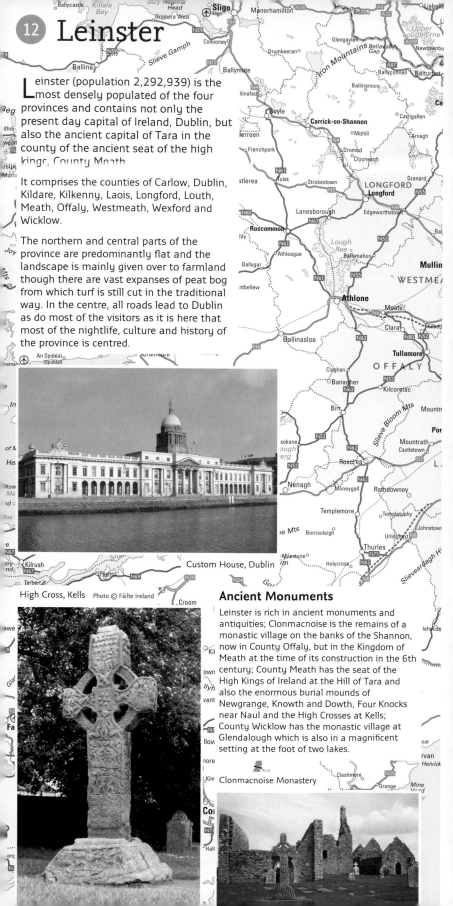

12 Leinster

Leinster (population 2,292,939) is the most densely populated of the four provinces and contains not only the present day capital of Ireland, Dublin, but also the ancient capital of Tara in the county of the ancient seat of the high kings, County Meath.

It comprises the counties of Carlow, Dublin, Kildare, Kilkenny, Laois, Longford, Louth, Meath, Offaly, Westmeath, Wexford and Wicklow.

The northern and central parts of the province are predominantly flat and the landscape is mainly given over to farmland though there are vast expanses of peat bog from which turf is still cut in the traditional way. In the centre, all roads lead to Dublin as do most of the visitors as it is here that most of the nightlife, culture and history of the province is centred.

Custom House, Dublin

High Cross, Kells   Photo © Fáilte Ireland

Ancient Monuments

Leinster is rich in ancient monuments and antiquities; Clonmacnoise is the remains of a monastic village on the banks of the Shannon, now in County Offaly, but in the Kingdom of Meath at the time of its construction in the 6th century; County Meath has the seat of the High Kings of Ireland at the Hill of Tara and also the enormous burial mounds of Newgrange, Knowth and Dowth, Four Knocks near Naul and the High Crosses at Kells; County Wicklow has the monastic village at Glendalough which is also in a magnificent setting at the foot of two lakes.

Clonmacnoise Monastery

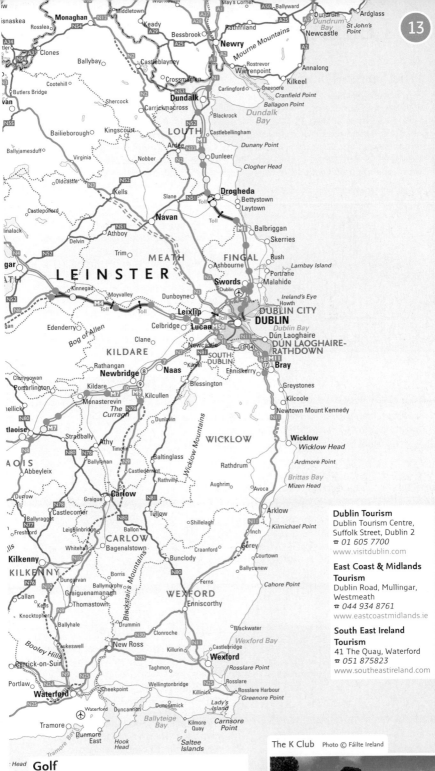

Dublin Tourism
Dublin Tourism Centre,
Suffolk Street, Dublin 2
☎ 01 605 7700
www.visitdublin.com

East Coast & Midlands
Tourism
Dublin Road, Mullingar,
Westmeath
☎ 044 934 8761
www.eastcoastmidlands.ie

South East Ireland
Tourism
41 The Quay, Waterford
☎ 051 875823
www.southeastireland.com

The K Club   Photo © Fáilte Ireland

Golf

Almost a quarter of all of the golf courses in the Republic of Ireland are within one hours travelling time of Dublin. Every variety of course is available from parkland to links and from championship to pitch & putt. The mild climate means that most courses are playable all the year round.

The K Club in County Kildare, designed by Arnold Palmer, hosted the Ryder Cup in 2006, the first time it was held in Ireland.

The Easter Rising 1916

On Easter Monday 1916 a group of Republicans seized the General Post Office, the Four Courts, the College of Surgeons and Boland's Mills in Dublin. From the steps of the GPO, the headquarters of the Rising, one of the leaders Padraig Pearse read a proclamation announcing the establishment of an Irish Republic in the hope that it would be the start of a national rebellion against the English. The forces in the Post Office resisted for five days before surrendering, followed by the others once word reached them of the surrender.

In fact the rising had little support at the time but the outrage at the execution at Kilmainham Gaol and subsequent martyrdom of the leaders was of greater significance than the rising itself – James Connolly and Sean MacDiermada were too sick to stand and were strapped to chairs before being shot. In 1921 the Irish Free State was created and gave independence back to the 26 counties.

Four Courts, Dublin

The Royal County of Meath

The ancient fifth province of Ireland and so named because the Hill of Tara, south of Navan, was the seat of the High Kings of Ireland.

For centuries Meath included the area that is now County Westmeath and evidence of habitation by man has been found dating back 9000 years.

The fertility of the soil has made this an important farming area to the present day and it is only recently that the tourism potential has been realised. The Boyne Valley is not only beautiful in its own right but also contains a wealth of archaeological treasures including the Hills of Slane and Tara, the ancient tombs of Newgrange, Dowth and Knowth and Trim Castle.

Newgrange & Knowth Tombs
Photo © Fáilte Ireland

Carlingford Lough

On the northern boundary of Leinster at the mouth of the Newry River lies Carlingford Lough, which is not only an important leisure centre for watersports, fishing and bird watching but also has a growing fisheries industry in the cultivation of oysters, mussels, crabs and lobsters. A large colony of Brent Geese overwinter on the Lough and seals are a common sight. It is also the site of a collision between the SS Connemara and the SS Retriever in November 1916 with the loss of 94 lives. Both ships sank and the wrecks lie in only 6m (20ft) of water. There are memorials commemorating the disaster in the cemetery in Kilkeel and in the stained glass window in Dundalk Cathedral.

Water sports, Carlingford Lough   Photo © Fáilte Ireland

River Boyne, Slane   Photo © Fáilte Ireland

Drogheda

Sitting astride the River Boyne at the lowest crossing point of the river, Drogheda is a bustling town within easy reach of the abundance of historic sites of the Boyne Valley including the Hills of Slane and Tara and the ancient sites of Monasterboice, Newgrange, Knowth and Dowth. The head of Oliver Plunkett, Archbishop of Armagh is preserved at the Catholic Church of St. Peter. He was martyred at Tyburn in London in 1681, near what is now Marble Arch, and was canonised in 1975, the first new saint to be created in Ireland for over 700 years. To the south of the river is Millmount, a motte on which sits a Martello Tower and barracks within which is housed the Millmount Museum. Little remains of the medieval fortifications though remnants of the town walls survived Cromwells onslaught in 1649 during which 2000 Drogheda folk were slaughtered. However, the 13th century St. Lawrence Gate survived and is one of the most complete town gates in Ireland.

The Royal Canal

Built by a disenchanted former shareholder of the Grand Canal Company in an effort to take business from the more established canal. The Royal Canal was fully completed in 1830 but at more than twice the cost per mile than the Grand Canal took to build. As a result, many of the investors, including its founder, were bankrupted and the canal was never commercially viable. Although it had fallen into disuse many years before, it was not until 1961 that the canal was officially closed to traffic.

The canal is now fully open from Dublin to Mullingar and ongoing restoration of the remaining sections to Clondra, where it meets the Shannon, and of the Longford branch has been in the hands of the Office of Public Works since 1986.

Counties Wicklow & Wexford

The Wicklow Mountains are within easy reach of Dublin and as a consequence the area is frequently busy. However, once off the beaten track and onto the hill slopes, the crowds are soon left behind to be replaced by the wonderful isolation that is so often encountered in Ireland's mountains. The Wicklow Mountains National Park visitor centre is at Glendalough which is also the site of an ancient monastic settlement.

The southernmost county, Wexford, is rich with history being the closest to the mainland of Britain and also Europe and subsequently the first place of landing of any invaders. It is also the warmest and sunniest part of Ireland and enjoys large stretches of sandy beach along both its southern and eastern coastlines.

Glendalough

Munster

Munster (population 1,172,170) is the largest of the four provinces of Ireland having an area of 24,000 sq kms but a population less than that of County Dublin.

It comprises counties Clare, Kerry, Limerick, Tipperary, Waterford and Cork which is the largest county in Ireland having an area of 7457 sq kms.

The peninsulas of the south west can be extremely busy in the summer months. In fact, it is advised that the Ring of Kerry that circumnavigates the Iveragh Peninsula is driven in an anti-clockwise direction in order to minimise traffic problems. The Burren in north west Clare is 300 sq km of karst limestone creating a moonscape that has to be seen to be believed.

Gaeltacht (Irish speaking) areas include the Dingle Peninsula, parts of the Iveragh Peninsula, the Muscerry Gaeltacht west of Macroom in County Cork, Clear Island and the area around Ring in County Waterford.

The Cliffs of Moher

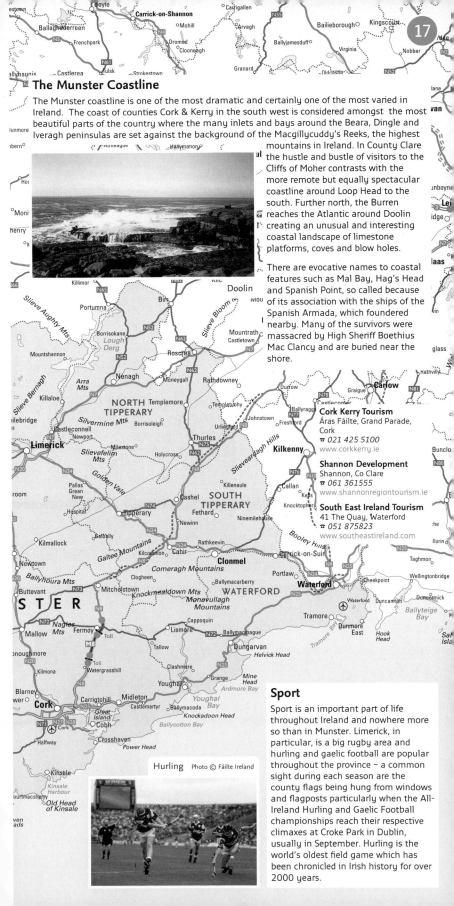

The Munster Coastline

The Munster coastline is one of the most dramatic and certainly one of the most varied in Ireland. The coast of counties Cork & Kerry in the south west is considered amongst the most beautiful parts of the country where the many inlets and bays around the Beara, Dingle and Iveragh peninsulas are set against the background of the Macgillycuddy's Reeks, the highest mountains in Ireland. In County Clare the hustle and bustle of visitors to the Cliffs of Moher contrasts with the more remote but equally spectacular coastline around Loop Head to the south. Further north, the Burren reaches the Atlantic around Doolin creating an unusual and interesting coastal landscape of limestone platforms, coves and blow holes.

There are evocative names to coastal features such as Mal Bay, Hag's Head and Spanish Point, so called because of its association with the ships of the Spanish Armada, which foundered nearby. Many of the survivors were massacred by High Sheriff Boethius Mac Clancy and are buried near the shore.

Cork Kerry Tourism
Áras Fáilte, Grand Parade, Cork
☎ 021 425 5100
www.corkkerry.ie

Shannon Development
Shannon, Co Clare
☎ 061 361555
www.shannonregiontourism.ie

South East Ireland Tourism
41 The Quay, Waterford
☎ 051 875823
www.southeastireland.com

Hurling   Photo © Fáilte Ireland

Sport

Sport is an important part of life throughout Ireland and nowhere more so than in Munster. Limerick, in particular, is a big rugby area and hurling and gaelic football are popular throughout the province – a common sight during each season are the county flags being hung from windows and flagposts particularly when the All-Ireland Hurling and Gaelic Football championships reach their respective climaxes at Croke Park in Dublin, usually in September. Hurling is the world's oldest field game which has been chronicled in Irish history for over 2000 years.

Munster

Killarney

Killarney is at the heart of the most popular tourist area in Ireland. The Iveragh Peninsula, encircled by the Ring of Kerry, the Dingle and Beara Peninsulas and the

Lakes of Killarney are all within easy reach. Sitting at the entrance to the Iveragh Peninsula are Macgillycuddy's Reeks, the highest mountain range in Ireland. At 1041m (3415ft) Carrantuohill is the highest peak and Beenkerragh the second highest at 1010m (3314ft).

The Lakes of Killarney – Lough Leane (Lower Lake), Muckross Lake (Middle Lake) and Upper Lake – form the major part of Killarney National Park. The three lakes join at 'the Meeting of the Waters' where there is the 400 year old Old Weir Bridge. Boat tours of the Lakes are available which can range from short trips to a full tour of the entire lake system. On the south of Muckross Lake a path can be climbed to the top of the 18m (60ft) high Torc waterfall where the Owengarriff River cascades off the flanks of Torc Mountain.

Lakes of Killarney   Photo © Fáilte Ireland

There is an exhilarating walk to the Gap of Dunloe to the west of the Killarney National Park and trips to and from the famous pass can be taken on horseback or by pony and trap.

The River Shannon

The Shannon is the longest river in Ireland and rises in County Cavan and flows south through County Leitrim to form the southern and eastern boundaries with Munster and Leinster respectively. There are over 100 bottlenose dolphins resident in the Shannon estuary – the only known group in Ireland and one of only five groups in Europe.

Gap of Dunloe   Photo © Fáilte Ireland

Cruising on the Shannon
Photo © Fáilte Ireland

Tralee

Race Week and the Rose of Tralee Festival are held in Tralee (population 21,000) every August. The Rose of Tralee beauty pageant has been held every year since 1959 and attracts entrants of Irish birth or ancestry from all over the world.

Irish National Folk Theatre
Photo © Fáilte Ireland

Tralee is also the headquarters of Ireland's National Folk Theatre (Siamsa Tíre) which presents performances of Irish culture throughout the year.

The Burren

The Burren (boireann meaning rocky place), is one of Ireland's most unique areas, being the largest area of Karst limestone in Europe. It almost resembles a lunarscape in it's most isolated areas and is a stark contrast to the mountains or lush green landscape most associated with Ireland. Apart from being of great interest to botanists and geologists, a wealth of archaeological interest is to be found in the Burren including the famous Poulnabrone Dolmen south of Ballyaughan dating back to 2500BC.

The Burren

Poulnabrone Dolmen

Romance in Lisdoonvarna

Lisdoonvarna is a small spa town famous for its annual Matchmaking Festival which runs throughout September and into October, mainly concentrated at weekends. Matchmaking originated by the desire of rich landowners that their children marry into a similar family. The Festival culminates in the selection of Mr and Miss Lisdoonvarna and also Queen of the Burren.

Although this is the main event in the calendar year, there is also an annual barbecue contest, marching band, and horse racing festivals. It is also known for its spring waters. The sulphur springs at the Spa Wells Health Centre are reputed to have healing qualities and has a pump house, sauna and massage room. The Burren Smokehouse gives tours showing the processes involved in smoking salmon and the town is also an ideal base for exploring the Burren. The Spectacle Bridge to the west is an unusual bridge which has a double arch supporting the road which is 25m (81ft) above the Aille River.

The Legend of Loop Head

The Clare coastline is spectacular and nowhere more so than at Loop Head, which has the advantage of being off the tourist routes and is relatively quiet. Loop Head (Ceann Léime) gets its name from Cúchulainn who leapt the chasm between the headland and the offshore rock in order to escape the pursuing hag, Mal. In trying to follow she fell to her death in the sea below. Her body was washed ashore further north in Mal Bay and her head at Hag's Head just south of the Cliffs of Moher.

Loop Head

Local telephone numbers are shown.

Abbey Theatre, *Dublin City* 147 B2
☎ 01 887 2200   www.abbeytheatre.ie
Ireland's National Theatre, founded by Lady Gregory and W.B. Yeats in 1904. The Abbey quickly became world renowned, staging plays by J.M. Synge and Sean O'Casey, and played a significant role in the renaissance of Irish culture. The present theatre was built in 1966 to replace the previous building which had been destroyed by fire. The Abbey stages classic Irish plays, while the Peacock theatre downstairs presents new and experimental drama.

Abbeyleix Heritage House, *Laois* 125 D2
☎ 057 873 1653
Located in a restored 1884 school building in the village of Abbeyleix. It tells the story of the village, which was built by the de Vesci family in the mid 1700s, as well as explaining much of the history of the county. The interior of the Abbeyleix carpet factory, which made carpets for the Titanic ship, has also been re-created here.

Adare Golf Club, *Limerick* 123 C2
☎ 061 605274   www.adaremanor.com
Opened in 1995 this is one of the last courses designed by the great Robert Trent Jones Senior and host of the Irish Open from 2007–09.

Adare Heritage Centre, *Limerick* 123 C2
☎ 061 396666   www.adareheritagecentre.ie
Situated beside the River Maguire, the picturesque village of Adare once belonged to the Kildare Fitzgeralds and then the Earls of Dunraven; the story of Adare from the arrival of the Normans is told at the centre through audiovisual displays and models. Several buildings of historic interest in the village are witness to its heritage; the remains of a 16th century Franciscan Friary, medieval Desmond castle and 19th century Adare Manor.

Ahenny High Crosses, *South Tipperary* 133 D1
☎ 051 640200
A pair of intricate high crosses dating from the 8th century carved in interlacing traditional Celtic patterns rather than the more usual style depicting Biblical stories.

Aillwee Cave, *Clare* 118 B3
☎ 065 707 7036   www.aillweecave.ie
Aillwee Cave was discovered in 1940 by a local shepherd. Well over 2 million years old, the 1km long tunnel is filled with stalagmites and stalactites and has an illuminated underground river and waterfall.

Alcock & Brown Monument, *Galway* 116 B2
☎ 095 21163
Commemorating the first non-stop flight across the Atlantic in 1919 by John Alcock & Arthur Brown. The monument overlooks the Derrygimla bog where they crash landed in their Vickers Vimy on this historic flight. Alcock died later the same year after crashing on the way to the Paris air show. Brown never flew again and died in 1948.

Altamont Gardens, *Carlow* 126 B3
☎ 059 915 9444   www.altamontgarden.com
Altamont Gardens contain trees planted in the mid 18th century, plus many exotic and native shrubs and trees planted since. The 40ha (100 acre) estate was inherited by Corona North in 1983, who restored and developed the gardens to their present splendid state. They include a formal garden adjacent to the house, a man made lake excavated in 1845, surrounded by rhododendrons and magnolias, a wild garden and an ice age glen with walks alongside the River Slaney.

Altamont Gardens   Photo © Fáilte Ireland

Altmore Fisheries & Open Farm, *Dungannon* 105 C1
☎ 028 8775 8977
Essentially a sheep farm but with rare breeds of domestic fowl and opportunities for pony trekking and fly fishing. Also a traditionally furnished thatched cottage museum and working water wheels.

An Creagán Visitor Centre, *Omagh* 104 B1
☎ 028 8076 1112   www.an-creagan.com
To be found in the foothills of the Sperrin Mountains, the centre interprets the archaeology, natural environment and culture of the area. Besides Irish language, archaeology and history courses and lectures, the centre includes traditional arts, crafts, music, song, dance and storytelling in its regular programme of events.

Andrew Jackson Centre, *Carrickfergus* 101 C4
☎ 028 9335 8049
Housed in a thatched Ulster-Scots farmhouse of 1750, the centre commemorates Andrew Jackson, 7th President of the US from 1829–1837 whose parents emigrated from Carrickfergus in 1765. The centre's homestead has been restored and furnished in traditional style. Besides exhibits relating to the life of Andrew Jackson, there are displays of Ulster patchwork quilts and farm implements. An exhibition dedicated to the First Battalion US Rangers raised in Carrickfergus in 1942 stands in the grounds.

Annalong Marine Park & Corn Mill, *Newry & Mourne* 106 B3
☎ 028 3026 8877
Follow the Marine Park Trail, visit the herb garden and view the exhibition at the visitor centre. The water-powered corn mill, which was built around 1830, has a restored grain drying kiln and three pairs of millstones. Also includes a café, play area & picnic area.

Annes Grove Gardens, *Cork* 123 D4
☎ 022 26145   www.annesgrovegardens.com
This 12ha (30 acre) garden was transformed to its current layout in 1907. It comprises a walled garden, water garden, the glen and the riverside garden. Rhododendron seeds collected by Kingdon Ward in the Himalayan region are a major feature of the woodland garden, and the riverside garden, set in a limestone gorge, has an island and bridges which were constructed before WWI by soldiers stationed at Fermoy.

Antrim Castle Gardens, *Antrim* 100 A4
☎ 028 9448 1338
Restored 17th century water gardens in Anglo-Dutch style including parterre with plants of the period, ornamental canals, round pond and riverside and woodland walks. An ancient motte stands in the grounds as well as the ruins of the castle which was destroyed by fire in 1922. The carriage house and stables of the former castle houses the Clotworthy Arts Centre where there are displays illustrating the development of the gardens.

Antrim Round Tower, *Antrim* 100 A4
☎ 028 9442 8331
The remains of a Celtic monastic settlement, the tower is around 1000 years old and over 28m (83ft) tall. Although possibly used as a bell tower, it would have served a defensive purpose for the monks.

Aran Islands   Photo © Ireland West

Aran Islands Heritage Centre (Ionad Árann), *Galway* 117 C4
☎ 099 61355   www.visitaranislands.com
The centre introduces the archaeology, history, landscape and geology, culture and marine traditions of the islands. The islanders traditional dress is displayed and there are examples of the world famous Aran style knitting.

Ardagh Heritage Centre, *Longford* 113 C2
☎ 043 42577
Housed in a schoolhouse dating from 1898, the heritage centre looks at the history of this pretty village from its roots in Irish mythology through to the present day.

Ardboe Cross, *Cookstown* 105 D1
☎ 028 8676 6727
Believed to be the first high cross of Ulster and dating from the 10th century, Ardboe Cross stands around 6m (19ft) high and is richly carved with biblical scenes. During the 18th century this National Monument became a place of pilgrimage.

Ardboe Cross   Photo © Northern Ireland Tourist Board

Ardfert Cathedral, *Kerry* 121 C3
☎ 066 713 4711   www.heritageireland.ie
'The Great Navigator' St Brendan, who, folklore has it, discovered America 900 years before Columbus, founded a monastery on this site in the 6th century. Today there are remains of two medieval churches, a friary and the Cathedral which dates from the 12th century. It has a well-preserved Romanesque doorway, interesting carvings and a row of nine lancets.

Ardgillan Castle, *Fingal* 115 D2
☎ 01 849 2212
Dating from 1738, this restored country manor house with 'castellations' includes a permanent exhibition of the Down Survey colour maps and text of 1658. The gardens comprise a formal garden, which has been restored to the layout of 1865 and a 1ha (2 acre) walled garden, an Irish garden and a 20 alcove free standing fruit wall.

Ardmore Round Tower & Cathedral, *Waterford* 132 B4
☎ 024 94444
Dominating the coastline, 12th century Ardmore Round Tower stands 29m (95ft) high on a monastic site which includes the ruins of a 12th century cathedral with a 9th century chancel. The west gable of the cathedral is decorated with a Romanesque frieze of carved figures depicting Biblical scenes and there are stones inscribed with Ogham writing, the first written Celtic language. Close by is a small stone church or oratory, possibly dating back to the 8th century, and reputed to be the site of St Declan's grave.

Ardress House, *Armagh* 105 D2
☎ 028 8778 4753
www.ntni.org.uk
Originally a 17th century farmhouse, Ardress became more of a small mansion after 18th century additions. Owned by the National Trust, the house has an Adam-style drawing room with fine plasterwork, a collection of paintings and 18th century furniture. Old farm tools are on display in the farmyard which is stocked with some rare breed farm animals. Examples of early Irish roses are found in the gardens and apple orchards are a particular feature of the estate.

Ards Forest Park, *Donegal* **97 D2**
☎ 074 912 1139
Situated on the Rosguill peninsula on Sheep Haven Bay, Ards Forest Park comprises sand-dunes and seashore, salt marsh, freshwater lakes and broadleaved and coniferous woodland and consequently has a great diversity of plant, bird and wildlife. Walks and trails through the forest have viewing points which offer spectacular views of the surrounding countryside. Several megalithic tombs and four ring forts are amongst the features of archaeological interest in the park.

Argory, The, *Dungannon* **105 D2**
☎ 028 8778 4753   www.ntni.org.uk
Set in wooded countryside and overlooking the Blackwater River, the house dates from 1824. Originally built for Walter McGeough, it remained in the same family until it was given to the National Trust in 1979 and is full of generations of family treasures. It is furnished as it would have been in 1900 and is still without electricity; the acetylene plant which made the gas to light the house can be seen in the courtyard. The 130ha (321 acre) estate is particularly notable for spring flowering bulbs.

Arigna Mining Experience, *Roscommon* **103 C4**
☎ 071 96 46466   www.arignaminingexperience.ie
An insight into 400 years of mining in the Arigna Valley. Underground tours of a disused mine, by guides who have mining experience, brings home the conditions that had to be endured up until production ceased in 1990. A talking telescope is a recent popular addition.

Ark Rare Breeds Open Farm, *Ards* **107 C1**
☎ 028 9182 0445   www.thearkopenfarm.co.uk
Situated in 16ha (40 acres) of countryside with picnic areas, this rare breeds farm has over 80 domestic species of cattle, sheep, goats, pigs and poultry. The young lambs and goats can be bottle fed. Other attractions include pony rides, llamas and red deer.

Arklow Maritime Museum, *Wicklow* **127 D3**
☎ 0402 32868
There has been a permanent port at Arklow since Viking times and, by the 20th century, Arklow was the premier fishing port of Ireland. The museum displays the port's maritime history, especially boat building, fishing and its life boat traditions. There are photographs from the mid 19th century, a working model of the wheelhouse controls of a trawler and models of vessels built in Arklow, including one of Gypsy Moth III.

Armagh County Museum, *Armagh* **105 D2**
☎ 028 3752 3070
www.armaghcountymuseum.org.uk
Reveals the varied history of both the city and the county of Armagh with archaeology, natural history, military, railway and costume collections; also an art gallery, library and annual programmme of temporary exhibitions.

Armagh Planetarium, *Armagh* **105 D2**
☎ 028 3752 3689   www.armaghplanet.com
Ireland's only planetarium with multimedia shows, interactive computers and a wide variety of astronomical exhibits displayed in the Hall of Astronomy and in the Eartharium. The 10ha (24 acre) landscaped Astropark features a scale model of the universe. Nearby is the Armagh Observatory, an astronomical research centre.

Arthur Ancestral Home, *Ballymena* **100 A3**
☎ 028 2563 8494
Restored ancestral home of Chester Alan Arthur, 21st US President 1881–1885, his father having emigrated from Dreen in 1816. An 18th century farmhouse with open flax straw thatched roof and an interior with open hearth, clay floor and open dresser. Displays illustrate Arthur's life; also traditional baking and craft demonstrations.

Askeaton Abbey, *Limerick* **122 B2**
☎ 061 392149
Sited on the River Deel, it is thought that this Franciscan abbey dates from 1400. It was founded by the 4th Earl of Desmond and features well-preserved cloisters. Tours by appointment.

Athassel Abbey, *South Tipperary* **132 B1**
☎ 052 41453
Built in the 12th century and burnt down in 1447, it is believed to be the largest medieval priory in Ireland. The original cloisters, gatehouse and chapter house are still standing as well as the 15th century tower.

Athenry Castle, *Galway* **119 C2**
☎ 091 844797   www.heritageireland.ie
Surrounded by a strong defensive wall, this three storey tower house was built by Meiler de Bermingham around 1250. The entrance to the restored castle is made through a first floor carved decorative doorway and the castle contains an exhibition and audiovisual display.

Athenry Castle   Photo © Ireland West

Athenry Heritage Centre, *Galway* **119 C2**
☎ 091 844661   www.athenryheritagecentre.com
Situated in the medieval St Mary's Church, the centre brings the medieval town of Athenry to life using models, static and interactive displays. The original mace and seal are amongst the displays tracing the history of the town.

Athlone Castle, *Westmeath* **112 B3**
☎ 090 649 2912
Built at a strategic fording point on the River Shannon, this 13th century castle has seen much action over the centuries, especially during the Cromwellian and Jacobite wars of the 17th century. It now contains exhibitions and presentations including the military history and Siege of Athlone and the history and ecology of the River Shannon.

Athlumney Castle, *Meath* **114 B2**
☎ 046 943 7111
This tower house, now a ruin, was built by the Dowdall family in the 15th century. It was enlarged in the 1630s and destroyed in 1649 in order to prevent its use by Oliver Cromwell who had just taken Drogheda.

Athy Heritage Centre, *Kildare* **126 A2**
☎ 059 863 3075
www.athyheritagecentre-museum.ie
Looks at the history of Athy with themes including WWI, the Royal Canal and the explorer Ernest Shackleton, who was born near Athy.

Atlantaquaria, *Galway* **118 B2**
☎ 091 585100   www.nationalaquarium.ie
Located on the promenade at Salthill, this National Aquarium of Ireland gives an insight into the deep sea world off the west coast of Ireland with a diverse collection of 170 species of marine life including lobster, rays, sea bass and conger eels. There are also tanks re-creating the habitats of native freshwater fish, touch tanks where visitors may handle creatures like crabs and starfish, a series of exhibits on the life of the Irish salmon and the 'fish-eye' view of life beneath a waterfall.

Audley's Castle, *Down* **107 C2**
☎ 028 9023 5000
On a rocky prominence overlooking Strangford Lough, Audley's Castle is a tower house with an enclosing 15th century bawn (courtyard). Latrines and window seats are still visible.

Aughnanure Castle, *Galway* **117 D2**
☎ 091 552214   www.heritageireland.ie
Aughnanure is a well preserved six storey Irish tower house of around 1500, probably built by de Burgos and then captured and retained by the O'Flahertys until confiscation in the 17th century, after which it fell into ruin. The castle has been restored and features of interest include a dry harbour, watch tower, unusual double bawn and bastions, a circular guard house with cupola roof and one remaining wall of a banqueting hall with floral carvings on the windows.

Avondale House & Forest Park, *Wicklow* **127 C2**
☎ 0404 46111   www.coillte.ie
Avondale House was built in 1777 and is a museum dedicated to the memory of one of Ireland's most famous political leaders, Charles Stewart Parnell, who was born here.

The Estate is 200ha (494 acres), bordering the west bank of the Avonmore river. It cotains miles of forest trails through a great variety of tree species, some of which are as old as the house.

Ballaghaderreen Cathedral, *Roscommon* **111 D3**
☎ 094 986 0011   www.achonrydiocese.org
The Cathedral of the Annunciation & St Nathy was built in the 1850s athough it was not until 1912 that the 57m (187ft) tower and spire was added, which is visible for miles around and tends to overpower the not insubstantial main building.

Ballaghmore Castle, *Laois* **124 B2**
☎ 0505 21453   www.castleballaghmore.com
Originally built by the Gaelic Chieftan MacGoillaphadraig (changed to Fitzpatrick by order of Henry VIII) in the late 15th century, Ballaghmore Castle was partially destroyed by the armies of Oliver Cromwell in the mid 1600s. The castle was restored in 1836 but was not lived in and was used as a granary, after which it fell into disuse until the present owners bought and restored it in 1990.

Ballance House, The, *Antrim* **106 A1**
☎ 028 9264 8492   www.ballance.utvinternet.com
John Ballance, Prime Minister of New Zealand 1891-1893, was born here in 1839; audiovisual presentations and a library highlight the many links between New Zealand and Ireland as a result of emigration and also illustrate pioneer life and Maorie culture. The parlour is furnished as it would have been in 1850.

Ballindoolin House & Garden, *Offaly* **114 A4**
☎ 046 973 1430   www.ballindoolin.com
The Georgian house was built in the early 1820s and contains original features, along with some unique furniture which was specifically designed for the house. The 1ha (2 acre) 19th century walled garden has been restored to include a working kitchen garden which supplies the restaurant. The rest of the gardens comprise of 200 year old trees, a Victorian rockery, many flowers and shrubs and woodland containing a nature trail, a tree folklore trail a limekiln and an iron age mound.

Ballinlough Castle Gardens, *Westmeath* **114 A2**
☎ 046 943 3268
These restored gardens contain a 1.2ha (3 acre) walled garden which includes an orchard,

Aughnanure Castle   Photo © Ireland West

lily pond, rose garden and herbaceous borders. There are walks through woodland, around the lakes and through a Water Garden which has an 18th century 'Rockbridge' and summerhouse.

Ballinrobe Racecourse, *Mayo* 117 D1
☎ 094 954 1052   www.ballinroberacecourse.ie
National Hunt and Flat racing course with six race days a year.

Ballintober Castle, *Roscommon* 111 D4
☎ 090 662 6342
The ruins of a massive castle, dating back to about 1300, which was the principal seat of the O'Connor dynasty from the time of the Anglo-Norman invasions until the 18th century when they moved to Clonalis. Many times besieged, rarely breached, it is without a keep, but retains its twin-towered gatehouse and corner towers.

Ballintubber Abbey, *Mayo* 117 D1
☎ 094 903 0934   www.ballintubberabbey.ie
Founded in 1216 by Cathal O'Conor, King of Connaught, for the order of St Augustine, the abbey has been in daily use almost without interruption ever since, which makes it unique in Ireland. The church includes an ancient cloister arcade and the tomb of Theobold, son of the 'pirate queen' Grace O'Malley. Major restoration took place in 1966. Tóchar Phádraig, an ancient pilgrims' path, runs past here to the holy mountain of Croagh Patrick.

Ballintubber Abbey   Photo © Mayo Naturally

Ballitore Quaker Village Museum, *Kildare* 126 A2
☎ 059 862 3344
Ballitore was founded by Quakers who arrived from Yorkshire in the 1700s and who transformed the valley into rich fertile farmland. The museum is housed in the library and contains artefacts from the Quaker families who lived here along with folk life and Quaker costume collections.

Ballybunion Golf Club, *Kerry* 121 D3
☎ 068 27146   www.ballybuniongolfclub.ie
A links course described by Tom Watson as 'one of the best and most beautiful tests of links golf anywhere in the world'. The Irish Professional, the Irish Matchplay and the Irish Open Championships have all been held here.

Ballycasey Crafts Centre, *Clare* 123 C1
☎ 061 362105
Only a few minutes from Shannon Airport, craftsmen can be observed making Aran knitwear, pottery, ironwork and jewellery in the courtyard of the 18th century Ballycasey House.

Ballycastle Museum, *Moyle* 100 A1
☎ 028 2076 2942
Located in Ballycastle's 18th century courthouse, the museum collection has items relating to the social history and folklore of the area.

Ballycopeland Windmill, *Ards* 107 C1
☎ 028 9054 6552
www.kingdomsofdown.com/ballycopelandwindmill/
Situated to the west of Millisle, this 18th century windmill was used until 1915 for milling oats and making animal feed and is still in working order. In the former miller's house there is an electrically operated model of the mill, audiovisual displays and the chance for visitors to have a go at milling.

Ballyhack Castle, *Wexford* 134 A3
☎ 051 389468   www.heritageireland.ie
Overlooking Waterford Estuary, this tower house castle is thought to have been built by the Knights Hospitallers of St John in 1450. Some of the building has been renovated to contain a small museum.

Ballyliffin Golf Club, *Donegal* 98 A1
☎ 074 937 6119   www.ballyliffingolfclub.com
Founded in 1947 and unusual in that the Glashedy links weaves across the Old Course. Hosted the 2002 North West of Ireland Open.

Ballymaloe Cookery School Gardens, *Cork* 132 A4
☎ 021 464 6785
www.ballymaloe-cookery-school.ie
Set on a working organic farm with its own animals. Most of the vegetables and herbs used in the school are grown in the adjoining gardens which are open to the public. The herb garden is the largest in Ireland and there is also a shell house, fruit and water gardens and a celtic maze.

Ballymena Museum, *Ballymena* 100 A3
☎ 028 2564 2166   www.mid-antrimmuseums.org
Currently housed in Wellington Square but due to move into a new complex on the site of the old Morrows Shop Museum during 2007. It will offer an auditorium of some 450 capacity, new arts facilities including workshop spaces and rehearsal areas, tourist office and a restaurant.

Ballymoney Museum, *Ballymoney* 99 D2
☎ 028 2766 0245
Situated at the rear of the town hall and featuring both permanent and frequently changing exhibitions including memorabilia about the legendary motorcycle racer Joey Dunlop who was born in Ballymoney.

Ballymore Historic Museum, *Wexford* 127 C4
☎ 053 938 3189
This museum is located in several buildings on a large family farm. There is a 1798 Exhibition, a 'Family' museum (the Donovans have lived here for 300 years) which includes old farm accounts, a picture gallery and a display of old farm equipment. Other features on the farmland which can be visited include an old church, a holy well, a mill pond and a Norman motte.

Ballymote Castle, *Sligo* 102 B4
☎ 071 966 2145
The remains of an Anglo-Norman castle built in 1300 by Richard de Burgo, the 'Red Earl' of Ulster. The Book of Ballymote, a compilation of manuscripts and documents put together in the castle in the late 14th century, has an important treatise on Ogham inscriptions, the ancient Celtic writing system of straight lines which can be seen on many standing stones.

Baltinglass Abbey, *Wicklow* 126 B2
☎ 0404 69117
Dermot McMurrough, King of Leinster founded this Cistercian Abbey in 1148, on the banks of the River Slaney just north of the town. The 12th century remains include a run of beautiful Gothic arches along the nave, supported on alternate round and square decorated pillars. The fragments of the cloisters and church are from this period, as are the three west windows and a doorway on the south side of the cloister. The Abbey ceased to be a monastery in the 16th century. The tower was erected in the middle ages but replaced with a Gothic style one in the 19th century.

Banagher Glen National Nature Reserve, *Limavady* 99 C3
☎ 028 7776 3982   www.ehsni.gov.uk
Mature oak and ash trees predominate in this steep sided glen with an abundance of wild flowers in spring; buzzards and sparrowhawks are amongst the birds which can be seen. A 5km (3 mile) track leads to Altnaheglish Reservoir.

Bantry House & Gardens, *Cork* 130 A3
☎ 027 50047   www.bantryhouse.ie
Home of the White family since 1765 and magnificently sited to overlook Bantry Bay. On display is furniture and art collected on the European travels of the 2nd Earl of Bantry. He was also responsible for the gardens which are in the process of being restored. In outbuildings is The French Armada Centre which tells the story of the attempted invasion by the French fleet and the United Irishmen led by Theobald Wolfe Tone in 1796.

Barnett Demesne Country Park, *Belfast* 106 B1
☎ 028 9032 0202   www.malonehouse.co.uk
Set in the heart of the Lagan Valley Regional Park comprising meadows, woodland and marsh. Fauna to be seen include red and grey squirrels, stoats, foxes, badgers, mink, otters, bats and long eared owls. Within the park Malone House, a late Georgian manor with colourful gardens, houses a restaurant and is available for functions.

Barryscourt Castle, *Cork* 132 A4
☎ 021 488 2218   www.heritageireland.ie
Barryscourt Castle was the seat of the Barry family for 500 years until the 17th century. The Tower house dates from the 15th century though it was added to in the 16th century. An exhibition of the history of the castle and of the arts in Ireland during the time of the Barrys is on the ground floor of the Keep.

Battle of Aughrim Interpretative Centre, *Galway* 119 D2
☎ 090 967 3939
The centre recreates the bloody battle of Aughrim on July 12th 1691 when 9000 lives were lost. It was the last battle fought for the English throne between the Protestant forces of King William of Orange and the Jacobite forces of the deposed Catholic King, James II and resulted in an overwhelming victory for William. Audiovisuals give a soldiers acount of the battle and the history which led up to the war and the effect of the outcome is explained.

Battle of Aughrim Interpretative Centre   Photo © Ireland West

Battle of Ballynahinch 1798, *Down* 106 B2
☎ 028 4461 2233
The last major battle in Ulster of the 1798 uprising by the United Irishmen. Irish forces led by Henry Munro were defeated on June 13th at Windmill Hill on the edge of the town by government troops under General Nugent.

Battle of Benburb 1646, *Dungannon* 105 D2
☎ 028 3752 1800
One of the biggest Irish victories over the Plantation settlers when Owen Roe O'Neill defeated the Scottish forces of General Monro on 5th June 1646 in the Drumflugh and Derrycreevy Hills to the west of Benburb.

Battle of Callan 1261, *Kerry* 130 A2
☎ 064 41233
Fought between an alliance of the O'Sullivan, McCarthy and O'Donahue clans and the Fitzgeralds. John Fitzgerald was killed, along with his son Maurice, resulting in 300 years of dominance in the South West for the MacCarthaigh (McCarthy) Clans.

Battle of Kinsale 1601, *Cork* 131 D3
☎ 021 477 2234
The struggle for independence was dealt an ultimately terminal blow when the Irish forces, led by Hugh O'Neill and Hugh O'Donnell, and their Spanish allies were defeated at the Battle of Kinsale in 1601. The Spanish landed at Kinsale and were surrounded by the English meaning that the Irish had to make a long march south to come to their aid. Despite having the greater numbers, the alliance was defeated and for many this signalled the end and the migration to the Americas began.

Battle of the Boyne 1690, *Louth* 115 C2
☎ 041 980 9950 / 984 9876
www.battleoftheboyne.ie
This famous battle took place on the 1st July 1690, when the deposed James II failed to regain the English throne from his son-in-law William of Orange at Oldgrange near Drogheda on the banks of the River Boyne. The site of the battle can be seen from a viewing point accessed by some steps opposite the Tullyallen turn off the N51. Today, the battle is recalled on the 12th of July, as eleven days were lost when the change was made to the Gregorian calendar.

Beaulieu House & Garden, *Louth* 115 C2
☎ 041 983 8557 www.beaulieuhouse.ie
The house was constructed between 1660–1666 for Sir Henry Tichbourne, of whom the present occupants are tenth generation descendants. Much of the original period decoration and furnishings are retained and the grounds include terraced lawns, a walled garden, churchyard and a classic car museum celebrating the racing career of the current owner Gabriel Konig.

Bective Abbey, *Meath* 114 B3
☎ 041 988 0305
Originally founded in 1147, although most of the impressive ruins date from the 15th century. The abbey was converted into a manor house in 1536 during Henry VIII's dissolution of the monasteries and handed over to civil servants as a reward for their loyal work. Used in the filming of 'Braveheart'.

Belfast Castle
Photo © Northern
Ireland Tourist Board

Belfast Castle, *Belfast* 106 B1
☎ 028 9077 6925 www.belfastcastle.co.uk
From its location on Cave Hill, Belfast Castle overlooks the city from 122m (400ft) above sea level. Completed in 1870 by the 3rd Marquis of Donegall, this magnificent sandstone castle was refurbished over a 10 year period by Belfast City Council at a cost of more than £2m and was reopened to the public in 1988.

Belfast City Hall, *Belfast* 106 B1
☎ 028 9027 0456 www.belfastcity.gov.uk
A striking classical Renaissance style building of Portland stone, built to commemorate Queen Victoria giving city status to Belfast in 1888 and completed in 1906. The great copper dome which crowns the City Hall rises to 53m (173ft), providing a landmark throughout the city. The impressive grand staircase is made of Italian marble.

Belfast City Hall
Photo © Northern Ireland Tourist Board

Belfast Zoo, *Belfast* 100 B4
☎ 028 9077 6277 www.belfastzoo.co.uk
Set in landscaped parkland on the slopes of Cave Hill, over 160 species are housed in family groups or colonies in enclosures designed to replicate their natural environment. Gorillas and chimpanzees, big cats, free-flight aviaries, underwater viewing of sea-lions and penguins and a children's farm are among the attractions. The zoo increasingly focuses on wildlife facing extinction and has specialised collections with breeding programmes for endangered species.

Bellaghy Bawn, *Magherafelt* 99 D4
☎ 028 7938 6812 www.ehsni.gov.uk
In 1622 Bellaghy became one of the first planned settlements in Ulster at the time of the Plantation of Ulster and parts of the original fortified enclosure remains together with a restored 18th century house. An interpretative centre presents the history of the Bawn and of south Londonderry. There is also an exhibition about contemporary Irish poetry and in particular that of Nobel Prize winning poet Seamus Heaney who was born in Bellaghy.

Belleek Pottery & Visitor Centre, *Fermanagh* 103 C2
☎ 028 6865 8501 www.belleek.ie
The pottery was established in 1857 by John Caldwell Bloomfield who had inherited nearby Castle Caldwell. A tour of the pottery demonstrates the continuing production of the award winning highly decorated lustrous parian ware and the museum exhibits many pieces from all periods of the pottery's working life.

Bellewstown Racecourse, *Meath* 115 C2
☎ 041 984 2111 www.bellewstownraces.ie
Bellewstown has an annual three day meeting with a carnival-like atmosphere. Flat and National Hunt racing.

Belvedere House, Gardens & Park, *Westmeath* 113 D3
☎ 044 934 9060 www.belvedere-house.ie
Belvedere House was the 18th century home of Robert Rochfort, Earl of Belvedere. It has been beautifully restored and is open to the public. The Estate covers 65ha (160 acres) on the shores of Lough Ennell and includes a walled garden and several follies – the 'Jealous Wall' is the largest man-made folly in Ireland. The visitor centre tells the story of the cruel imprisonment of the Earl's second wife and the scandalous seduction of Lady Cloncurry.

Belvoir Park Forest, *Castlereagh* 106 B1
☎ 028 4377 2240 www.forestserviceni.gov.uk
On the banks of the River Lagan, Belvoir Forest was formerly an estate and contains mixed woodland. Forest walks, a nature reserve, a small arboretum and a Norman motte are among the attractions of the park. The RSPB is based here and the park is ideal for bird watching.

Benburb Heritage Centre, *Armagh* 105 D2
☎ 028 3754 9885
19th century linen weaving factory beside the old Ulster canal with displays of linen and other industrial machinery from 1850-1950, including two steam engines. Nearby is the site of the 1646 Battle of Benburb; a scale model of the battle can be seen in the centre.

Belfast Zoo   Photo © Northern Ireland Tourist Board

Benburb Valley Park, *Dungannon* 105 D2
☎ 028 3754 8241
Riverside walks along the wooded Blackwater river valley and limestone gorge, past the ruins of 17th century Benburb Castle and derelict parts of the former Ulster canal.

Benvarden, *Ballymoney* 99 D2
☎ 028 2074 1331   www.benvarden.com
One of the oldest estates in Northern Ireland dating back to the 1630s. Most of the landscaping was carried out by the Montgomery family in the early 19th century with grounds stretching down to the River Bush. The walled garden originated in 1788 and there are herbaceous borders, shrubs, roses and a kitchen garden. Other features include a Victorian woodland pond and an 18th century cobbled stable yard with cart and coach houses and a small collection of garden and farm tools.

Binevenagh National Nature Reserve, *Limavady* 99 C2
☎ 028 7776 3982   www.ehsni.gov.uk
Binevenagh mountain towers above the flat coastal plain and from the basalt outcrops there are panoramic views over Magilligan Strand, Lough Foyle and the hills of Inishowen. The area supports a rich variety of plant life while buzzards, fulmars and kittiwakes can be seen overhead.

Birr Castle Demesne & Ireland's Historic Science Centre, *Offaly* 124 B1
☎ 057 912 0336   www.birrcastle.com
Birr Castle has been occupied by the Parsons family since 1620 when Sir Laurence Parsons built most of the current building. Twice beseiged in the late 17th century, the Gothic façade was added in the 19th century. Although the castle is only occasionally opened to the public, the gardens are open daily and consist of a beautifully landscaped collection of trees and shrubs, the tallest box hedge in the world, and a kitchen garden, all set around a lake and waterfalls. An unusual feature is the case of the Great Telescope, built in the 1840s by the 3rd Earl of Rosse and the largest in the world until 1917.

Bishop's Palace, *Limerick* 157 B1
☎ 061 313399   www.limerickcivictrust.ie
Formerly the home of the Protestant Bishops of Limerick, the English Palladian style building with classical façade is now occupied by the Limerick City Trust.

Blarney Castle, *Cork* 131 D2
☎ 021 438 5252   www.blarneycastle.ie
The keep, standing on a rocky outcrop, amid 18th century parkland, was built in 1446. The Blarney Stone lies just beneath the battlements. According to the rhyme 'A stone that whoever kisses, O he never misses to grow eloquent' but the origin of this bizarre piece of hokum is unknown, although it is said that Dermot MacCarthy was expert in using honeyed language to keep the English at bay in the 16th century.

Blarney House, *Cork* 131 D2
☎ 021 438 5252   www.blarneycastle.ie/house.php
Situated next to Blarney Castle, Blarney House is as good an example of a Scottish baronial mansion as can be found. The landscaped gardens include an arboretum and views of Blarney Lake.

Blasket Centre, The (Ionad an Bhlascaid Mhóir), *Kerry* 120 A4
☎ 066 9156444 / 9156371   www.heritageireland.ie
The Centre at Dunquin (Dún Chaoin) tells the story of the Blasket Islands off the tip of the Dingle Peninsula which were abandoned in 1953. The rich literary history and the traditional Irish culture of the islands are told and there are regular boat trips to Great Blasket Island in the summer, weather permitting.

Blennerville Windmill, *Kerry* 121 D4
☎ 066 712 1064
Built in the late 18th century by Sir Rowland Blennerhasset, the windmill was restored in 1984 and is the largest working windmill in Ireland at 21.5m (70 ft) high. The visitor is guided through the flour making process and the visitor centre has audiovisuals and exhibitions giving an insight into the history of the industry and of the area.

Boathouse Centre, *Moyle* 100 A1
☎ 028 2076 2024
Exhibition relating to the history, culture and ecology of Rathlin Island, with a growing collection of photographs, documents and artefacts. The Rathlin Community Quilt, created by the women of Rathlin, depicts many of the special features and events of the island.

Bog of Allen Nature Centre, *Kildare* 114 A4
☎ 045 860133   www.ipcc.ie
Based at Lullymore in Rathangan, this fascinating centre has a museum, housed in a restored 19th century courtyard, with a series of trails around it where guided walks can be offered to visitors. The museum explains the history, development, ecology, exploitation and future importance of bogs. Formerly known as Peatland World.

Bohill Forest Nature Reserve, *Down* 106 B2
☎ 028 4461 2233   www.ehsni.gov.uk
A small reserve of deciduous woodland comprising oak, holly, birch, rowan and hazel. Bohill was first established to protect the Holly Blue butterfly and a colony still exists here. Native woodland birds are joined by summer migrants such as the blackcap and chiffchaff and red deer may also be seen.

Bonamargy Friary, *Moyle* 100 A1
☎ 028 2076 2024
Substantial ruin of a Franciscan friary founded by Rory McQuillan in about 1500 and occupied until the mid 17th century. The vault contains the coffins of several McDonnell chiefs.

Boyle Abbey   Photo © Ireland West

Book of Kells, The, *Dublin City* 147 B2
☎ 01 896 1000   www.bookofkells.com
An elaborate copy of the four Gospels from around AD800. It was stolen in 1007 but recovered without its elaborate binding. Around sixty pages of the manuscript appear to have been lost but what remains is 680 pages of lavishly decorated text. Created by Columban monks at Kells in county Meath and perhaps partially on Iona, an island off the west coast of Scotland. It is now on permanent display in the library of Trinity College Dublin (courtesy of the Board of Trinity College Dublin).

Boyce's Gardens, *Limerick* 122 B2
☎ 069 65302   www.boycesgardens.com
This one acre garden overlooking the Shannon is a ten times regional winner in the All Ireland gardens' competition. Curved paths link small, intimate gardens including rockeries, herbaceous borders, sunken garden, water garden, rose garden and vegetable garden containing many plants from the southern hemisphere. There is also a glasshouse and conservatory.

Boyle Abbey, *Roscommon* 103 C4
☎ 071 966 2604   www.heritageireland.ie
The impressive remains of the 12th century Cistercian abbey are on the north side of the market town of Boyle and are the burial place of Ireland's most famous medieval religious poet, Donnchadh Mor O'Daly. Although badly damaged in the 17th and 18th centuries when it housed a military garrison, the abbey is one of the best preserved in the country. The church is a fine example of the transition from Romanesque to Gothic; this is illustrated in the nave where there are rounded arches on one side and pointed arches on the other.

Bray Heritage Centre, *Wicklow* 127 D1
☎ 01 286 6796
This Old Court House, originally built in 1841, now houses a permanent exhibition on the history of the town. Downstairs is a re-creation of the inside of 12th century Bray Castle, whilst upstairs is a railway theme, commemorating the work of the engineer William Dargan.

Breen Oakwood Nature Reserve, *Moyle* 100 A2
☎ 028 2076 2024   www.ehsni.gov.uk
One of the last areas of the extensive oak woodlands that covered much of north east Antrim. Ferns and mosses thrive in the shady, boggy conditions which attract dragonflies, frogs and newts. Sparrowhawks and buzzards hunt among the trees.

Brigit's Garden, *Galway* 117 D3
☎ 091 550905   www.brigitsgarden.ie
4.5ha (11 acres) of woodland and wildflower meadows representing the four Celtic festivals: Samhain, Imbolc, Bealtaine and Lughnasa. A nature trail runs through woodlands, meadows and the Ogham trees. There is a thatched roundhouse at the centre of the gardens, ringfort, children's trail and play area and nature trail. The calendar sundial is 16m (50ft) in diameter and gives not only the time but also the month.

Brontë Homeland Interpretive Centre, *Banbridge* 106 B3
☎ 028 4063 1152
Drumballyroney Church and School where Patrick Brontë first preached and taught has been converted into a centre to illustrate the life of the literary family in this area; Patrick being the father of the novelist sisters, Emily, Anne and Charlotte. Starting at the centre is a signposted 16km (10 mile) Brontë Homeland drive through the Bann valley which takes in Patrick's birthplace at Emdale.

Brookhall Historical Farm, *Lisburn* 106 B1
☎ 028 9262 1712
Rare breeds animals, a farm museum and a wildlife pond are among the attractions at this family-run farm. A holy well, reputed to have healing properties, is found within the grounds and the enclosed landscaped gardens were once an ancient burial ground.

Brownshill Dolmen, *Carlow* 126 A3
☎ 059 913 1554
Constructed between 4,900 and 5,500 years ago with a capstone weighing around 100 tonnes, which is the largest in Europe. A short walk is necessary to reach the dolmen.

Brú Ború Cultural Centre, *South Tipperary*
124 B4 ☎ 062 61122
Located at the foot of the Rock of Cashel, the Centre is named after Brian Ború, the 10th century king of Ireland. Many facets of Irish life including music, dance, theatre and genealogy are celebrated.

Brú na Bóinne Visitor Centre
(Newgrange & Knowth Megalithic Tombs),
Meath **115 C2**
☎ 041 988 0300 / 982 4488   www.knowth.com
Access to the Newgrange and Knowth tombs, both World Heritage Sites, is only by guided tour from the Visitor Centre. The Centre includes a full size replica of the chamber at Newgrange, which is naturally lit by the sun during the Winter Solstice, a time so popular that bookings need to be made in advance.

Bruce's Cave, *Moyle* **100 A1**
☎ 028 2076 2024
Robert the Bruce is alleged to have hidden here for three months in 1306 after his defeat by the English at Perth. Reputedly it was only by watching the perseverance of a spider spinning its web that stopped him giving up the fight against the English. He returned to gather his army and defeated the English at Bannockburn in 1314 to claim his throne. Situated under the East Lighthouse and can only be reached by boat.

Buncrana Castle, *Donegal* **98 A2**
☎ 074 936 2600
These ruins date back to the 16th century but the castle was largely re-built in 1718. Wolfe Tone is reputed to have been imprisoned here following his capture in 1798 after the Anglo-French naval encounter in Lough Swilly.

Bunratty Castle & Folk Park, *Clare* **123 C1**
☎ 061 361511 / 472523   www.castlesireland.com
The magnificent keep has been restored to how it looked at the time of its construction in 1460. Widely admired in its heyday, the three storeyed keep retains its corner towers and massive arches. Inside is the vaulted entrance hall, with so-called 'sheela-na-gig' (female fertility figure) in the wall, chapel and cellars with 16th century stucco work. Many rooms contain period furniture whilst mock banquets regularly evoke the castle's colourful past. The nearby folk park has examples of traditional Irish houses and agricultural machinery and demonstrations of ancient skills.

Bunratty Castle   Photo © Fáilte Ireland

Burren Centre, *Clare* **118 A4**
☎ 065 708 8030   www.theburrencentre.ie
An introduction to the rich diversity of flora, fauna and geology of the Burren which has created the magnificent landscape of limestone pavement into which ruins, monuments and tombs naturally blend .

Burren Heritage Centre, *Newry & Mourne*
106 A3
☎ 028 4177 3378
Housed in a restored 1839 National School, the centre presents the archaeology and social history of the locality from Neolithic times to the 19th century.

Burren Perfumery & Floral Centre, *Clare*
118 B4
☎ 065 708 9102   www.burrenperfumery.com
The oldest working perfumery in Ireland producing such fragrances as Man of Aran, Fronde, Fraoch and Ilaun. The distillation and blending processes can be observed and a herb garden has recently been opened.

Burren Smokehouse, *Clare* **118 A4**
☎ 065 707 4432   www.burrensmokehouse.ie
The processing of fresh Atlantic salmon, mackerel, trout and eels can be seen including the sorting, salting and smoking over oak chips. The Visitor Centre gives an overview of the whole process in several languages and a craft shop sells locally produced goods.

Cahir Castle, *South Tipperary* **132 B1**
☎ 052 41011   www.heritageireland.ie
A pretty town, Cahir boasts this impressive castle, the largest of its type in the country, which sits on a rocky outcrop in the middle of the River Suir at the foot of the Galty Mountains. It dates back to the 15th century and was inappropriately restored in 1840. However, behinds its walls are a huge keep, a furnished great hall and two courts. Notwithstanding its solid appearance it was frequently overrun and in 1650 surrendered to Cromwell without coming to battle.

Cardinal O'Fiaich Heritage Centre,
Newry & Mourne **105 D3**
☎ 028 3086 8757   www.ofiaichcentre.co.uk
An exhibition depicting the life of Cardinal O'Fiaich 'Father Tom' (1923–1990), who was born near Cullyhanna. O'Fiaich, a professor of modern history, was appointed Archbishop of Armagh in 1977 and Cardinal and Primate of all Ireland in 1979. The items displayed include photographs, video interviews as well as personal memorabilia.

Carlow Castle, *Carlow* **126 A3**
☎ 059 913 1554
This Norman castle was built in 1208 by William Marshall, Earl of Pembroke. Half the keep still remains but originally there would have been outer curtain walls, perhaps two towered gate buildings with other associated towers and buildings, with a basement and a great hall on the first floor.

Carlow Cathedral, *Carlow*
126 A3
☎ 059 913 1554
The driving force behind the original construction came from James Doyle, the Bishop of Kildare and Leighlin, who died the year after its completion in 1834 and is interred in the walls. The inspiration of the Belfry Tower in Bruges on the designer Thomas Cobden can be seen in the 46m (150ft) tower and lantern.

Carrick-a-Rede Rope Bridge

Photo © Northern Ireland Tourist Board

Carnfunnock Country Park, *Larne* 100 B3
☎ 028 2827 0541
Woodland and gardens which feature a maze in the shape of Northern Ireland and a collection of sundials; also miniature railway, golf and a driving range. Situated on Drains Bay, the park encompasses beaches and coastline with panoramic views of the Antrim coast.

Carrick-a-Rede Rope Bridge, *Moyle* 100 A1
☎ 028 2076 9839
www.northantrim.com/carrick_a_rede.htm
A 20m (66ft) bridge of planks with wire handrails which swings 24m (80ft) above the sea and rocks, separating Larrybane Cliffs from a small rocky island. Now in the care of the National Trust, this bridge has been erected here every spring for at least 200 years by the salmon fishermen of the island.

Carrick-on-Suir Heritage Centre, *South Tipperary* 133 D1
☎ 051 640200
The converted former Protestant church of St Nicholas of Myra which includes many interesting gravestones, amongst the many exhibits of local interest and a celebration of basketmaking which was once commonplace in the area.

Carrickfergus Castle, *Carrickfergus* 101 C4
☎ 028 9335 1273   www.ehsni.gov.uk
Dating back to the end of the 12th century when it was built by John de Courcy, the castle is well preserved with three remaining medieval courtyards within the walls, a massive keep with barrel-vaulted chambers and a Great Hall. Standing on a rock overlooking the harbour, the castle dominates the town's skyline. Among the historical events associated with the castle are the landing of William of Orange in 1690 and the first action by an American ship in European waters in 1778. It was garrisoned until 1928.

Carrowkeel Megalithic Cemetery, *Sligo* 102 B4
☎ 071 966 2145
A Bronze Age passage tomb cemetery with 14 chambered cairns situated on hilltops in the Bricklieve Mountains above the west shore of Lough Arrow. It is also the site of an ancient village consisting of some 70 circular huts, but it is not known if it is from the same era as the cemetery.

Carrowmore Megalithic Cemetery, *Sligo* 102 B3
☎ 071 916 1201   www.heritageireland.ie
One of the oldest and most important megalithic cemeteries in Europe and the largest in Ireland with over 40 tombs in various states of preservation clustered around a central cairn covered monument. Some archaeologists have suggested a date of around 4840–4370BC for their original construction and ongoing excavations on the site have provided evidence they were used for secondary burials in the late Neolithic, Bronze and Iron Ages.

Carton House Golf Club, *Kildare* 114 B4
☎ 01 505 2000   www.carton.ie
Host to the 2005 and 2006 Irish Open and home of the National Golf Academy and the Golfing Union of Ireland, which is the oldest golf union in the world. Both the O'Meara and Montgomerie courses play over 7000 yards, the latter being awarded the 'Best New Design of the Year 2004' by Golf World.

Cashel Folk Village, *South Tipperary* 124 B4
☎ 062 62525
A reconstruction of a traditional thatched village including a butchers, public house and a blacksmiths. There are also exhibitions about the Great Famine, traditional trades including turf cutting and the 1916 Rising and the War of Independence.

Cashel Heritage Centre, *South Tipperary* 124 B4
☎ 062 62511   www.cashel.ie
This award winning heritage centre includes a delightful scale model of Cashel in the 1640s and a multimedia presentation. The craft shop sells locally produced products including pottery, carvings, cheeses, preserves and woollen clothing.

Casino Marino, *Dublin City* 115 C4
☎ 01 833 1618   www.heritageireland.ie
A miniature 18th century neo-classical masterpiece designed by Sir William Chambers. Casino means 'small house'. It is a compact building containing 16 rooms, with many interesting architectural features. The interior circular hall, ringed by columns, is crowned by a coffered dome. The graceful roof urns disguise chimneys while the columns conceal drainpipes.

Castle Archdale Country Park, *Fermanagh* 103 D2
☎ 028 6862 1588   www.ehsni.gov.uk
Featuring an exhibition which explains how the loughs of the area were formed and illustrates how Lough Erne has influenced the people who live around its shore. The archaeological heritage of the area is presented along with the rich diversity of landscape.

Castle Balfour, *Fermanagh* 104 A3
☎ 028 6632 3110
The substantial ruin of a three storey tower house overlooking the town of Lisnaskea which has undergone recent restoration. Built in about 1618 by Sir James Balfour, a Scottish planter, the castle was occupied continuously until the 19th century.

Castle Caldwell, *Fermanagh* 103 D2
☎ 028 6634 3032   www.forestserviceni.gov.uk
The ruined 17th century Caldwell family castle is situated on a wooded peninsula on the shores of Lower Lough Erne and the three sheltered bays here are now a RSPB reserve. There are inspiring views across the lough from the estate, where wildfowl hides give visitors the opportunity to view the flocks of waterfowl. Way-marked walks and nature trails lead from an exhibition centre through beech and conifer forest to the shoreline.

Castle Coole, *Fermanagh* 104 A2
☎ 028 6632 2690   www.ntni.org.uk
Restored by the National Trust, this elegant mansion was designed in neo-classical style at the end of the 18th century. The interior has ornate plaster work by Joseph Rose, marble chimney pieces carved by Westmancott and rooms filled with original Regency furnishings and furniture. A visit includes the servant's tunnel, ice house and the Belmore private coach in the original coach house. Castle Coole is set in beautiful landscaped parkland with mature oak woodland and a lake, which is home to a breeding colony of Greylag Geese.

Castle Espie Wildfowl and Wetlands Trust, *Ards* 107 C1
☎ 028 9187 4146   www.wwt.org.uk
Castle Espie on the shores of Strangford Lough has the largest collection of geese, ducks and swans in Ireland. In autumn and winter the birds are increased in great numbers by migrants such as Brent geese and godwits. Hides allow visitors to watch birds undisturbed and there are woodland walks and wildfowl gardens with ponds and lakes.

Castle Leslie, *Monaghan* 105 C2
☎ 047 88109   www.castle-leslie.ie
Set in wooded parkland overlooking a lake, Castle Leslie has been home to the Leslie family since 1665, although the present house was built in 1870. The interior has Italian Renaissance features while the exterior is in Scottish Baronial style. Castle Leslie is now run by the family as a hotel and conference venue.

Castle Matrix, *Limerick* 122 B2
☎ 069 64284
Built in 1440 by the 7th Earl of Desmond, the castle contains original furnishings, objets d'art, a fine library and historic documents. Walter Raleigh is reputed to have met Edmund Spencer here in the 1580s and begun a lifelong friendship. During the 17th century the castle was taken by Irish rebels and then in 1642 by Cromwell's forces. The castle has been fully restored and is now a venue for banquets and conferences.

Castle Ward, *Down* 107 C2
☎ 028 4488 1204   www.ntni.org.uk
Situated in over 200ha (490 acres) of walled parkland on the shores of Strangford Lough, Castle Ward is a half Gothic, half Palladian masterpiece built in 1765 for the first Viscount Bangor and his wife, who both favoured different styles. There is a Victorian laundry, a working cornmill driven by water and old sawmill on the estate. Close to the house is Old Castle Ward, a small Plantation tower house built in 1610, and there are walks through the woodland and alongside Strangford Lough. A National Trust property.

Castlecomer Estate, *Kilkenny* 125 D3
☎ 056 444 0707   www.cdem.ie
Castlecomer House was the seat of the family of Sir Christopher Wandesforde, who laid out the town of Castlecomer, for over 300 years. The house was destroyed by fire in the 1960s and the site is undergoing restoration. The grounds include man-made lakes with bridges and cascades, children's playground and woodland walks. The stables house a thriving craft centre and 'Footsteps in the Coal' looks at the history of Leinster Coalfield and the geological heritage of the area.

Castlederg Visitor Centre, *Strabane* 98 A4
☎ 028 8167 0795
A celebration of Castlederg and its people through the presentation of several stories on an innovative video wall. Connections with the town are found to include Davy Crocket and the creator of Irish Coffee, Joe Sheridan.

Castle Coole   Photo courtesy of The National Trust Northern Ireland

Castlerea Railway Museum, *Roscommon* 111 D3
☎ 094 96 20181   www.hellskitchenmuseum.com
Next to the Hells Kitchen Bar, the museum houses the largest private collection of railway memorabilia in Ireland. On display are bells, lamps, shunting poles, signal equipment, station boards and a fully restored A55 Diesel Locomotive.

Castleruddery Stone Circle, *Wicklow* 126 B2
☎ 059 913 1554
A circle of 29 stones approximately 30m (100ft) in diameter surrounded by an earth bank. Two large quartz entrance stones which reflect the sunlight are the most striking feature.

Castletown, *Kildare* 114 B4
☎ 01 628 8252   www.heritageireland.ie
Built in 1722 for the Speaker of the Irish House of Commons, William Connolly, it is perhaps the largest private house in Ireland. Consisting of a central block flanked by colonnades, Castletown was designed by the Florentine, Alessandro Galilei, and Edward Pearce, architect of the Dublin Parliament. The house has been restored through the work of the Irish Georgian Society.

Castlewellan Forest Park, *Banbridge* 106 B3
☎ 028 4377 8664   www.forestserviceni.gov.uk
Mixed woodland predominates at Castlewellan which is the location of the national arboretum, first established in 1740. The park also has gardens with Queen-Anne style courtyards, a glasshouse with tropical birds, a 4km (3 mile) sculpture trail around the lake and the hedged Peace Maze, the largest maze in the world opened in 2001. Castlewellan offers opportunities for outdoor activities such as fishing, canoeing and pony trekking.

Cathedral of St Mary & St Anne, *Cork* 143 B1
☎ 021 430 4325
The Cathedral was built in 1808 and features a 55m (180ft) high tower built over the Great West Door. It was extensively renovated in 1996, the reordination of which was the last public function performed by Bishop Michael Murphy before he died 8 days later. The funeral of former Taoiseach Jack Lynch was held in the Cathedral in October 1999.

Cathedral of Saints Patrick and Felim, *Cavan* 104 B4
☎ 049 433 1942
Built between 1938 and 1942, this was one of the last huge Roman Catholic cathedrals built in Ireland. Neo-classical in style with a single spire rising to 70m (230 ft). The cavernous interior has fine marble pillars, pulpit and statues by Italian craftsmen although there is variation in the quality of finish in other areas which may indicate financial problems during the construction.

Causeway School Museum, *Moyle* 99 D1
☎ 028 2073 1777
Re-creation of a 1920s classroom in a former National School designed by Clough Williams Ellis where visitors try out copperplate handwriting and playground games from a past era. Located next to the Giant's Causeway Centre.

Cavan & Leitrim Railway, *Leitrim* 112 B1
☎ 071 963 8599   www.irish-railway.com
The narrow gauge railway line has a vintage steam train and diesel railcars operational on 1km of track; work is ongoing to extend the railway 8km (5 miles) to Mohill where the station is also being restored. The railway first opened in 1887 but closed in 1959 and the ticket office and waiting room at Dromod have been restored as well as the workshops, engine shed and water tower. There is also a collection of rolling stock and vintage buses.

Cavan County Museum, *Cavan* 113 D1
☎ 049 854 4070   www.cavantourism.com
Housed in a splendid 19th century building set within extensive grounds, the museum presents the history and heritage of Cavan from earliest times. Among the rare artefacts is the Killycluggin stone dating back 4000 years, the 1000 year old Lough Errol Log Boat, medieval Sheela-na-gigs (carved female figures set into church and castle walls) and the 18th century Cavan Mace. For sports enthusiasts there is a recently opened Gaelic Athletic Association gallery reflecting the history of the GAA in Cavan.

Cavan Crystal, *Cavan* 104 B4
☎ 049 433 1800   www.cavancrystaldesign.com
Visitors are given an insight into the production of the crystal which is mouth-blown and hand-cut, and the audiovisual theatre also presents a brief history of Cavan and the surrounding area. The work of innovative craft and design artists from all over Europe is displayed in the showroom as well as the locally handcrafted crystal.

Cavan Crystal   Photo © Fáilte Ireland

Cavanacor Gallery, *Donegal* 98 A3
☎ 074 914 1143   www.cavanacorgallery.ie
The art gallery is located in the grounds of the 17th century Cavancor House and exhibits the works of both international and resident artists. In April 1689 James II is reputed to have dined at Cavancor which was later to become the ancestral home of James Knox Polk, the 11th U.S. President between 1845 and 1849.

Cave Hill Country Park, *Belfast* 106 B1
☎ 028 9077 6925   www.belfastcastle.co.uk
The park comprises heath and moorland, meadows and woodland and is rich in wild plants and birdlife. Walks to McArt's Fort opens up panoramic views. Other archaeological sites include Neolithic caves and the remains of a stone cairn and crannog. The Heritage Centre explains the archaeology, natural history and folklore of the area.

Céide Fields & Visitor Centre, *Mayo* 109 D1

☎ 096 43325   www.heritageireland.ie

Céide Fields consists of an area of 1500ha (3705 acres) containing field systems, enclosures and megalithic tombs dating back 5000 years. Preserved beneath the bogland of North Mayo and now coming to light through excavation, it is the most extensive Stone Age monument in the world. The visitor centre, an award winning pyramid structure of limestone and peat, has displays and exhibitions which interpret the geology, archaeology, botany and wildlife of the area and there are guided tours of the site.

Céide Fields Visitor Centre   Photo © Mayo Naturally

Celbridge Abbey, *Kildare* 114 B4

☎ 01 628 8350

The abbey was built in 1697 by Bartholomew Van Homrigh. His daughter Vanessa planted the grounds, which are situated on the rivers Liffey and Millrace, for her friend Jonathan Swift. The St John of God Order are developing the grounds for the public to enjoy; they include a garden centre, model railway, tea rooms, theme walks, children's playground, crafts and gifts and woodland gardens.

Celtic Furrow Visitor Centre, The, *Mayo* 117 D1

☎ 094 903 0934

A visitor centre which explores Ireland's cultural heritage by tracing the development of customs and festivals from Neolithic times to the 20th century. It shows the importance of the winter and summer solstices and the two equinoxes and how pagan festivals were absorbed into Christian practice.

Celtic Park & Gardens, *Limerick* 122 B2

☎ 061 394243

Situated on the site of an original Celtic settlement, Celtic Park and Gardens was a renowned estate in the 17th century. Now re-created with authentic features such as stone circles, dolmens, cooking sites, and an early ring fort which give a perspective on the way of life of the pre-Christian Celts. Meanwhile, the classic style gardens with roses, flowering shrubs, lily ponds, and herbaceous beds afford panoramic views of the surrounding countryside, and the adjoining parkland is home to a variety of wild orchids.

Charles Fort, *Cork* 131 D3

☎ 021 477 2263   www.heritageireland.ie

A classic 17th century example of a star-shaped fort which has five bastions, two of which face the sea. It was built by the English to protect the harbour but was poorly protected from landward attack and was taken by the forces of William of Orange in 1690. It remained in service until The Irish Civil War of 1922-23 and was declared a National Monument in 1973 and subsequently renovated.

Charleville Castle, *Offaly* 113 C4

☎ 057 932 3040   www.charlevillecastle.com

Built in the late 18th century, this is regarded as the finest neo-Gothic house in Ireland. It has many turrets and spires along with 55 rooms and a gallery which runs the full length of the building. The 12ha (30 acres) of grounds include a medieval grotto, an oak tree reputed to be 700 years old and five avenues flanked with Irish Yews radiating from the house.

Chester Beatty Library, *Dublin City* 147 B2

☎ 01 407 0750   www.cbl.ie

Situated in the Clock Tower building of Dublin Castle, the library is a treasure of manuscripts, books, prints and textiles collected by American scholar Sir Alfred Chester Beatty. It has some of the rarest original manuscripts still in existence. With many Early Christian papyri, the library is a major resource for the study of the Old and New Testaments. European Museum of the Year 2002.

Chimney, The, *Dublin City* 146 A2

☎ 01 817 3838   www.smithfieldvillage.com

Originally built in 1895 as part of the Jameson Distillery, this 56m (185ft) tower now has viewing galleries that offer a 360 degree panoramic view of Dublin. Access to the viewing galleries is by either a glass fronted elevator running up the outside of the chimney or by a climb of 257 steps. Located on the site of the old area of Smithfield which has been developed as a thriving tourist and residential area which includes the Jameson Distillery, bars, restaurants and craft shops.

Christ Church Cathedral, *Dublin City* 147 B2

☎ 01 677 8099   www.cccdub.ie

The Cathedral was established by Strongbow and Archbishop Laurence O'Toole in 1173 on the site of the cathedral founded around 1030 by the Norse King Sitric Silkenbeard. Lambert Simnel, pretender to the English throne, was crowned here as Edward VI in 1487. It was extensively restored between 1871-78 by George Edmund Street and is one of the best examples in Ireland of early Gothic architecture. The medieval crypt is one of the oldest and largest in Ireland.

Christ Church Cathedral, *Waterford* 163 C2

☎ 051 874 119   www.christchurchwaterford.com

Originally, a Norman Gothic Cathedral built in 1210 stood on this site but was considered too old fashioned, so a new design was commissioned from John Roberts who also designed the Catholic Holy Trinity Cathedral. It is said that the bishop needed some persuasion so it was arranged for pieces of rubble to fall sufficiently close to him as he walked through the old cathedral. It was completed in 1779. Concerts and exhibitions are frequently held.

Church of St Anne Shandon, *Cork*
143 B1
☎ 021 450 5906   www.shandonsteeple.com
A landmark visible from most of the city with a distinctive salmon weather vane and a clock on all four sides of the tower. Built on the site of a medieval church in 1722 from a combination of red sandstone and limestone taken from the ruins of Shandon Castle and a Franciscan Friary nearby. A climb up the 120 steps to the top of the tower is rewarded with good views of the city and visitors get the opportunity to ring the Shandon bells.

Clare Heritage & Genealogical Centre, *Clare* **118 B4**
☎ 065 683 7955   www.clareroots.com
Housed in the former St Catherine's Church which was previously an old barn before being converted in 1715. The original Tau Cross is on display and the 19th century Irish history of famine, disease and mass emigration is explored in some detail. The Genealogical Centre has all available registers for the 47 parishes in Clare and offers professional help for those wishing to trace their family roots.

Clare Island Abbey, *Mayo* **108 B4**
☎ 098 25711
Founded in the 13th century as a cell of the Cistercian Abbey at Knockmoy in Galway, these ruins are of simple design with just a nave and chancel divided by an arch. The present abbey is 15th century with traces of medieval paintings on the ceiling and east wall. A canopied tomb is reputed to be the burial site of Granuaile, Grace O'Malley Pirate Queen of Connaught.

Clare Museum, *Clare* **122 B1**
☎ 065 682 3382   www.clarelibrary.ie
The Museum is housed in what was originally a Sisters of Mercy primary school built in 1865. Amongst documents, photographs and artefacts of local interest is The Riches of Clare, a thematic exhibition looking at the history of Clare through the themes of Earth, Power, Faith, Water and Energy and includes objects on long-term loan from the National Museum of Ireland.

Clay Pipe Visitor Centre, *Roscommon* **112 A3**
☎ 090 666 1923   clay-pipe.irishop.de
The village of Knockcroghery has a history of 300 years of clay pipe or 'Dúidín' manufacture. Production ceased after the village was burnt down by the Black and Tans in 1921 but has now been revived on the site of the original factory using traditional tools and methods.

Clay Pipe
Visitor Centre   Photo ©
Ireland West

Clew Bay Heritage Centre, *Mayo* **109 C4**
☎ 098 26852   www.museumsofmayo.com
Housed within a 19th century building, the heritage centre illustrates the history and marine traditions of Westport and the Clew Bay area from prehistoric times to the present

day. Themes include Grace O'Malley and Ireland's struggle for independence. A genealogical service is also available with an extensive database which includes census returns, church and civil records, school registers, local newspapers and rent rolls.

Clifden Castle, *Galway* **116 B2**
☎ 095 21163
Clifden Castle was built in 1815 by John D'Arcy who also laid out the town of Clifden at around the same time. The lands were eventually purchased by the government and divided out among the tenants but as there was no outright owner the castle became the ruin we see today.

Cliffs of Moher & O'Brien's Tower, *Clare* **118 A4**
☎ 065 708 1171 / 1565   www.cliffsofmoher.ie
The hustle and bustle of the car park are a marked contrast to the spectacular cliffs a short walk away which rise to over 200m (660ft) and extend for 8kms (5 miles). Seabirds nest on the numerous ledges on the headlands and stacks that have been created from the constant pounding of the Atlantic. The 19th century O'Brien's Tower is a Victorian viewpoint on the highest point of the cliffs. The new visitor centre has been built into the hillside to blend in with the local contours and includes restaurant, exhibition centre, interactive displays and 'The Ledge' - a bird's eye CGI journey along the cliffs.

Clonalis House, *Roscommon* **111 D3**
☎ 094 962 0014   www.clonalis.com
Ancestral home of the O'Connor clan, high kings of Ireland and Connaught, who can be traced back to AD75. Built in 1878, Clonalis replaced an earlier 18th century house and is furnished with Sheraton and Louis XV furniture and hung with family portraits. Georgian silver and fine china are displayed in the house and exhibits include the inauguration stone of the kings of Connaught, family documents and manuscripts, costumes, uniforms and laces, as well as the 18th century harp of the Gaelic bard, Turlough O'Carolan.

Clonalis House   Photo © Ireland West

Clonfert Cathedral, *Galway* **112 A4**
☎ 057 935 1269
12th century cathedral church on the site of a monastery founded in 557 by St Brendan the Navigator who was interred here in 577. The cathedral has a highly decorated Irish Romanesque west doorway consisting of six large arcs and the east window is an equally fine example of Romanesque architecture. Inside there is a notable carved oak pulpit and Bishop's chair.

Clonmacnoise, *Offaly* 112 B4
☎ 090 967 4195   www.heritageireland.ie
The remains of one of Ireland's first and most
holy monasteries sit on a ridge on the banks
of the Shannon. Founded in 545 by St Kiaran,
a few months before his death, his tomb
became an object of pilgrimage and the
monastery grew to become a centre of Irish
art and literature. Clonmacnoise has endured
many fires and numerous pillagings by Irish,
Viking and English. The remains consist of two
fine High Crosses, 400 memorial slabs from
the 8th, 9th and 10th centuries, two Round
Towers and eight churches. The 10th century

West cross,
with its frieze
depicting St
Kiaran and
the local king
from whom
he obtained
the
monastery
land, and the
magnificently
carved
doorway of
the Cathedral
church are of
particular
interest.

Clonmacnoise

Clonmacnoise & West Offaly Railway,
Offaly 112 B4 ☎ 090 967 4450   www.bnm.ie
This train runs on a 9 km (5.5 mile) circular
route through Blackwater Raised Bog. On the
guided tour learn about the 6000 year old bog
oaks and the past, present and future of the
area, in terms of industry and ecology. There
is a stop to see traditional turf cutting
methods.

Clonmel Racecourse, *South Tipperary* 133 C1
☎ 052 22611   www.clonmelraces.ie
National Hunt and Flat racing course of 2kms
(1.2 miles) with a history of more than 100
years.

Clough Castle, *Down* 107 C2
☎ 028 9054 6522   www.ntni.org.uk
Clough is an Anglo Norman motte-and-bailey
earthwork castle with an added stone tower.
Excellent views can be enjoyed from the top of
the mound.

Coach & Carriage Museum, *Dungannon*
104 B2 ☎ 028 8952 1221
Coaches on display include an impressive

1825 London-to-Oxford stagecoach while the
diverse carriage collection exhibits range in
age from 1790 to 1910. Horse drawn farm
machinery and costumes are also on show.

Cole Monument, *Fermanagh* 104 A2
☎ 028 6632 5050
Located in Forthill Park in Enniskillen, it stands
in memory of Sir G. Lowry Cole G.C.B. Opened
in 1857 after taking 12 years to build, over
100 steps lead up to a platform giving
magnificent views of the town and the
surrounding area.

Colin Glen Forest Park, *Lisburn* 106 B1
☎ 028 9061 4115   www.colinglentrust.org
80ha (198 acres) of beautiful broadleaved
woodland, grassland, waterfalls and ponds in
West Belfast, reclaimed from a landfill site and
disused brickworks. The Forest Park Centre
provides information about the history of the
park, which was originally a game estate and
the wide variety of flora and fauna to be
found.

Collegiate Church of St Mary, *Cork* 132 B4
☎ 024 94444
Alleged to have been founded by St Declan in
the 5th century it was rebuilt in the 13th
century and has been substantially altered
since then. Contains the grave and a
monument to Sir Richard Boyle, Earl of Cork,
who died in 1643 and a 14th century stone
font.

Colmcille Heritage Centre, *Donegal* 97 D3
☎ 074 913 7306
An exhibition about the life and work of St
Colmcille (St Columba) who is said to have
been born in the area around AD521. He
founded his monastery on Iona in AD563 from
where he introduced Christianity to the north
of England. He died in AD597.

Cong Abbey, *Mayo* 117 D2
☎ 094 950 6542
Founded in the 6th century by St Féichín and
superseded by an Augustinian monastery in
the 12th century founded by Turlough
O'Connor, High King of Ireland. The remains of
the chancel and cloister of the abbey church
are to be found to the south west of the
village. The abbey church has a beautiful
north door but most appealing of all are the
three doorways in the remaining convent
buildings. The gold Cross of Cong is now in the
National Museum in Dublin.

Connemara Heritage & History Centre   Photo © Ireland West

Connemara National Park
Photo © Ireland West

Connemara Heritage & History Centre, Galway 116 B2
☎ 095 21808   www.connemaraheritage.com
Includes a homestead is built on the original site of the cottage of Dan O'Hara who was evicted from his home and emigrated to America. O'Hara's wife and three of their children died during the journey, the four remaining children were taken into care and he ended up selling matches on the streets of New York. A tractor drawn carriage gives tours of a reconstructed 19th century farm and to several sites of archaeological interest including the 5000 year old Upland burial site and a crannog, ring fort and clochan.

Connemara National Park Visitor Centre, Galway 116 B2
☎ 095 41054 / 41006   www.heritageireland.ie
Comprising 2000ha (4949 acres) of scenic countryside including mountain, bog and grassland, the park is particularly rich in wildlife and there are herds of red deer. Part of the Twelve Bens range of mountains lies within the area and the River Polladirk runs through the Glanmore valley at the centre of the park. There are several sites of archaeological interest and two nature trails.

Coole Park, Galway 119 C3
☎ 091 631804   www.heritageireland.ie
Once the home of the co-founder of the Abbey Theatre in Dublin, Lady Augusta Gregory, Coole Park is now a nature reserve and wildlife park. Coole House was demolished in the 1950s, although the ruined walls and garden with its yew walk remain and it is the stables that have been converted into the visitor centre. In the walled garden stands a copper beech known as the 'autograph tree' on which are carved the initials of Coole's famous visitors.

The Autograph Tree at Coole Park
Photo © Ireland West

Corcomroe Abbey, Clare 118 B3
☎ 065 682 8366
A peaceful and tranquil site at the edge of the Burren it is thought to have been founded by Dónal O'Brien, King of Limerick, in the 12th century. Contains the grave of the great Irish chieftain Conor na Siudaine Ua Briain.

Cork City Gaol, Cork 131 D2
☎ 021 430 5022   www.corkcitygaol.com
The Gaol closed after the Civil War in 1923 and is now a museum with furnished cells and life size figures showing the life of the inmates during the 19th and 20th century. The Radio Museum Experience is located in the Governor's House which housed the original studios of the 6CK radio station set up in 1927.

Cork Heritage Park, Cork 131 D2
☎ 021 435 8854
Set in 2.5ha (6 acres) of grounds originally part of the estate of the prominent Pike family in the 19th century. There are audio tours of the history and development of Cork, fire fighting and maritime exhibitions.

Cork Public Museum, Cork 142 A2
☎ 021 427 0679
The history of Cork is traced and archaelogical finds from recent digs around the town walls are on display. Letters exchanged between Michael Collins and Kitty Kiernan are a recent addition to the exhibits.

Cork Racecourse, Cork 131 C1
☎ 022 50207   www.corkracecourse.ie
A round, right handed, National Hunt and Flat racing course with 17 race days a year.

Corlea Trackway Visitor Centre, Longford 112 B2
☎ 043 22386   www.heritageireland.ie
This Visitor Centre is built on a raised bog and houses an 18m (58ft) section of the largest Iron Age Oak Bog Road in Europe. It has been dated to 148BC and is preserved in the Centre in climatically controlled conditions. A display tells its story. The road continues in the surrounding bog which is being conserved by Bord na Mona and the Heritage Service to make sure it remains wet.

Cornmill Heritage Centre, Dungannon 105 D1
☎ 028 8774 7215
Local history and the industrial development of Coalisland is brought to life through photographs, paintings, recordings of people's memories and by means of audiovisual presentations.

Correl Glen, *Fermanagh* 103 D2
☎ 028 6632 3110   www.ehsni.gov.uk
The Sillees River runs through Correl Glen and a nature trail follows the river up through shady native woodland to a panoramic viewpoint on heathland above. Meadow pipits and curlews nest on the reserve from April to July. Correl Glen is just part of the extensive Largalinny National Nature Reserve which contains some rare plants and most of the Irish native species of butterfly.

Costello Chapel, *Leitrim* 112 A1
☎ 071 962 0170
At 5m x 3.6m (16ft x 12ft) this is the smallest chapel in Ireland. It was built in the 19th century by merchant Edward Costello in memory of his wife. He died in 1891 and lies beside her in the church.

County Louth Golf Club, *Louth* 115 C2
☎ 041 988 1530   www.countylouthgolfclub.com
Host of the 2004 Irish Open, the club was founded in 1892 with the present course being designed in 1938. This is Irish links golf at its finest with towering sand dunes, superb greens and not a weak hole on the course.

Crag Cave, *Kerry* 122 A4
☎ 066 714 1244   www.cragcave.com
Crag Cave is a network of limestone caves some 4kms (2.5 miles) in length, only opened to the public in 1989. Over a million years old, they are festooned with stalactites and stalagmites, many of which have joined to form curtains and pillars. The Crystal Gallery is so called because of the white straw stalactites that glitter in the light. Crazy Cave is a separate indoor play area for children up to 12 years old.

Craggaunowen, *Clare* 123 C1
☎ 061 360788   www.shannonheritage.com
Created in the 1960s in the grounds of Craggaunowen Castle, the centre is a recreation of a prehistoric site where traditional crafts and trades are carried out by people in the costume of the period. A Crannog, an artificial island containing clay huts, has been created in the lake and an original iron age timber road is also included.

Cratloe Woods House, *Clare* 123 C1
☎ 061 327028
Dating from the 17th century, this is the only example of an inhabited longhouse in Ireland. Of interest are numerous works of art, displays of horse drawn farm machinery and a pets' corner. Garranon Oak Wood, which provided the timbers for Westminster Hall in London, is part of the estate.

Crawfordsburn Country Park, *North Down*
101 C4 ☎ 028 9185 3621   www.ehsni.gov.uk
16km (10 miles) east of Belfast on Helen's Bay and alongside the North Down Coastal Path, Crawfordsburn Country Park has two fine sandy beaches, stretches of rocky coastline, meadows and a wooded glen with a waterfall at its head. Walks and nature trails cross the park and there is a countryside centre with interactive natural history exhibits. Grey Point Fort, a defensive gun site built to protect Belfast Lough, is situated within the park and has a small military museum.

Creevelea Friary, *Leitrim* 102 B3
☎ 071 962 0170
Creevelea was founded in 1508 by Margaret, wife of Owen O'Rourke and was the last such foundation before the suppression of the monasteries by Henry VIII. Accidentally burned down in 1536 but subsequently restored, it was occupied by the English in 1598. Standing in a picturesque setting beside the River Bonet, the ruins are well preserved and include a cloister, transept, east window and a kitchen and refectory in the north wing.

Creevykeel Court Cairn, *Sligo* 102 B2
☎ 071 916 1201
The 55m (180ft) long trapeze-shaped cairn encloses an oval courtyard, where ritual rites would have been performed, and a burial chamber of two compartments. It is one of the best examples of a court tomb in Ireland. The eastern entrance end is 25m (82ft) wide and there are additionally three single chamber tombs set in the west end of the monument.

Croagh Patrick Visitor Centre, *Mayo*
109 C4 ☎ 098 64114   www.croagh-patrick.com
Known locally as the Reek, Croagh Patrick rises to 762m (2515ft). St Patrick is said to have spent 40 days on the summit in AD441, fasting and praying for the people of Ireland. Since early Christian times a pilgrimage has taken place every July when the devout climb the mountain in the footsteps of the saint. A Celtic hill fort encircles the summit and a dry stone oratory is one of the oldest stone churches in Ireland.

Croke Park & GAA Museum, *Dublin City*
147 C1 ☎ 01 855 8176   www.crokepark.ie
The Gaelic Athletic Association (GAA) is dedicated to promoting the games of hurling, Gaelic football, handball, rounders and camogie. The museum is at Croke Park, home of Irish hurling and football, and traces the history of Gaelic sports and their place in Irish culture right up to the present day. Interactive exhibits allow visitors the chance to try out the skills of the games for themselves.

Croagh Patrick

Crom Estate, *Fermanagh* 104 A3
☎ 028 6773 8118 / 8174 www.ntni.org.uk

Comprising 770ha (1901 acres) of oak woodland and parkland on the SE shores of Upper Lough Erne, Crom is an important nature conservation area in the care of the National Trust. Abundant wildlife includes fallow deer and pine martens whilst spotted flycatchers and curlews are amongst the birds to be seen; there is the facility of an overnight woodland hide. The area supports many rare plants and the estate is notable for flowering shrubs in Culliaghs Wood in spring. The landscape is enhanced by several old buildings including the ruin of Crom Old Castle. The visitor centre has a wildlife exhibition.

Croom Mills Visitor Centre, *Limerick* 123 C2
☎ 061 397130 www.croommills.com

The history of grain milling in the Croom area and the impact it had on the local community is illustrated in the restored 19th century corn mill beside the River Maguire, where wheat is milled once more. Working conditions for 19th century millers are portrayed in the restored granary and visitors can try out grinding corn on an old quern stone with model milling equipment.

Crown Liquor Saloon, *Belfast* 139 B2
☎ 028 9027 9901
www.crownbar.com

Dating from Victorian times and one of the most famous public houses in Belfast. Mosaic floor tiles, a burnished ceiling of yellow, red and gold, wood carvings and etched glass throughout make a visit a unique experience . A National Trust property.

Crown Liquor Saloon
Photo © Northern Ireland Tourist Board

Cruachan Aí, *Roscommon* 112 A1
☎ 071 963 9268 www.cruachanai.com

Cruachan Aí heritage centre interprets the mythology, archaeology and history of Rathcrogan, the best preserved Celtic Royal site in Europe where the kings of Connaught were inaugurated. Over an area of 518ha (1279 acres) there are countless archaeological remains from the Stone Age with 60 national monuments including ring forts, burial mounds and megalithic tombs, the most notable of which, Rathcrogan Mound is 88m (290ft) in diameter.

Culkin's Emigration Museum, *Sligo* 111 C1
☎ 096 47152

Displays in the museum illustrate the era in Irish history when emigration was part of the every day life of the people of Ireland as many sought a better life abroad. Daniel Culkin's Shipping and Emigration Agency operated on this site from the 19th century until the 1930s; the restored office is now incorporated into the purpose built modern museum.

Curfew Tower, *Moyle* 100 B2
☎ 028 2076 2024

Built in the 19th century in the centre of Cushendall by land owner John Turnly, who originally built the tower to hold any undesirables in the dungeon until they had repaid their debt to society. It is now an arts centre with artists in residency.

Curragh Racecourse, The, *Kildare* 136 A1
☎ 045 441205 / 441105 www.curragh.ie

The headquarters of Irish Flat Racing, this 3.2km (2 mile) course hosts meetings between March and November, almost every fortnight. Classic races include the 1000 Guineas and the 2000 Guineas in May, followed by The Derby, The Oaks and the St Leger.

Curragh Racecourse
Photo © Fáilte Ireland

Curraghchase Forest Park, *Limerick* 123 C2
☎ 061 337322

A 240ha (593 acre) plantation which features a lake, arboretum and garden surrounding the ruins of the 18th century home of the de Vere family which included the poet, Aubrey de Vere.

Curraghmore House & Gardens, *Waterford* 133 D2
☎ 051 387102

Home of the Marquis of Waterford and his ancestors since 1170. The current mansion was built in 1700, the grounds of which include a shell house which took seven years to build. A bridge across the River Clodagh dates from 1205.

Custom House, *Dublin City* 147 C2
☎ 01 878 7660

An architectural masterpiece designed by James Gandon and completed in 1791. Exhibits relate to James Gandon and the history of the Custom House itself, with illustrations of how the building was restored after it was gutted by fire in 1921. The building is best viewed from the south bank of the River Liffey.

Dalkey Castle & Heritage Centre, *Dún Laoghaire-Rathdown* 115 D4
☎ 01 285 8366 www.dalkeycastle.com

This 15th century castle with its battlements, turrets and garderobe even includes a murder hole! It has been restored to include a heritage centre, showing the development of the town from medieval to Victorian times. There is also information on notables such as Shaw and Joyce, and modern day writers who live in this area. The centre frequently houses exhibitions of art and crafts from the best artists in Ireland.

Dartfield Horse Museum & Park, *Galway* 119 D3
☎ 091 843968   www.dartfieldhorsemuseum.com
Housed in the renovated workers' cottages and stables, this modern museum is dedicated to the Irish horse and its contribution to society. Divided into separate dedicated areas, exhibits include farm machinery, veterinary displays, carriages and life size models. The mechanised horse tests the visitors' riding skills and there are also rocking horses and computer games, as well as demonstrations by blacksmiths and saddlers. The 140ha (350 acre) parkland has horses, cattle, deer and sheep and can be explored on foot, horseback or even by horse-drawn carriage.

Davagh Forest Park, *Cookstown* 99 C4
☎ 028 8676 6727
Wilderness area of mixed conifer forest covering 1200ha (2964 acres) a on the north facing slope of Beleevamore Mountain; abundant wildlife including a herd of sika deer. Nature trails and a scenic forest drive.

De Valera Museum & Heritage Centre, *Limerick* 123 C3
☎ 063 90900
Dedicated to the memory of Eamon De Valera (1882–1975), freedom fighter, statesman and President of Ireland, the museum is housed in his former school and contains a collection of his personal belongings. The history and heritage of the local area is also illustrated with artefacts relating to rural life in Bruree in the early 20th century.

Delamont Country Park, *Down* 107 C2
☎ 028 4482 8333   www.delamontcountrypark.com
Comprising gardens, woodland and parkland adjoining Strangford Lough, Delamont also has the longest miniature railway in Ireland, an adventure playground and opportunities for boat trips. Standing within the park is the tallest megalith in Ireland, the Strangford Stone.

Derreen Garden, *Kerry* 129 C3
☎ 064 83588   www.gardensireland.com
Located on the north coast of the Beara Peninsula, these woodland gardens were created by the 5th Marquess of Lansdowne in the 1870s at a time when exotic plants imported by travellers were in fashion. Sixty feet high Arborerum Rhododendrons, planted in the original garden, are amongst the plants which thrive in the moist climate warmed by the Gulf Stream.

Derrymore House, *Newry & Mourne* 106 A3
☎ 028 8778 4753   www.ntni.org.uk
This elegant thatched house, dating back to the 18th century, is set in picturesque parkland laid out in the style of Capability Brown. Once home to Isaac Corry, who represented Newry in the Irish House of Commons for 30 years from 1776 and was General in Chief of the Irish Volunteers. A National Trust property.

Derrynane House, *Kerry* 128 B3
☎ 066 9475113   www.heritageireland.ie
The former home of Daniel O'Connell 'The Liberator' (1775–1847) who fought for civil rights for Catholics and was later elected MP for County Clare. The simply constructed house contains much of his furniture and possessions as a memorial to the great statesman. The grounds of 120ha (300 acres) give access to attractive coastal scenery.

Deserted Village, The, *Mayo* 108 B3
☎ 098 47353   www.achilltourism.com
Almost 100 stone cottages on the lower flanks of Slievemore, Achill Island's highest mountain. Megalithic tombs from 5000 years ago have been found on the site and settlement dates back to medieval times. However, some dwellings have only relatively recently been abandoned having been used as 'booley' settlements - temporary dwellings close to pasture land.

Desmond Castle, *Cork* 131 D3
☎ 021 477 4855   www.desmondcastle.ie
Also known as the 'The French Prison' due to a tragedy in 1747 when 54 French prisoners died in a fire. Built in the 16th century by the Earl of Desmond for use as a custom house, the castle was subject to occupation by the Spanish in 1601 and was also used to imprison captured American sailors during the American War of Independence. Also houses the International Museum of Wine.

The Deserted Village

Devenish Island   Photo © Northern Ireland Tourist Board

Desmond Hall, *Limerick* 122 B3
☎ 069 77408   www.heritageireland.ie
An imposing medieval hall used by the Earls of Desmond which includes a restored oak musician's gallery and a limestone hooded fireplace. The 15th century building consists of the hall, vaulted lower chamber and adjoining tower built on the site of a 13th century structure.

Devenish Island, *Fermanagh* 104 A2
☎ 028 6862 1588   www.ehsni.gov.uk
Devenish is remarkable for its well preserved 12th century round tower which belonged to a monastic settlement originally founded by St Molaise in the 6th century. This island in Lower Lough Erne also has the remains of an Augustinian abbey and an intricately carved medieval cross still standing in the graveyard.

Dixon Gallery, *Donegal* 97 C1
☎ 074 913 5502   www.oileanthorai.com
A legacy of the encouragement given to the islanders in the 50s and 60s by the internationally acclaimed artist Derek Hill. Mainly displaying the work of local artists from Tory Island, though mainland artists also exhibit here.

Doagh Visitor Centre, *Donegal* 98 B1
☎ 074 937 8078   www.doaghvisitorscenter.com
An outdoor museum which recreates the life and traditions of the people of Inishowen from the 1840s and the time of the Great Famine through to the 1970s. Scenes from past times are re-enacted including a Presbyterian meeting and an eviction and there are several reconstructed buildings ranging from a turf house to a landlord's mansion.

Dr. Douglas Hyde Interpretative Centre   Photo © Ireland West

Dr. Douglas Hyde Interpretative Centre, *Roscommon* 111 D3
☎ 094 987 0016
Dr. Douglas Hyde (1860–1949) was co-founder of the Gaelic League and first President of Ireland. A scholar, profoundly interested in the Irish language and culture, Hyde published many works which are acknowledged to be a major source for the Irish Literary Renaissance. Photographs, documents, letters, personal items and books of his work illustrate the political and literary contribution he made to Ireland. The Centre is housed in the church where his father was rector and Hyde's grave is in the churchyard.

Doe Castle, *Donegal* 97 D2
☎ 074 913 8445   www.doecastle.com
A ruined medieval fortress well protected on three sides by the sea and on the other by a moat hewn from rock. The castle did not fall to the English until 1650 when it was attacked from the sea. Once guarded by a drawbridge and portcullis, the moat is now spanned by a bridge. Considerable alterations to the castle were made in the 19th century by General Vaughan Harte.

Donaghmore Famine Workhouse Museum, *Laois* 125 C2
☎ 086 829 6685   www.donaghmoremuseum.com
Originally built in the 1850s, this workhouse could, and did, take up to 400 people at any one time, following the famine years of 1845 to 1849. Today, there is an agricultural museum displaying artefacts which were in use by the rural community during the 19th and 20th centuries. Life in the workhouse has also been depicted by the renovation of the original dormitories and workrooms.

Donaghmore Round Tower & Church, *Meath* 114 B2
☎ 041 988 0305
The Round Tower is probably 10th century and in good condition, having been restored in the 19th century. The ruined 15th century church is built on the site of an earlier structure, where St Patrick is said to have founded the first monastery, leaving it in the care of his disciple St Cassanus.

Donegal Ancestry Centre, *Donegal* 98 A2
☎ 074 915 1266   www.donegalancestry.com
Ramelton's story from the time it was a Gaelic stronghold through to its prosperity in the

Georgian era is portrayed in an exhibition housed in a restored quayside warehouse, while the adjacent warehouse is a genealogical centre providing a service for people who wish to research their family history. Since the 1600s there has been widespread emigration from Donegal which was accelerated in the mid 19th century as a result of the Great Famine and compounded by evictions and clearances.

Donegal Castle, *Donegal* 103 C1
☎ 074 972 2405   www.heritageireland.ie
Overlooking the River Eske, the restored late 15th century castle is just off the main square of this market town. Originally the seat of the O'Donnells, the castle was built by Red Hugh II O'Donnell in 1505, whilst additions, including the magnificent fireplace in the banqueting hall, were made in the 17th century by Sir Basil Brooke, who was responsible for the fine Jacobean fortified house that forms part of the castle. The castle furnishings include French tapestries and Persian rugs.

Donegal Castle

Donegal County Museum, *Donegal* 97 D3
☎ 074 912 4613
The museum has a wide range of exhibits which illustrate all aspects of life in Donegal from prehistoric times to the 20th century and is housed in buildings which were once part of the Letterkenny Workhouse which functioned between 1846 and 1922.

Donegal Craft Village, *Donegal* 103 C1
☎ 074 972 2225
Resident professional craftspeople can be seen at work in their workshops which are clustered round a central courtyard. Pottery, sculpture, metalwork, batik and jewelry are among the crafts on view.

Donegal Historical Society's Museum, *Donegal* 103 C1
☎ 071 985 1342 / 985 1267
www.donegalhistory.com
Housed in a room in a Franciscan friary, the museum documents Irish history from the Stone Age to World War II with a collection which includes prehistoric artefacts, items from the Spanish Armada including an anchor, coins and medals and Belleek pottery. There is also a genealogical section.

Donegal Railway Heritage Centre, *Donegal* 103 C1
☎ 074 972 2655   www.countydonegalrailway.com
Located in the old Donegal Town Station, the centre displays restored carriages, models and memorabilia from the time when Donegal was served by an extensive narrow gauge rail network.

Doneraile Park, *Cork* 123 D4
☎ 022 24244   www.heritageireland.ie
160ha (400 acres) of landscaped parkland in a natural 'Capability Brown' style. A number of red deer herds can be seen amongst the mature deciduous trees. The building of a dam, originally in the mid 1750s, created a number of islands in the River Awbeg and also a weir which includes a fish pass allowing trout and salmon to gain access to spawning grounds upriver.

Donkey Sanctuary, The, *Cork* 123 C4
☎ 022 48398   www.thedonkeysanctuary.ie
Part of the UK registered charity The Donkey Sanctuary. Over the years the sanctuary has taken in over 2,200 donkeys. For many it would be the first time that they have been lovingly cared for after their working life has ended. Also has walks, a picnic area and an iron age ring fort.

Donore Castle, *Meath* 114 A3
☎ 046 943 7111
This three storey round-cornered tower house is likely to have been built in response to an offer made by Henry VI in 1629. He requested that anyone castles of certain dimensions be built in order to help quell the rebellious Gaelic lords. After it was captured in 1650 by John Reynolds for Cromwell, James MacGeoghegan and over 40 members of his household, including women and children, were executed.

Doonamo Fort, *Mayo* 108 B2
☎ 096 70848
The remains of a prehistoric promontory fort near Erris Head with a 60m (200ft) wall across the headland that rises to a height of 5m (18ft) in some places. It contains the remains of a ring fort and three clochans.

Dorn Nature Reserve, *Ards* 107 C2
☎ 028 4272 9882   www.ehsni.gov.uk
An extensive area of sheltered bays, saltmarsh and mud-flats on the east side of Strangford Lough supporting a remarkable diversity of marine life including sponges, sea squirts, anemones and star fish. The channel which connects several bays to the lough has rock sills which hold back the water as the tide falls, creating saltwater rapids. Common seals and large numbers of wintering wildfowl can be seen on the foreshore. At the north end of the reserve a spit of shingle and bedrock extends over 1km (0.6 mile) into the lough.

Down Cathedral, *Down* 107 C2
☎ 028 4461 4922   www.downcathedral.org
A fine Gothic cathedral of the Church of Ireland with beautiful stained glass windows; originally built in 1183 as part of a Benedictine monastery, substantially destroyed in the 14th century, restored and remodelled in the late 18th century and the interior comprehensively renovated in 1987. The organ, one of the finest in Ireland, has a magnificent oak case. In the grounds lies a grave reputed to be that of St Patrick.

Down County Museum, *Down* 107 C2
☎ 028 4461 5218   www.downcountymuseum.com
Housed in an 18th century gaol with restored cells, the museum's changing exhibitions and activities bring to life the history of County Down. There is a room dedicated to St Patrick and carved stones from Saul, the traditional site of St Patrick's first church.

Down Royal Racecourse, *Lisburn* 106 B1
☎ 028 9262 1256   www.downroyal.com
National Hunt and Flat racing course with 12 race meetings a year including the Ulster Oaks and the Ulster Derby in June, and the Northern Ireland Festival of Racing held in November. Down Royal was first established by royal charter in 1685.

Downhill Castle & Mussenden Temple, *Coleraine* 99 C2
☎ 028 7084 8728   www.ntni.org.uk
Now a ruin, this massive palace was built in 1780 by the eccentric Frederick Hervey, Earl of Bristol and Bishop of Derry. The temple folly, inspired by the Tivoli Temple of Vesta, is perched on the clifftop and from the landscaped Downhill estate and ornamental gardens there are stunning views over the north coast. A National Trust property.

Downpatrick & County Down Railway, *Down* 107 C2
☎ 028 4461 5779   www.downrail.co.uk
Steam and diesel locomotives, carriages and working engines on display; also a model railway in the station house. Train rides take place along 2km (1mile) of a restored section of the BCDR Belfast-Newcastle main line.

Downpatrick Racecourse, *Down* 107 C2
☎ 028 4461 2054   www.air.ie
National Hunt and Flat racing course with eight race days a year. 1685 saw the first race meeting in Downpatrick and racing has taken place on the present course for over 200 years.

Dowth Megalithic Tomb, *Meath* 115 C2
☎ 041 988 0300 / 982 4488
www.knowth.com/dowth.htm
This passage tomb is thought to have been built around 5000 years ago and is the oldest of its type in the Boyne Valley. Although much plundered and damaged over the centuries, the mound is still impressive, being about 85m (290ft) in diameter and 15m (49ft) high. It contains two prehistoric tombs and an early Christian chamber. The name 'Dowth' translates as 'darkness' and the main chamber faces the setting sun. At the winter solstice, the rays of the sun shine into the tomb.

Dromberg Stone Circle, *Cork* 130 B4
☎ 028 21766
Originally consisting of 17 stones of which 13 remain in a good state of preservation, this 9.1m (30ft) diameter stone circle is almost certainly Bronze Age and could date as early as 2000BC. Human remains were discovered in the 1950s that have been dated to 150BC – AD130. The flat western stone and the entrance align with the sunset at the winter solstice. To the west are two 1st or 2nd century stone huts and an ancient cooking area which was still in use in the 5th century.

Dromoland Castle   Photo © Fáilte Ireland

Dromoland Castle, *Clare* 122 B1
☎ 061 368144   www.dromoland.ie
Constructed in the 16th century by the Earls of Thomond and converted to a five-star luxury hotel in the 1960s. In the castle grounds is Moghane Fort, the largest hill fort site in the country from which there are fine views of the Shannon Estuary.

Dromore Wood, *Clare* 118 B4
☎ 065 683 7166   www.heritageireland.ie
Covering an area of 400ha (990 acres) Dromore Wood includes a variety of habitats – wetlands, limestone pavement, woodland and peatland – that enables the diverse flora and fauna to thrive. The 17th century O'Brien Castle stands on the lake side and there are also sites of a castle, church, ring forts and lime kiln.

Mussenden Temple   Photo © Northern Ireland Tourist Board

Druids Glen Golf Resort, *Wicklow* 127 D1
☎ 01 287 3600   www.druidsglen.ie
Host of the 2002 Seve Trophy and the 2006 Irish PGA Championship. The 'Augusta of Europe' features a Celtic Cross on the 12th hole and the 18th century Woodstock House clubhouse overlooks the 18th green. The newer Druids Heath course is no less of a challenge than the Druids Glen course.

Drum Manor Forest Park, *Cookstown* 105 C1
☎ 028 8676 2774
A 92ha (227 acre) forest with 11km (7 miles) of walking trails and an interpretative centre. Drum Manor no longer exists but the tower and outside walls remain. Two ornamental ponds have various species of waterfowl, a butterfly garden, an arboretum and demonstration forest plots planted with both evergreen and deciduous trees.

Drumcliffe High Cross & Round Tower, *Sligo* 102 B2
☎ 071 914 4956
The remains of the round tower and a 10th century high cross are all that remains of a monastic settlement founded by St Colmcille (St Columba) in 574. The monastery was flourishing in the 13th century but went into decline soon afterwards. Irish poet W.B.Yeats, who spent much of his childhood in Sligo, is buried in the churchyard here.

Drumena Cashel, *Down* 106 B3
☎ 028 4372 2222
Measuring 40m x 33m (131ft x 108ft) with walls that are over 3m (10ft) thick, one of the main features is a T-shaped souterrain with two entrances. Substantial repairs have taken place with concreting of the roof of the souterrain and the outer wall rebuilt in the 1920s.

Dublin Castle, *Dublin City* 147 B2
☎ 01 645 8813   www.dublincastle.ie
Originally built between 1204–1228, the Record Tower is the principal remnant of the 13th century Anglo-Norman fortress and has walls 5m (16ft) thick but what remains today is largely the result of 18th and 19th century re-building. The 15th century Bermingham Tower was once the state prison and was rebuilt in the 18th century. Within the State Apartments are the magnificent throne room and St Patrick's Hall, 25m (82ft) long with a high panelled and decorated ceiling which are now used for Presidential Inaugurations and state receptions. In the undercroft can be seen the remains of a Viking fortress and parts of the original moat and old city walls.

Dublin Civic Museum, *Dublin City* 147 B2
☎ 01 679 4260
Housed in the former Georgian City Assembly House, the museum illustrates the history of Dublin and has a large collection of maps, prints and newspapers. Among the artefacts is the head of the statue of Lord Nelson, blown off its pillar in O'Connell Street in an IRA explosion in 1966.

Dublin Writer's Museum, *Dublin City* 147 B1
☎ 01 872 2077
Tracing the history of Irish literature from its earliest times to the 20th century. Writers and playwrights including Jonathan Swift, George Bernard Shaw, Oscar Wilde, W.B. Yeats, James Joyce and Samuel Beckett are brought to life through personal items, portraits, their books and letters. There is also a room dedicated to children's authors. The museum is housed in a restored 18th century Georgian mansion with decorative stained-glass windows and ornate plaster-work.

Dublin Zoo, *Dublin City* 115 C4
☎ 01 474 8900   www.dublinzoo.ie
Dublin Zoo is well known for its captive-breeding programme and is committed to the conservation and protection of endangered species. The zoo doubled in size in 2000 and an African Plains area has been developed providing greater space and freedom for giraffe, hippo, rhino and other African animals and birds. Other attractions include a zoo train, discovery centre, and 'meet the keeper' programme.

Dublinia, *Dublin City* 147 B2
☎ 01 679 4611   www.dublinia.ie
A multimedia re-creation of Dublin life in medieval times from the Anglo-Norman arrival in 1170 to the dissolution of the monasteries in 1540. There is a scale model of the medieval city, a life size reconstruction of a merchant's house and numerous Viking and Norman artefacts from excavations at nearby Wood Quay. The building is the old Synod Hall and is linked to Christ Church Cathedral by an ornate Victorian pedestrian bridge which spans the road.

Duiske Abbey, *Kilkenny* 126 A4
☎ 059 972 4238
Built at the start of the 13th century, this Cistercian Abbey was the largest of its kind in Ireland. Restored in the late 1970s, it contains exhibitions of local artefacts, contemporary Christian art and a large carved Norman knight. In the grounds there are two crosses, dating from the 8th and 9th centuries. The Abbey takes its name from the local river Duiske, which means 'Black Water'. Guided tours are available on request.

Duleek Cross, *Meath* 115 C2
☎ 041 988 0305
This 1.8m (6ft) high cross dates from the 9th or 10th century on a site that also includes a priory and church built much later. Unusually it contains many different themes used in Celtic art – mazes, knots, spirals – and is a popular subject for jewellers and artists.

Dún Aonghasa (Dún Aengus)

Dún Aonghasa (Dún Aengus), *Galway* 117 C4
☎ 099 61008   www.heritageireland.ie
The 2500 year old Dún Aengus is one of the most important prehistoric stone forts in

Europe. It is spectacularly sited on a desolate clifftop with a 76m (250ft) drop to the Atlantic Ocean. There are three enclosures with dry stone walls up to 5m (18ft) high. The middle wall is defended by tall jagged limestone blocks (chevaux-de-frise) set vertically into the ground. The inner fort is 45m (148ft) in diameter and contains wall chambers, stairways and terraces. The visitor centre, about 1km away, gives information about the site

Dún a'Ri Forest Park, *Cavan* 114 A1
☎ 049 433 1942
Located in the River Cabra glen, the forest comprises 229ha (565 acres), more than half of which is managed commercially to produce Norway spruce and oak. The park has a wide variety of plants and animals including squirrels, stoats, Irish hares, pigmy shrews, mink and otters. Forest walks pass many places associated with the legends and history of the valley; a holy well, the ruins of Fleming's Castle, a flax mill, lake and an old ice house.

Dún Dúchathair, *Galway* 117 C4
☎ 099 61263   www.visitaranislands.com
The 'Black Fort' sits on cliffs on the south coast of Inis Mór though, due to coastal erosion, would probably not have been in such an exposed location when it was constructed. Not as easily accessible and therefore quieter than the more famous Dún Aonghasa to the north west.

Dunbrody Abbey & Visitor Centre, *Wexford* 134 A3
☎ 051 388603   www.dunbrodyabbey.com
The ruins of this Cistercian Monastery date back to the late 12th century and are reputedly the finest example of medieval architecture in the county. The visitor centre includes a small museum with a dolls house. There is also a hedge maze, golf pitch and putt and a craft gallery.

Dunbrody Ship, *Wexford* 134 A2
☎ 051 425239   www.dunbrody.com
At the quayside in New Ross is a full scale sea-going replica of a three masted barque famine ship of the 19th century. Visitors can board the ship, explore it, and look through the huge database of passengers recorded as having sailed from Ireland during this time. An interactive exhibition shows shipboard life as it would have been 150 years ago and traces the

success stories of families such as the Kennedys.

Duncannon Fort, *Wexford* 134 A3
☎ 051 389454
Located on a promontory in Waterford Harbour, this star shaped 16th century military fort is one of four in Ireland. Its purpose was to defend against an attack by the Spanish Armada. Of interest is the grisly story of the 'Croppy Boy', the dry moat and the massive exterior walls. It now houses an art gallery and studio, craft centre and marine museum.

Dundalk Racecourse, *Louth* 106 A4
☎ 042 71271 / 01 825 6618
www.dundalkstadium.com
This redeveloped 2 km track opened in 2006 and is Ireland's first all-weather floodlit track in use for flat and national hunt racing.

Dundonald Old Mill, *Castlereagh* 107 C1
☎ 028 9048 5030
A 300 year old former linen & flour sandstone mill with exposed beams which now houses the tea shop selling home baked cakes and snacks. The fully restored waterwheel is one of largest in Ireland and is in working operation.

Dundrum Castle, *Down* 107 C3
☎ 028 9054 6518   www.ehsni.gov.uk
Built by John de Courcy in about 1177 and later occupied by the Magennises, Dundrum is one of the finest Norman castles in Northern Ireland. A massive circular stone tower is enclosed by stone walls and further protected by a ditch hewn from rock. The castle affords panoramic views of the Mourne Mountains and across Dundrum Bay.

Dundrum Plantarum, *South Tipperary* 124 A4
☎ 062 71303
A Celtic theme runs through this 3.2ha (8 acres) woodland with walks, water features, dolmens and crannogs.

Dungannon Park, *Dungannon* 105 D1
☎ 028 8772 7327
A 28ha (70 acres) park, the centrepiece of which is the 5ha (12 acres) Stillwater Lake which was created in the 1790s by Viscount Northland. Tennis, football, cricket and angling are all catered for - disabled anglers have use of the 'wheelyboat'. There is also a children's play area, barbeque site and miles of paths running through the park.

Dunguaire Castle

Dungarvan Castle, *Waterford* 133 C3
☎ 058 48144
Built by Prince John of England in 1185 but considerably altered at various later periods, the castle consists of a 12th century shell keep with an enclosing curtain wall, gate tower and corner tower. Within the curtain wall stands an early 18th century two storey military barracks which has been restored and now houses an exhibition and visitor facilities. Access is by guided tour only.

Dunguaire Castle, *Galway* 118 B3
☎ 061 360788
www.shannonheritage.com/Dunguaire_Day.htm
Dunguaire Castle is a restored fortified tower house built by the O'Hynes in 1520. It was bought in 1924 by Oliver St John Gogarty, surgeon, poet and wit, who was involved with the Irish Literary Revival; W.B Yeats, Lady Gregory, George Bernard Shaw and J.M.Synge were among visitors to the castle. Now the venue for medieval banquets, the castle also has exhibits giving an insight into the lives of the people who have lived there since the 16th century.

Dunhill Castle, *Waterford* 133 D2
☎ 051 381572
Built by the la Poer family in the 13th century from where many attacks on Waterford were launched resulting in the capture and hanging of many family members. Not deterred, the remaining family joined forces with the O'Driscoll family and continued the attacks for the next 100 years. It was attacked and taken by Cromwell in 1649 and fell into disuse as a consequence.

Dunluce Castle, *Coleraine* 99 D1
☎ 028 2073 1938
www.northantrim.com/dunlucecastle.htm
An extensive dramatic cliff top ruin on a rocky headland, the site of which has been fortified for over 1500 years. The mainly 16th and

17th century remains of the castle incorporate two Norman towers dating from 1305. Successively occupied by Ulster clans, the McQuillens, O'Neills and McDonnells, until the 17th century when, during a storm, the kitchens fell into the sea and all the servants were killed.

Dunluce Castle   Photo © Northern Ireland Tourist Board

Dunluce Centre, *Coleraine* 99 D1
☎ 028 7082 4444   www.dunlucecentre.co.uk
Indoor family entertainment centre which includes a multimedia display of the folklore of the surrounding area, interactive nature exhibits, a soft play area and a viewing tower. '4D Turbo Tours' is Ireland's only 4D effects theatre where action on a giant screen is synchronised with moving seats. The 'Treasure Fortress' is a high-tech treasure hunt set in a simulated castle environment.

Dunmore Cave, *Kilkenny* 125 D3
☎ 056 776 7726   www.heritageireland.ie
These limestone caves contain magnificent calcite formations along almost a quarter of a mile of passageways. Many of these are now lit and stairs and walkways have been installed for visitors (guided tours). In AD928, the cave was the site of a Viking massacre and the bones of 44 individuals have been identified. In late 1999, 43 silver and bronze artefacts dating to around AD970 were found by a tour guide in the caves. The caves are a National Monument and the visitor centre houses exhibitions and displays.

Dunseverick Castle, *Moyle* 99 D1
☎ 028 2076 2024
Ruins dating from the 16th century sitting on a small peninsula just east of the Giant's Causeway. All that remains is part of the tower after being destroyed by the Scottish army in 1642 to put down the Irish rebellion threatening English and Scottish settlers. Dunseverick was visited by St Patrick on several occasions.

Dunsoghly Castle, *Fingal* 115 C3
☎ 01 605 7755
Dunsoghly Castle consists of a stately residential keep-like tower on three floors buttressed by rectangular corner turrets. It was built in the 15th century by Thomas Plunkett, Chief Justice of the King's Bench, whilst the nearby chapel was built in 1573 by Sir John Plunkett, also Chief Justice but for the Queen's Bench.

Durrow Abbey, *Offaly* 113 C4
☎ 057 935 2617
Founded by St Columba in the 6th century though the earliest surviving relics are a High Cross and inscribed gravestones from the 9th century. Such is the similarity of design to the crosses at Monasterboice and at Clonmacnoise that the same artist may have been responsible. A motte built by Hugh de Lacy, 1st Lord of Meath, in the 1180s is also on the site and it was here that he was killed in 1186.

Dwyer McAllister Cottage, *Wicklow* 126 B2
☎ 0404 45325   www.heritageireland.ie
This is an excellent example of a traditional thatched Irish cottage, built of local stone and now whitewashed outside and in. It was from here that the famous Irish rebel Michael Dwyer escaped from British troops in 1799.

Dysert O'Dea Archaeology Centre, *Clare* 118 B4
☎ 065 683 7794 / 683 7401
Built in 1480 the castle now houses the Clare Archaeological Centre which contains a museum and exhibitions about the twenty five archaeological monuments that fall within a 6km (3.7 mile) radius of the castle. These include two stone forts, a 12th century High Cross, a 'fulacht fiadh' (an ancient cooking site), Romanesque Churches and Holy Wells.

Eagles Flying, *Sligo* 102 B4
☎ 071 9189310   www.eaglesflying.com
Ireland's largest sanctuary for birds of prey with twice daily free-flying displays. The Irish Raptor Research Centre serves as a hospital for injured birds and runs breeding and release programmes. There are also farm animals and a pet corner.

Enniskillen Castle   Photo © Northern Ireland Tourist Board

Earhart Centre & Wildlife Sanctuary, *Londonderry* 98 B2
☎ 028 7135 4040
Commemorates Amelia Earhart, the first woman to fly solo across the Atlantic, who landed unexpectedly in the field here on 21st May 1932.

ECOS Environmental Centre, *Ballymena* 100 A3
☎ 028 2566 4400   www.ecoscentre.com
Standing in a 60ha (150 acre) park which can be explored by hiring a solar-powered bike. Interactive displays focus on the environment and alternative energy production from renewable sources. On site willow coppicing, wind turbines and solar energy account for 60% of the centre's energy requirements.

Elizabeth Fort, *Cork* 142 B2
☎ 021 427 3251
Built in the 16th century it has been used as a prison, barracks and now houses the Garda. The outer walls are 5–9m (16–30ft) high and the view from them is impressive showing the strategic importance of the location. The Gateway Bar, the oldest pub in Cork, is next to the fort.

Emo Court & Gardens, *Laois* 125 D1
☎ 057 862 6573   www.heritageireland.ie
Emo Court is a neo-classical style building designed by James Gandon for the Earl of Portarlington in 1790. Subsequently owned by the Jesuits, it was acquired by Mr. Cholmeley-Harrison in 1960 and extensively restored. The gardens contain formal lawns, parkland and woodland walks, along with a 9ha (22 acre) lake and a 1.5km (1 mile) tree lined avenue dating from the late 19th century.

Ennis Friary, *Clare* 122 B1
☎ 065 682 9100   www.heritageireland.ie
Founded in 1242 by the O'Briens, though most of the building dates from the 14th century. In the 15th century over 300 monks and 600 pupils resided here as it was one of the finest seats of learning in Ireland. The decorated tombs and carvings are of most interest especially the St Francis carving and the 15th century MacMahon tomb.

Enniscoe Gardens, *Mayo* 109 D3
☎ 096 31112   www.enniscoe.com
Enniscoe, situated on Lough Conn, is an 18th century Georgian house with gardens dating back to the 1840s. The walled garden contains organic vegetables and is separated from an ornamental garden by a decorative stone archway planted with hardy ferns. Paths run through the parkland to the lake and many of the trees in the Victorian pleasure gardens are 150 years old.

Enniscorthy Castle, *Wexford* 134 B2
☎ 053 923 5926
This Norman castle is a well preserved example of its kind. In spite of several onslaughts and alterations in the 16th century, it retained its three distinctive round towers. Overlooking the Slaney River, in the centre of the town, it now houses the County Wexford Historical and Folk Museum. There are two rooms containing memorabilia from the 1798 and 1916 uprisings.

Enniskillen Castle, *Fermanagh* 104 A2
☎ 028 6632 5000   www.enniskillencastle.co.uk
Overlooking the River Erne, Enniskillen Castle dates back to the 15th century and was once the stronghold of the Gaelic Maguire chieftains. The medieval keep remains intact and is surrounded by 18th and 19th century barracks buildings, while the 17th century turrets of the Water-gate give the castle its distinctive appearance. The keep houses the Royal Inniskilling Fusiliers museum which explains the history of the regiment from its formation in 1689. The Heritage Centre, located in a modern purpose built building within the castle, houses the Fermanagh County Museum and Fermanagh's archaeological heritage is portrayed in the curved barracks building.

Erne Gateway Centre, *Fermanagh* 103 C2
☎ 028 6865 8866
Featuring an exhibition which explains how the loughs of the area were formed and illustrates how Lough Erne has influenced the people who live around its shore. The archaeological heritage of the area is presented along with the rich diversity of landscape and wildlife.

Exploris, *Ards* 107 C2
☎ 028 4272 8062   www.exploris.org.uk
Aquarium attraction with some of the largest tanks in Britain, simulating the experience of underwater exploration of Strangford Lough and the Irish Sea. Attractions include a touch tank, marine discovery lab and a recently opened seal sanctuary where sick or orphaned seals are rehabilitated to return to the wild.

Fairyhouse Racecourse, *Meath* **115 C3**
☎ 01 825 6167 / 8 / 9
www.fairyhouseracecourse.ie
Fairyhouse has hosted the Irish Grand
National since the late 1900s. 19km (12
miles) north west of Dublin, there are frequent
fixtures for both National Hunt and Flat
Racing.

Famine Museum, *North Tipperary* **124 B4**
☎ 0504 21133
A fascinating look at the 1840s Great Famine
located in St Mary's Church of Ireland in
Thurles town centre.

Famine Warhouse 1848, *South Tipperary*
125 C4
☎ 087 908 9972   www.ballingarry.net
The Warhouse was the scene of the principal
action of the 1848 Rebellion by the Young
Irelanders led by William Smith O'Brien, MP for
County Limerick. The local police
commandeered the house taking hostage the
five young McCormack children who lived
there and from this impregnable position, and
with reinforcements arriving, broke the back of
the resistance. O'Brien and the other leaders
were captured, found guilty of high treason
and sentenced to be hanged, drawn and
quartered. However, the sentences were
commuted to life imprisonment in Tasmania
in Australia. A full pardon followed in 1856
and O'Brien returned to Ireland where he lived
until his death in 1864.

Fantasy Island, *Coleraine* **99 D1**
☎ 028 7082 3595
Indoor adventure play area for young children
with ball ponds and climbing frames.

Farney Castle, *North Tipperary* **124 B4**
☎ 0504 43281
Built in 1495 this Round Tower is currently
occupied by the designer Cyril Cullen. The
naturally coloured wool from the rare Jacob
Sheep that graze in the surrounding fields is
used to make the world-famous Jacob
sweaters which, along with the home
produced Parian Porcelain, are retailed from
the shop on the premises.

Father McDyer's Folk Village, *Donegal*
96 A4
☎ 074 973 0017   www.glenfolkvillage.com
The museum is built in the form of a village
where each cottage is a replica dwelling used
by local people in one of the 18th, 19th or
20th centuries with period furnishings and
artefacts. A 19th century National School is
also featured and has a collection of old
photographs, books and items of local history
on display. The folk village was established by
Father James MacDyer in the 1950s to help
ease unemployment and maintain the
traditional culture of the area.

Fernhill Gardens, *Dún Laoghaire-Rathdown*
115 C4
☎ 01 295 6000
Overlooking Dublin Bay, these 16ha (40 acres)
of gardens, laid out in a 'Robinsonian' style,
contain many fine Himalayan trees and
shrubs, spring bulbs, ferns and heathers, as
well as a kitchen garden, water garden and
numerous other features. The original layout
was created in the mid 17th century.

Ferns Castle, *Wexford* **127 C4**
☎ 053 936 6411 / 056 772 4623
www.heritageireland.ie
Half of this Norman castle remains, with two
towers and some curtain wall still standing,
one of which contains a lovely circular chapel,
several fireplaces and a vaulted basement.

Fethard Folk Farm & Transport Museum,
South Tipperary **132 B1**
☎ 052 31516
Housed in the former 19th century railway
station near the town walls, there are over
1200 exhibits many of which sit in recreations of authentic surroundings.

Fintown Railway, *Donegal* **97 C3**
☎ 074 954 6280
The only operational narrow gauge railway in
Donegal which was re-opened in 1995. Once
part of the Stranorlar to Glenties branch line of
the County Donegal Railway, visitors can take
a 6km (4mile) return journey along the shore
of Lough Finn. It is the intention of the
volunteers to reopen the line all the way to
Glenties where there are still original stone
bridges, a platform at Shallogans Halt and the
privately owned station buildings at Glenties.

Flight of the Earls Heritage Centre,
Donegal **98 A2**
☎ 074 915 8178 / 915 8131
In 1607 the O'Neill and O'Donnell chieftains
fled the country for Spain in what became
known as The Flight of the Earls. The heritage
centre traces the history of these times and
their consequences with lively and interesting
displays including works of art and costume.

Florence Court, *Fermanagh* **103 D3**
☎ 028 6634 8249   www.ntni.org.uk
Once the home of the Earls of Enniskillen,
18th century Florence Court was built in the
Palladian style and is one of the finest historic
houses in Ulster. It was named after Florence,
the wife of the first Earl of Enniskillen.
Beautiful rococo ceilings and panels decorate
the interior which has original furniture,
paintings and artefacts. Within the estate is a
1780s walled garden, ice house, summer
house and water-powered sawmill. A National
Trust property.

Fernhill Gardens   Photo © Fáilte Ireland

Florence Court Forest Park, *Fermanagh* 103 D3

☎ 028 6634 3032   www.forestserviceni.gov.uk

Adjoining Florence Court House, the forest park covers over 1200ha (2964 acres) encompassing a wide variety of habitats including open blanket bog, coniferous forest and the old estate woodland featuring many oak trees planted around 200 years ago.

Folklife Display, *Fermanagh* 104 A3

☎ 028 6772 1222

An exhibition in Lisnaskea Library depicting rural life in Fermanagh, made up from the bric-a-brac collection of a retired local publican.

Fore Abbey, *Westmeath* 113 D2

☎ 044 966 1780

Originally built as a monastery in AD630, by St Fechin, the remains seen today are of the nearby 13th century Benedictine priory, with 15th century fortifications. The ruins of the church of St Fechin are 11th and 13th century and above this is an anchorite's cell, occupied by hermits until the 17th century. One of the 'Seven Wonders of Fore'.

Fort Dunree Military Museum, *Donegal* 98 A2

☎ 074 936 1817   www.dunree.pro.ie

The museum is set within the old military fort at Dunree Head which had a strategic role in defending the entrance to Lough Swilly. With an audiovisual theatre, an extensive collection of military artefacts and large artillery pieces in their original location, the museum explains the role of coastal artillery and the military history of the area. The Old Fort Hospital has a wildlife exhibition illustrating the flora and fauna of the surrounding area.

Fota House, Gardens & Arboretum, *Cork* 131 D2

☎ 021 481 5523   www.fotahouse.com

Originally a two-storey lodge which was converted to this elegant residence in the 19th century by John Smith-Barry. The billiard room was used for meetings of the Royal Cork Yacht Club where, legend has it, the term 'black-balled' originated where, if a proposal was rejected, the black ball was rolled down the table. Covering an area of 13ha (32 acres) the excellent soil and mild climate allows a wide range of exotic trees and shrubs from every continent to thrive. There is an orangery, terraces and four walled gardens which include stone ornamental gateways and a summer house in the Italian Garden.

Fota Island Golf Club, *Cork* 131 D2

☎ 021 4535 2031   www.fotaisland.com

Championship course on the 350ha (780 acre) island in Cork Harbour. The Irish Open & Seniors Open Championships have been held here in recent years.

Fota Wildlife Park, *Cork* 131 D2

☎ 021 481 2678   www.fotawildlife.ie

The park holds over 90 species of animal including giraffes, bison and cheetahs and is important in the conservation and breeding of endangered species. Wherever possible the animals are encouraged to thrive in unrestricted areas and some, such as lemurs, kangaroos and wallabies, are allowed to roam free through the park.

Fourknocks Megalithic Tomb, *Meath* 115 C2

☎ 01 849 5208

www.knowth.com/fourknocks.htm

Built around 5000 years ago, Fourknocks Passage Chamber Tomb contains a rare example of the image of a human face, just inside the entrance.

Foxford Woollen Mills, *Mayo* 110 B2

☎ 094 925 6756

Working mills where skilled craftspeople produce tweed, rugs and blankets. The mills were founded in 1892 by a nun, Mother Agnes Morrogh Bernard, whose life story is told in the visitor centre with a three dimensional audiovisual presentation incorporating animated life size models.

Foynes Flying Boat Museum, *Limerick* 122 B2

☎ 069 65416   www.flyingboatmuseum.com

During the 1930s and 1940s Foynes was the base for flying boats operating between the United States and Europe. The museum commemorates the operational staff and many of the passengers on the transatlantic flights and an audiovisual show brings to life Foynes during the war time era. Features of interest include the original terminal building, weather and radio room with original transmitters, receivers and morse code equipment, a 1940s style cinema and wartime radio.

Francis Ledwidge Museum, *Meath* 114 B2

☎ 041 982 4544   www.francisledwidge.com

The local poet Francis Ledwidge was born in this labourer's cottage, at Janeville near Slane, in 1887. Though a Nationalist, he enlisted in the British Army during WWI. It was while recovering from his wounds in a military hospital, he heard of the Easter Rising and wrote possibly his best known poem in honour of Thomas MacDonagh, one of the leaders of the Rising, who was executed in 1916. He survived Gallipoli and also a time in Serbia before he was killed in Belgium in 1917. The cottage comprises four rooms with a small garden and contains original and period furnishings depicting the simple life of the poet. Some of his original manuscripts are also on display.

Francis Ledwidge Museum   Photo © Fáilte Ireland

Fry Model Railway, *Fingal* 115 D3

☎ 01 846 3779

Covering 233 sq m (2500 sq ft) this is one of the world's largest working miniature railways. Besides the track, the railway has stations, bridges, trams, buses and barges and includes the Dublin landmarks of Heuston station and O'Connell Bridge. On display are the hand constructed models of Irish trains by Cyril Fry, draughtsman and railway engineer.

Gallarus Oratory, *Kerry* 120 A4
☎ 066 915 5333
On the beautiful Dingle peninsula, at Lateevmore is Gallarus oratory, a corbel-roofed dry-stone structure of remarkable perfection and completely waterproof. A thousand year old Christian chapel lacks only the crosses that once decorated the roof. Access is free but a charge applies for the visitor centre.

Gallery, The, *Donegal* 97 D2
☎ 074 9136224
Located in the 19th century fever hospital for Dunfanaghy Workhouse which was then used from the 1930s until the 60s as the National School for the Roman Catholic Children. Original oil and watercolour paintings are on display together with art & craft materials. The shop offers local and national crafts for sale.

Galway Cathedral, *Galway* 153 B2
☎ 091 563577   www.galwaycathedral.org
Located by the Salmon Weir Bridge on the River Corrib, the Cathedral was completed in 1965 and is dedicated to Our Lady Assumed into Heaven and St Nicholas. The 45m (145ft) high green dome is prominent on the city's skyline.

Galway Cathedral   Photo © Ireland West

Galway City Museum, *Galway* 153 B3
☎ 091 532467
Located in the medieval docks area of Galway and adjoining the Spanish Arch, the museum presents the folklife and social history of Galway. Redeveloped and reopened in 2006 and now including a restaurant. Exhibits include 17th century stone carvings, farm implements and tools, military exhibits relating to the 1916 Rising and the civil war, maps, photographs and engravings.

Galway Crystal, *Galway* 118 B2
☎ 091 757311   www.galwaycrystal.ie
The production of traditionally hand cut Irish lead crystal is shown in the context of the history, culture and landscape of Galway which has inspired the craftsmen. Visitors have the opportunity to see the craftsmen at work producing the intricately designed tabletop stemware and giftware; tours begin in the elegant Great Hall of Merlin Park House with its grand staircase and crystal chandeliers.

Galway Racecourse, *Galway* 118 B2
☎ 091 753870   www.galwayraces.com
National Hunt and Flat racing course with 12 race days a year including the six day Summer Racing Festival meeting, one of Ireland's premier racing festivals and a time of great celebration in Galway itself.

Garden of Europe, *Kerry* 121 D3
☎ 068 22590
The Garden of Europe in Childers Park, Listowel, contains over 2,500 plantings from across Europe and also a monument to the memory of the victims of the Holocaust.

Garden of Remembrance, *Dublin City* 147 B1
☎ 01 874 3074   www.heritageireland.ie
The Garden of Remembrance, opened in 1966, is dedicated to all those who died in the cause of Irish Freedom. There is a sculpture by Oisín Kelly representing the Irish legend, Children of Lir.

Gash Gardens, *Laois* 125 C2
☎ 057 873 2247
1.6ha (4 acres) garden on the banks of the River Nore. Features an impressive rock garden, heath garden, vibrant herbaceous borders, rhododendrons, moon house, pools, waterfall and a passageway leading to a riverside walk. Note that it is not suitable for children or dogs.

Giant's Causeway, *Moyle* 99 D1
☎ 028 2073 1855
www.northantrim.com/giantscauseway.htm
Thousands of layered basalt columns, mostly hexagonal, stretching for almost 1km (0.6 mile) into the ocean and resulting from the cooling of molten lava about 60 million years ago. Legend tells it was built by the giant Finn MacCool to enable him to cross to Scotland. The visitor centre has an audiovisual theatre and exhibition area which outlines the geological history of the Causeway and also illustrates the flora and fauna of the area and local history. An UNESCO World Heritage Site in the care of the National Trust.

Giant's Causeway   Photo © Northern Ireland Tourist Boar

Giant's Ring, *Lisburn* 106 B1
☎ 028 9266 0038   www.ntni.org.uk
One of Ireland's most important Neolithic sites consisting of a high circular earthbank 183m (600ft) in diameter which encloses a megalithic tomb. Situated beside the River Lagan, the enclosure was used as a horse racing circuit in the 18th century.

Giant's Ring   Photo © Northern Ireland Tourist Board

Glebe House & Gallery, *Donegal* 97 D3
☎ 074 913 7071   www.heritageireland.ie
Glebe House is a Regency house built in 1828 with an interior decorated with William Morris wallpaper and textiles and Japanese and Islamic art. Set in woodland gardens, the house is home to the Derek Hill Collection of over 300 works by leading 20th century artists including Picasso and Kokoshka. Many Irish and English artists are also represented in the collection.

Glebelands & Glebewood Gardens, *Meath* 115 C3
☎ 01 825 6015
'Glebelands' was created in 1813 and consists of low retaining walls with mature native trees along the boundaries, all set in gently rolling countryside. 'Glebewood', influenced by Lutyens, was only constructed in 1990. It required much sculpting to reflect the characteristics of the older garden, and aims to create a relaxing and interesting atmosphere.

Glenariff Forest Park, *Moyle* 100 B2
☎ 028 2955 6000   www.forestserviceni.gov.uk
Paths and trails lead through the narrow wooded gorge cut by the Glenarrif River to mountain viewpoints. Three spectacular waterfalls cascade down the river and the damp conditions support a variety of mosses and ferns; the woodland comprises oak, hazel, ash and willow. A visitor centre provides information about the park.

Glenariff Forest Park   Photo © Ireland West

Glencar Waterfall, *Leitrim* 102 B2
☎ 071 916 1201
Falling into Glencar Lake, this 50ft high waterfall is by no means the largest in Ireland but is certainly one of the most beautiful. Visible from the road near the Sligo/Leitrim border.

Glendalough & Visitor Centre, *Wicklow* 127 C2
☎ 0404 45325 / 45352   www.heritageireland.ie
Glendalough ('the valley of two lakes') is so named because of the two lakes, Upper Lake and Lower Lake. On the banks of Lower Lake stands a 6th century Christian monastic site founded by St Kevin which flourished before being largely destroyed in the 16th century. There are, however, many important remains, including the impressive 1000 year old 31m (100 ft) high round tower which is still in near perfect condition, several stone churches and decorated crosses. The Visitor Centre is set at the gateway to Glendalough Valley and the National Park. It contains a model of the site as it would have appeared in 1080 and an audiovisual presentation. Steep slopes surround the Upper Lake to give quite breathtaking scenery and a cave, St Kevin's Bed, on the south side of the lake is said to be a place of meditation for the monk.

Glendeer Open Farm, *Roscommon* 112 A4
☎ 0906 437147   www.glendeer.com
A family run 2.5ha (6 acres) farm with deer, donkeys, ostrich, pot bellied pigs, goats, llamas and many more breeds. There is a nature walk, indoor and outdoor picnic areas, restored 19th century cottage and children's playground. December sees Glendeer transformed into Ireland's Lapland.

Glengarriff Bamboo Park, *Cork* 129 D3
☎ 027 63570   www.bamboo-park.com
Created in 1999 by Serge de Thibault and his wife Claudine to the same pattern as the Bambouseraie in the South of France, although parts date back to the turn of the 20th century. There are thirty different species of bamboo surrounded by palms, tree ferns, hydrangeas, fuchsias and 15 different species of Eucalyptus. Also of interest are 13 mysterious stone pillars, the significance of which is unknown but are believed to be of ancient origin.

Glengowla Mines, *Galway* 117 D2
☎ 091 552021   www.glengowlamines.com
Historic silver and lead mine abandoned in 1865 after only 14 years production. A museum and guided underground tours give an idea of the conditions and methods used in 19th century mining. Restored buildings include the powder magazine, blacksmith's workshop and the agent's cottage.

Glenroe Open Farm, *Wicklow* 127 D1
☎ 01 287 2288   www.glenroefarm.com
Get close to the sika deer, sheep, cattle, pigs, goats, ducks, geese, turkeys, peacocks and hens and handle the more cuddly animals in pets' corner. A 1 km nature walk to coastal marshlands passes through sensory gardens and secret garden. A 350 year old thatched farmhouse houses the museum and there are both indoor and outdoor picnic areas. The long-running RTE television series 'Glenroe' used the farm as a location throughout its 18 years run.

Gosford Forest Park   Photo © Northern Ireland Tourist Board

Glenveagh Castle, *Donegal* 97 D2
☎ 074 913 7090
Set within the Glenveagh National Park, the Scottish style castle with its rectangular keep was built between 1870 and 1873 and is surrounded by celebrated gardens. An important collection of trees and shrubs is found at Glenveagh and there are a variety of garden styles skillfully set against the beautiful and rugged Donegal landscape. A formal Italian terrace has antique sculpture and terracotta pots while a fruit, vegetable and flower garden is surrounded by clipped hedges and overlooked by a neo-gothic conservatory.

Glenveagh National Park, *Donegal* 97 C2
☎ 074 913 7090   www.heritageireland.ie
Home to a large herd of red deer, the park comprises 16,500ha (40,755 acres) of mountains, lakes, glens and woods. Glenveagh Castle and gardens are found within the park and a visitor centre at the castle has exhibitions and an audiovisual show about the area.

Glenview Folk Museum, *Leitrim* 103 D4
☎ 071 964 4157
A private collection of over 3000 exhibits including farmyard equipment, tools and household items. A recreation of a 19th century street scene has a number of shops and a pub equipped as they would have been at the time.

Glin Castle, *Limerick* 122 A2
☎ 068 34173   www.glincastle.com
The Fitzgeralds, Knights of Glin, have lived here for over 700 years, first in a castle in the village itself, of which little remains, and then in Glin Castle, a Georgian house which dates from the 1780s. Set in formal gardens, Glin also has a beautiful kitchen garden and many specimen trees and shrubs amongst the woodland. The house interior is decorated with fine plasterwork and is hung with interesting Irish paintings and family portraits. There is also a collection of 18th century furniture by Irish craftsmen.

Gortin Glen Forest Park, *Omagh* 104 B1
☎ 028 8164 8217   www.forestserviceni.gov.uk
The park has an 8km (5 mile) scenic drive through the forest, walking and bike trails. All afford breathtaking views. Also within the park is a sika deer enclosure, wildfowl enclosure and visitor centre.

Gosford Forest Park, *Armagh* 105 D2
☎ 028 3755 1277   www.forestserviceni.gov.uk
The former estate of Gosford Castle, a mock-Norman castle built by Sir Arthur Acheson in 1839. Features include an arboretum with 200 year old broadleaved trees and a deer park. Traditional breeds of poultry in open paddocks, ornamental pigeons, nature trails and a walled garden are amongst other attractions.

Gougane Barra Forest Park, *Cork* 130 A2
☎ 026 43280
The lake on the edge of this 142ha (350 acre) park is the source of the River Lee. Holy Island sits in the lake and is linked to the shore by a causeway and it is here that the patron saint of Cork, St Finbarr, founded a monastery. Unusually, the ring road allows the motorist to drive around the park.

Gowran Park Racecourse, *Kilkenny* 126 A4
☎ 056 772 6120 / 772 6225   www.gowranpark.ie
13kms (8 miles) from Kilkenny hosting both Flat and National Hunt racing. It is home to the Thyestes Chase, a Group 1 Steeplechase.

GPA-Bolton Library, *South Tipperary* 124 B4
☎ 062 61944
Founded in 1744 by Theophilus Bolton, Archbishop of Cashel. Houses a collection of 12th century books, maps and manuscripts including extracts from Chaucers 'Book of Fame'.

Grand Opera House   Photo © Northern Ireland Tourist Board

Grand Opera House, *Belfast* 138 B2
☎ 028 9024 1919   www.goh.co.uk
Designed by architect Frank Matcham and opened by J F Warden in 1895, the theatre has always seen a rich variety of entertainment from opera to pantomime and serious drama to comedy. Its declining opulence was restored in 1980; transformed into a premier modern theatre whilst retaining the lavish Victorian interior.

Granny Castle, *Kilkenny* 133 D2
☎ 051 875823
Originally built by the 3rd Earl of Ormonde but occupied by the le Poer family in the 13th century until the execution of Eustace le Poer for treason in 1375. It fell victim to Cromwell's assault on Ireland in 1650.

Grant Ancestral Home, *Dungannon* 105 C2
☎ 028 8555 7133
Ancestral home of Ulysses Simpson Grant who became 18th President of the United States (1869–1877). The typical 19th century thatched cottage has original mud walls reinforced with reeds; the farmyard has a turf store, byre and display of agricultural implements. Exhibitions and audiovisual shows tell the story of the Simpson family and their early years in Ireland, of Irish emigration to America and of the American Civil War. A pond and wildlife garden has been created in the grounds of the homestead.

Granuaile Visitor Centre, *Mayo* 109 C4
☎ 098 66341
An audiovisual presentation of the fascinating story of the 'pirate queen' Grace O'Malley (Granuaile). With a base on Clare island, O'Malley achieved control of the area around Clew Bay and the visitor centre explores her political, diplomatic and commercial achievements in the male-dominated society of 16th century Ireland. A woman of outstanding determination and drive, O'Malley travelled to London to meet with Elizabeth I to plea protection from the English suppression of local chieftains, a wish that was granted.

Granuaile's Tower, *Mayo* 108 B4
☎ 098 47353   www.achilltourism.com
This 3 storey, 12m (40ft) high tower house is thought to have been constructed by the O'Malleys in about 1429. However, it is more closely associated with their descendant, the pirate queen Grace O'Malley or Granuaile who is thought to have been born in 1530 and died in 1603. A church and graveyard thought to date from at least the 12th century are adjacent.

Granuaile's Tower Photo © Mayo Naturally

Gray's Printing Press, *Strabane* 98 A4
☎ 028 7188 4094   www.ntni.org.uk
With a unique Georgian façade, the building houses an 18th century printing press (National Trust) thought to have been used by John Dunlap who was later to print the American Declaration of Independence. An impressive selection of 19th century hand printing machines are also displayed and there are compositor demonstrations from time to time. In the same building is Strabane's local history museum.

Greenan Farm Museums & Maze, *Wicklow* 127 C2
☎ 0404 46000   www.greenanmaze.com
Comprises three museums and two mazes as well as nature walks, tearoom, craft shop and sculpture trail. The 16th century Old Farmhouse was a safe-house for Irish rebels in the 1798 rebellion and has authentic furniture and utensils. The Farm Museum exhibits implements and tools from over 200 years of local agricultural history. The Bottle Museum displays bottles and vessels, some over 100 years old. The Solstice Maze has 21 perimeter stones with four large standing stones representing the seasons at the centre. The older Greenan Maze has a celtic theme and has a stream flowing to the pond in the centre.

Greencastle, *Newry & Mourne* 106 B4
☎ 028 9054 3037   www.ehsni.gov.uk
In medieval times this royal castle on the north shore of the narrow mouth to Carlingford Lough guarded the entrance to the lough and had an eventful history. Greencastle was besieged by Edward Bruce in 1316 and later became a garrison for Elizabeth I. The castle today is substantial, consisting of a curtain wall with a tower at each corner enclosing a large rectangular keep.

Grey Abbey Physic Garden, *Ards* 107 C1
☎ 028 4278 8585   www.ehsni.gov.uk
Set within beautiful parkland, Grey Abbey is the substantial remains of a Cistercian abbey founded by Affreca, the wife of John de Courcy, in 1193. Monks made use of many herbs in their medicines and a herb garden has been recreated here as it may have existed in medieval times.

Grianan Ailigh

Grianan Ailigh, *Donegal* 98 A3
☎ 074 936 8080   www.griananailigh.ie
A huge round stone fort or cashel dating back to 1700BC which stands at the centre of a series of three earthen banks from either late Bronze or early Iron Age. An important stronghold of the kingdom of Ailigh, it retained a mythological importance long after its strategic value had passed away. Restored in the 1870s, the cashel has walls measuring 4m (13ft) thick and 5m (16ft) high with terraces along their interior to allow access to the top of the wall. Situated on a hilltop 242m (800ft) above sea level, there are wonderful views across the Foyle and Swilly.

Grianan Ailigh Experience, The, *Donegal* 98 A2
☎ 074 936 8080   www.griananailigh.ie
Housed within a restored church, the centre provides information about the history of the ancient round stone fort of Grianan Ailigh; there is also an interpretative display of the ecosystem of the nearby woodland and wetland habitat, home to Hooper swans, wild geese and many woodland birds and animals.

Guillemot Maritime Museum, The, *Wexford* 134 B3
☎ 053 912 1572 / 051 561144
The lightship Guillemot is the last Irish Lights Vessel. Now beached at Kilmore Quay, it contains all of its original features. Also on board are many interesting nautical artefacts, model ships and a collection of pictures. Both the Hook and Barrels lights can be seen from the deck, as well as excellent views of the Saltee Islands.

Guinness Storehouse, *Dublin City* 146 A2
☎ 01 408 4800   www.guinness-storehouse.com
This attraction tells the story of Guinness from its beginnings in 1759, how it is made and the advertising campaigns used to make it internationally famous. Recently rehoused in St James's Gate Brewery, on six floors, the entrance is through a pint glass shaped atrium capable of holding 10,000 pints!

Harbour Museum, *Londonderry* 160 A2
☎ 028 7137 7331
Maritime museum which includes a replica of the curragh in which St Columba sailed to Iona in AD563.

Hennigan's Heritage Centre, *Mayo* 110 B2
☎ 094 925 2505   www.henniganheritage.com
Overlooking Creagaballa Lake, this small farm of less than 4ha (10 acres) was tilled by generations of the Hennigan family for 200 years. Visitors can see inside the original farmhouse and visit the theme farm where animals and poultry roam freely. Fishing and boating is available on the lake.

Heraldic Museum, *Dublin City* 147 C2
☎ 01 603 0311
The first permanent Heraldic Museum in the world was set up in 1909 and moved to its present location in 1987. The development and application of heraldry is traced throughout Ireland and Europe.

Heywood Gardens, *Laois* 125 D2
☎ 056 772 1450   www.heritageireland.ie
These gardens comprise parkland and interlinked elements designed by Sir Edwin Lutyens in the early 20th century. There is a formal lawn with herbaceous borders and several pools with associated features, such as a hidden pergola and a pavilion with planted terraces. Other planted areas are enclosed with yew hedges.

Hezlett House, *Coleraine* 99 C2
☎ 028 7084 8567   www.ntni.org.uk
Thatched house dating from 1600s, one of few remaining of this age in Ireland, with simple Victorian furnishings. The cruck-truss roof construction may be viewed from the attic and there is a display of farm implements. A National Trust property.

Hilden Brewery Visitors Centre, *Lisburn* 106 B1
☎ 028 9266 3863
A working brewery with restaurant and visitor centre. The Tap Room is the only bar in Ireland to exclusively serve draft real ale.

Hill of Slane, *Meath* 114 B2
☎ 041 988 0305
This site is most famous for its 5th century legend. St Patrick lit a fire here at Easter, which was against the pagan law of the time, as the High King of Tara had decreed that no fire should be lit until the one on the Hill of Tara was ablaze. Luckily, St Patrick was able to convert the King to Christianity by daybreak. There are ruins of buildings from various dates here, including those of a 16th century church with a tower that can still be climbed; the views are magnificent.

Hill of Tara, *Meath* 114 B3
☎ 046 902 5903   www.heritageireland.ie
In the late stone age, a passage tomb was built here and later, an Iron age hill fort. It is best known, however, for being the seat of the legendary 'Kings of Ireland', reaching the height of its success with Cormac MacAirt in the third century. Its importance gradually declined with the coming of Christianity, although it was not finally abandoned until the 11th century. Excavations continue and there are guided tours and a visitor centre.

Hillsborough Castle, *Lisburn* 106 B2
☎ 028 9268 2244 / 1309
The official residence of the Secretary for State for Northern Ireland and formerly the home of the Governor of Northern Ireland. It was the venue of the signing of the 1985 Anglo-Irish Treaty by the UK and Irish Prime Ministers, Margaret Thatcher and Garret FitzGerald. Built in the 1770s by Wills Hill, first Marquess of Downshire, the mansion is set in impressive grounds with a rose garden and lakeside walks. The state drawing room, dining rooms and the Candlestick Hall are open to visitors. Hillsborough displays silver from H.M.S Nelson and has many items of Georgian furniture.

Hillsborough Fort, *Lisburn* 106 B2
☎ 028 9268 3285
Set in the Hillsborough Forest Park, the fort was completed in 1650 by Colonel Arthur Hill and substantially renovated in the 18th century. The 82m (270ft) square fort is surrounded by an earthen rampart with outer parapet wall. It was made a Royal Fort by Charles II after the restoration and William of Orange spent several nights at the Fort on his way to the Boyne in 1690. A lone bugler can be heard at 11am on Sundays.

Holy Cross Abbey, *North Tipperary* 124 B4
☎ 0504 43241
Founded in the 12th century by Donal Mor O'Brien. Picturesque and in a lovely setting, the abbey is named after the true cross believed to have been presented to the grandson of Brian Ború in AD1100.

Holy Trinity Cathedral, *Waterford* 163 B2
☎ 051 875166   www.waterford-cathedral.com
Ireland's oldest Catholic Cathedral built in 1793 and designed by John Roberts who also designed Christ Church Cathedral in Waterford. Recent renovations include a new floor in the 1990s, ornate chandeliers donated by Waterford Crystal and, in 1977, a new altar enabled mass to be taken facing the congregation.

Holy Trinity Heritage Centre, *Louth* 106 A4
☎ 042 937 3454
The Heritage Centre is located in the Church of the Holy Trinity. It was restored in 1804 and has recently been refurbished to house an exhibition, including video presentations, showing how the town has developed from Norman times.

Hook Lighthouse, *Wexford* 134 A4
☎ 051 397055　　　www.thehook-wexford.com
This 13th century lighthouse is one of the
oldest working examples in the world and was
opened to the public when it was fully
automated in 1996. 115 steps snake up the
two tiered 36.6m (120ft) high building, almost
all of which is original. The café and craft shop
are situated in the former keeper's house.

Hook Lighthouse　　　Photo © Fáilte Ireland

Hospital of St John the Baptist, *Meath* 114 B3
☎ 046 943 7111
The remains of a 13th century Augustine
Friary which was converted to a hospital in the
18th century.

Hugh Lane Gallery, *Dublin City* 147 B1
☎ 01 222 5550　　　www.hughlane.ie
19th and 20th century paintings, mainly
Impressionist works, bequeathed by Sir Hugh
Lane who was drowned in the Lusitania in
1915, form the nucleus of this collection. The
Lane Collection is split with the Tate Gallery in
London; each half is alternated between the
galleries every five years. The exhibition area
includes the London studio of Dublin-born
artist Francis Bacon, which was carefully
dismantled and reconstructed here.

Hunt Museum, *Limerick* 157 B1
☎ 061 312833　　　www.huntmuseum.com
Works of Irish and European art and
antiquities collected by John and Gertrude
Hunt housed in the elegant 18th century
custom house. There are paintings by Renoir,
Picasso, O'Connor and Yeats, the personal seal
of Charles I of England, the cross worn by
Mary, Queen of Scots on the day of her
execution, a coin revered since the Middle ages
as being one of the '30 pieces of silver' and a
bronze horse by Leonardo da Vinci.

Irish Linen Centre & Lisburn Museum　　Photo © Northern Ireland Tourist Board

Ilnacullin (Garinish Island), *Cork* 129 D3
☎ 027 63040　　　www.heritageireland.ie
The gardens were created in 1910 by the
owner Annan Bryce and the garden designer
Harold Peto. A particularly mild climate allows
plants from all around the world to flourish.
Included is an Italian Garden with ornamental
lily pool, a New Zealand fernery, a Japanese
rockery and a number of follies including a
clock tower and a Grecian temple. Access to
the island is by boat for which there is a
separate charge.

Inch Abbey, *Down* 107 C2
☎ 028 9054 6552　　　www.ehsni.gov.uk
Situated on an island in the River Quoile and
reached by a raised causeway, Inch Abbey is
the ruin of a Cistercian monastery founded by
John de Courcy in the 1180s. Some
earthworks survive from a church which pre-
dated the abbey.

Inchagoill Monastic Site, *Galway* 117 D2
☎ 091 552808
One of over 360 islands on Lough Corrib. Ruins
include St Patrick's Church, the 10th century
Saint's Church and an obelisk gravestone
which has the oldest Christian carved
inscription in Latin in Ireland. Mass is held on
the last Sunday in June and is attended by
hundreds of people who also take part in
'Agape' - traditional feasting after Mass. Boats
run from Oughterard and from Cong.

Inishowen Maritime Museum & Planetarium, *Donegal* 99 C1
☎ 074 938 1363　　　www.inishowenmaritime.com
Located in the old coastguard station beside
the harbour, the museum illustrates the
traditions of the community which has one of
the busiest fishing fleets in Ireland. The
planetarium traces the history of navigation
and visitors have the opportunity to view the
stars as they would have looked before the
birth of Christ and as they are today.

Ionad Cois Locha, *Donegal* 97 C3
☎ 074 953 1699　　　www.dunleweycentre.com
Situated beside Dunlewey Lake in a restored
farmhouse, this centre presents an insight into
life in this Irish speaking area in the 19th
century. There are demonstrations of
traditional crafts such as spinning, weaving
and carding and a programme of cultural
events and concerts. Boat trips, a farm
museum and a large variety of animals are
also amongst the attractions.

Irish Agricultural Museum, *Wexford* 135 C3
☎ 053 914 2888
The Museum is housed in the farm buildings
of Johnstown Castle and depicts all aspects of
Irish rural and agricultural life.
There is a permanent exhibition
telling the story of the potato
and of the Great Famine of
1845–47.

Irish Harp Centre, *Limerick* 123 D1
☎ 061 372777
www.irishharpcentre.com
Music school in a mid 19th
century listed School House in a
magnificent location on the
shores of the River Shannon.

Irish Linen Centre & Lisburn Museum, Lisburn 159 B2
☎ 028 9266 3377
Linen weaving workshop with working hand looms recreates one of Ulster's greatest industries; also an exhibition on how linen has been produced through the ages and a textile collection. Established in the town's 17th century Market House along with the Lisburn Museum which has a changing programme of local history and art exhibitions.

Irish Museum of Modern Art & Royal Hospital, Dublin City 146 A2
☎ 01 612 9900   www.modernart.ie
Opened in 1991 in the building and grounds of the 17th century Royal Hospital, the museum is an important institution for the collection of modern and contemporary art. A wide variety of work by major established 20th century figures and that of younger contemporary artists is presented in an ever changing programme of exhibitions, drawn from the museum's own collection and from public and private collections world-wide.

Irish National Heritage Park, Wexford 135 C2
☎ 053 9120733   www.inhp.com
This Park traces the social development of the Irish people from 7000BC to the Norman Conquest. It does this by means of full size reconstructions of homes, farmsteads, places of worship and burial grounds on this 14ha (35 acre) site of woodland, open fields and other appropriate environments. There is an audiovisual introduction to the site and in summer, there are demonstrations of tasks such as spinning and cookery .

Irish National Stud, Japanese Gardens & St Fiachra's Garden, Kildare 126 A1
☎ 045 521617 / 522963
www.irish-national-stud.ie
The 400ha (1000 acre) farm has been used as stud farm since the turn of the century. Guided tours run throughout the day and there is a museum and video showing the birth of a foal. The Japanese Gardens were completed in 1910 and symbolise the 'Life of Man' and are a realistic re-creation of the type of gardens being produced in Japan at that time. St Fiachra's Garden was created as a millennium project to celebrate the Irish

landscape in its most natural state and contains woods, wetlands, lakes and islands.

Irish World, Dungannon 105 D1
☎ 028 8774 6065   www.irish-world.com
The centre offers the facility to research family history with the aid of a large computerised database. There are also collections of photographs, documents, land registration ledgers, maps, name scrolls and coats of arms along with arts and crafts memorabilia and artefacts from local industries.

Isaac Butt Heritage Centre, Donegal 97 D3
☎ 074 913 1858
Isaac Butt (1813–1879), born in Cloghan, was a civil rights activist and regarded as founder of the Home Rule party. Exhibitions about his life and times are housed in the restored old school.

James Joyce Centre, Dublin City 147 B1
☎ 01 878 8547   www.jamesjoyce.ie
A museum in a restored Georgian town house, built in 1784, devoted to the great novelist and run by members of his family. The centre hosts readings, lectures and debates on all aspects of Joyce and his literature and conducts guided city tours.

James Joyce Tower & Museum, Dún Laoghaire-Rathdown 115 D4
☎ 01 280 9265
The museum is housed in the Martello Tower which Joyce used as the setting for the opening chapter of Ulysses, his great work of fiction which immortalised Dublin. Joyce stayed here briefly in 1904 and the living room and view from the gun platform remains much as he described it in the novel. The museum collection includes personal possessions, letters, photographs, first editions and items that reflect the Dublin of Joyce.

Jameson Heritage Centre, Cork 132 A4
☎ 021 461 3594   www.whiskeytours.ie
Contains the world's largest pot still with a capacity of 32,000 gallons and a working waterwheel dating from 1825. Guided tours start with an audiovisual presentation, continue through the production process of Irish Whiskey and culminates with a tasting session in the Jameson Bar.

St Fiachra's Garden at the Irish National Stud   Photo © Irish National Stud

Janus Stones, *Fermanagh* 103 D1
☎ 028 6632 3110
The two-faced Janus Stones are thought to be over 2000 years old and are located on the west side of Boa Island, which is easily accessible by car.

Jerpoint Abbey, *Kilkenny* 133 D1
☎ 056 772 4623   www.heritageireland.ie
A superb example of Cistercian monastic life, as many of the domestic areas are still recognisable. Founded in the late 12th century, it had its own gardens, kitchens, infirmary, watermills, granary and cemetery (which is still used today). The Irish-Romanesque transepts and chancel are the oldest parts, where faded wall paintings can still be seen. The central tower is a 15th century addition. The cloister piers have been restored and show carvings representative of drawings found in Medieval manuscripts.

Jerpoint Abbey

John F. Kennedy Arboretum, *Wexford* 134 A3
☎ 051 388171   www.heritageireland.ie
Dedicated to the memory of John Fitzgerald Kennedy, this arboretum covers 252ha (622 acres) and contains over 4500 species of trees and shrubs, all planted in botanical sequence. The many paths and nature trails lead to 200 forest plots grouped by continent and several picnic areas. There is a lake, miniature railway, visitor centre with audiovisual presentations and a tea room.

Johnstown Castle Gardens, *Wexford* 135 C3
☎ 053 914 2888
The impressive Gothic Revival Johnstown Castle itself is not open to the public but the 20ha (50 acres) of gardens are. They contain lakes, hot houses, woodland (which includes the ruins of Rathlannon Castle), a walled garden and masses of rhododendrons. The Museum is housed in the castle's farm buildings and depicts all aspects of Irish rural and agricultural life. There is a permanent exhibition telling the story of the potato and of the Great Famine of 1845–47.

Johnstown Castle   Photo © Fáilte Ireland

Jordan's Castle, *Down* 107 C3
☎ 028 9054 6552   www.ehsni.gov.uk
One of several tower house castles built around the port of Ardglass in the 15th century. The four storey ruin is well preserved and houses a local exhibition centre.

K Club, The, *Kildare* 114 B4
☎ 01 601 7300   www.kclub.ie
Opened in 1991, these Arnold Palmer designed courses feature water on most of the 36 holes. Hosts the European Open and was the venue for the 2006 Ryder Cup, the first time the tournament had been held in Ireland.

Kanturk Castle, *Cork* 122 B4
☎ 021 425 5100
An early 17th century four storey semi-fortified Tudor style mansion house. In generally good condition despite the fact that the castle is reputed to have never been roofed – there is little difference in the amount of decay inside and outside of the walls. The fireplaces have been removed and installed at the nearby Lohort Castle.

Kate Kearney's Cottage, *Kerry* 129 D1
☎ 064 44146   www.katekearneyscottage.com
Located at the entrance to the Gap of Dunloe, this cottage was the home of Kate Kearney who flouted the law by distilling her famous poitín, 'Kate Kearney's Mountain Dew', and invited weary travellers to partake of her hospitality. Nowadays a bar, restaurant, craft shop and traditional Irish nights greet visitors. Trips to the Gap of Dunloe can be taken from here on horseback or by pony and trap.

Kebble Nature Reserve, *Moyle* 100 A1
☎ 028 2076 3948   www.ehsni.gov.uk
Situated at the west of Rathlin Island where the cliffs rise more than 100m (328ft) above the rocky seashore, Kebble is renowned for breeding birds. Guillemots, razorbills, kittiwakes, fulmars, peregrine falcons, buzzards and ravens breed on the cliff ledges whilst puffins rear their chicks in burrows in cliff grassland. Breeding waterfowl are found on the lake and marshy areas of the heathland which stretches inland from the cliffs.

Kells Heritage Centre, *Meath* 114 A2
☎ 046 924 7840
A multi-media exhibition, gift shop and Tourist Information Office are housed in the restored courthouse. The monastic history of the town is examined and facsimile copies of The Book of Kells are on display. The original is housed in Trinity College, Dublin (see page 28).

Kells High Crosses, *Meath* 114 A2
☎ 041 988 0305
There are five crosses here, decorated with biblical scenes and regarded by many as the most important in Ireland. Apart from the Market Cross, at the crossroads of Castle Street and John Street, the rest are in the churchyard of St Columba. The oldest is 9th century (the South Cross), a 10th century cross (the West Cross) has the best decoration, the East Cross has incomplete carvings, known as 'the unfinished' cross and only the base remains from the North Cross.

Kells Priory, *Kilkenny* 125 D4
☎ 056 772 8255
In 1193 a priory was founded in Kells, for

Canons Regular of St Augustine from Bodmin in Cornwall. The impressive remains are divided into two courts by a branch of the river, in the northernmost of which are the remains of the church, with traces of medieval paving tiles, and the ruined claustral buildings. Substantial medieval fortified walls surround the site, with mostly complete 15th century dwelling towers.

Kenmare Heritage Centre, *Kerry* 129 D2
☎ 064 41233
Opened in 1994 and covering much of local interest including the history of the traditional lace making industry for which Kenmare is famous. The Kenmare Lace and Design Centre above the Heritage Centre gives an opportunity to see the lace being made.

Kenmare Stone Circle, *Kerry* 129 D2
☎ 064 41233
An unusual egg-shaped stone circle comprising 13 standing and two prostrate stones. At the centre is a dolmen with a capstone weighing about seven tons.

Kennedy Homestead, *Wexford* 134 A2
☎ 051 388264   www.kennedyhomestead.com
The birthplace of President John F. Kennedy's great-grandfather Patrick Kennedy. Still owned by Kennedy family descendants, the visitor centre looks at how the Great Famine caused the emigration of Patrick Kennedy to the United States setting in motion the chain of events which had such an impact on American politics.

Kerry Alternative Technology, *Kerry* 129 C2
☎ 064 45563   www.kerryat.com
A 16ha (40 acre) farm, home to ten permanent residents dedicated to reusable energy and green methods using wind & water turbines, solar panels and reed beds. There are vegetable gardens and a cold store for wine, fruit and vegetable storage dug into the side of the hill. Courses on all aspects of the green lifestyle are available.

Kerry Bog Village Museum, *Kerry* 129 C1
☎ 066 976 9184   www.kerrybogvillage.ie
A recreation of a 19th century village and turf cutting which is still used as domestic fuel. Thatched cottages, a blacksmith's forge with authentic tools, a hen house and vegetable garden are amongst the buildings on display. There are also Kerry Bog Ponies of which there were less than 50 by the mid 20th century. A breeding program is in place.

Kerry County Museum, *Kerry* 121 D4
☎ 066 712 7777   www.kerrymuseum.ie
Housed in the Ashe Memorial Hall, this museum includes displays, slides, models and audiovisuals showing the lifestyle of settlers through the ages. Includes 'Kerry in Colour', an audiovisual tour of the Kerry landscape stretching back 7000 years and 'Geraldine Tralee', a reconstruction of Tralee in the 1450s when the Geraldine family ruled Kerry.

Kerry Geopark, *Kerry* 129 C2
☎ 064 45700   www.sccird.com
Kerry Geopark is an area of great geological and archaeological interest towards the southwest of the Iveragh peninsula with a wide variety of flora and fauna. The heritage centre houses an information centre and gives an overview of the history of the area.

Kia Ora Mini Farm, *Wexford* 127 C4
☎ 053 942 1166
Unaffected by the weather as most of the animals are indoors. Animals include tropical birds, pheasants, deer, turkeys, mules, pigs, chipmunks, ducks and geese. There are tractor rides, a touch barn and play area with sand pits.

Kilbeggan Racecourse, *Westmeath* 113 C4
☎ 057 933 2176   www.kilbegganraces.com
Situated 1.6kms (1 mile) from Kilbeggan, National Hunt racing takes place here during the summer.

Kilclooney Dolmen, *Donegal* 96 B4
☎ 074 9721148
Two 1.8m (6ft) high uprights support a huge capstone measuring 4m x 6m (13ft x 20ft). Simple Neolithic pottery are the only finds from the site. A smaller, collapsed tomb is in the next field but were both once covered by a huge cairn which is in line with a standing stone 40m (130ft) away.

Kilcooley Abbey, *North Tipperary* 125 C4
☎ 062 61333
Kilcooley was founded by Donal O'Brien in the 12th century. It has a fine east window and many decorative carvings.

Kilfane Glen & Waterfall, *Kilkenny* 126 A4
☎ 056 772 4558
Listed as an Irish Heritage Garden, this is an excellent example of a romantic garden, dating from the late 18th century. At that time it was designed to provide 'VIPs' with a setting for tea parties and outings. There are winding woodland paths, seats, bridges, fountains, a grotto, and a thatched summerhouse (cottage orne). The beautiful 9m (30 ft) waterfall was created by diverting a stream to a rock face. In the upper garden are commissioned works of art.

Kilfane Glen & Waterfall   Photo © Fáilte Ireland

Kilkee Waterworld, *Clare* 121 D1
☎ 065 905 6855   www.kilkeewaterworld.com
A modern leisure pool with crystal tower slide, water jets, bubble pool, sauna and baby pool.

Kilkenny Castle, *Kilkenny* 125 D4
☎ 056 772 1450   www.heritageireland.ie
A wooden tower was built on this site by Richard de Clare in 1172, followed by a stone castle constructed twenty years later by his son-in-law. In the late 14th century, the castle was bought by the powerful Butler family, the Earls of Ormonde, who lived there until 1935.

Killarney National Park

The Butlers restored it after damage in the mid 17th century and it was significantly rebuilt by the Victorians in the early 19th century. Bought by the state in 1967 for £50, it now includes a Long Gallery which has brightly painted ceilings and portraits of the Butler family, a library, drawing room and bedrooms. The Butler Gallery hosts art exhibitions and the old kitchens now serve teas in summer.

Killaloe Heritage Centre, *Clare* 123 D1
☎ 061 376866
www.shannonheritage.com/Killaloe.htm
Sited on a bridge on the Shannon, water plays an important part of the Centre's displays as does Brian Ború, High King of Ireland, who was born here in AD940.

Killarney Cathedral, *Kerry* 154 A2
☎ 064 31023
St Mary's Cathedral was designed by the famous architect Welby Pugin who died before it could be completed. It was built in the Gothic Lancet arched style with long slender windows and pointed arches and a spire 85m (280ft) high. Work ceased during the Great Famine when it was used as a hospital and shelter. It was finally completed in 1912.

Killarney National Park, *Kerry* 129 D1
☎ 064 31440   www.heritageireland.ie
The National Park covers an area of over 10,000ha (24,700 acres) most of which is given over to the beautiful three lakes of Killarney. The Visitor Centre at Muckross House gives information on the flora and wildlife in the Park, including Killarney Fern, Strawberry Tree, Northern Emerald Dragonfly and a flock of Greenland Whitefronted Geese which reside in the bogs over the winter months. There is also an information point at the 18m (60ft) high Torc Waterfall. Ladies View is a viewpoint on the N71 near Upper Lake so named because of the pleasure it gave to Queen Victoria's ladies-in-waiting in 1861. The Gap of Dunloe is a spectacular mountain pass just to the west of the National Park.

Killarney Racecourse, *Kerry* 129 D1
☎ 064 31125   www.air.ie
National Hunt and Flat racing course with seven race days a year.

Killeter Forest, *Strabane* 97 D4
☎ 028 8224 7831   www.ehsni.gov.uk
An extensive area of conifer forest with hill loughs and expanses of blanket bogland in the upper Derg valley. Grouse, skylarks and curlew are native birds while Greenland white fronted geese are seen flying overhead in winter; the bogs support a rich variety of specialised plants including sphagnum mosses and bog cotton.

Killruddery House & Gardens, *Wicklow* 127 D1
☎ 01 286 3405   www.killruddery.com
This early 17th century house was remodelled in the 1820s and reduced in size in the 1950s to its current proportions. It is one of the earliest Elizabethan-Revival mansions in Ireland, and is still home to the Earls of Meath. The statue gallery contains a collection of mid 19th century Italian statuary. The gardens are the oldest in Ireland and are still largely in their original 17th century style. There are a pair of canals, 170m (550 ft) long with the house at one end and an avenue of lime trees at the other. To the left of the canals are radiating walks (The Angles) flanked by hedges of beech, hornbeam and lime. On the other side is the only known Sylvan Theatre in Ireland, with terraced banks and a high bay hedge. Finally, there is an 18m (60ft) diameter pond with a French style fountain in the centre.

Kilmacduagh Monastic Site   Photo © Ireland West

Killykeen Forest Park, *Cavan* 104 A4
☎ 049 433 2541 www.coillte.ie
The park comprises 240ha (593 acres)of mixed woodland rich in wildlife at the south end of Lough Oughter, the lough forming part of a labyrinth of waterways known as the Erne River system. Lough Oughter and Killykeen are renowned for coarse angling and the forest park also has walking and cycle trails and facilities for watersports.

Kilmacduagh Monastic Site, *Galway* 119 C3
☎ 091 631436
The remains of a monastic settlement founded in the early 7th century by St Colman with a notable 10th or 11th century round tower 33m (111ft) high which leans almost 50cm (19.5 inches) from the perpendicular. The site has extensive remains of several churches and of a small cathedral which contains two finely carved crosses. In addition, there is a two storey 13th century building known as Glebe House, thought to be the abbot's house.

Kilmacurragh Arboretum, *Wicklow* 127 C2
☎ 01 647 3000
This arboretum was planted by curators of the National Botanic Gardens in Glasnevin, in the 19th century. The soil and climate at Kilmacurragh was very favourable for many of the less hardy conifers from around the World for which this garden is famous.

Kilmainham Gaol, *Dublin City* 115 C4
☎ 01 453 5984 www.heritageireland.ie
After its closure in 1924 Kilmainham re-opened in 1966 as a museum dedicated to the Irish patriots imprisoned there from 1792–1924. Two of the leaders of the 1916 Rising, Patrick Pearse and James Connolly, were executed in the prison yard and Eamon de Valera, later Prime Minister and then President of Ireland, was one of the last inmates. It is one of the largest unoccupied gaols in Europe with tiers of cells and overhead catwalks. Access is by guided tour only and features an exhibition and audiovisual show.

Kilmallock Museum & History Trail, *Limerick* 123 D3
☎ 063 91300
A small museum collection reflecting life in the area in the 19th century and 20th century, including aspects of industry and farming. There are also scale models of prehistoric houses excavated in the area and a large model of medieval Kilmallock. The self guiding history trail comprises thirteen points of interest in Kilmallock which are marked by information plaques. The town has retained many of its historic buildings including the early 13th century Collegiate Church and Dominican Friary, and one of the remaining 16th century town gates.

Kilmokea House & Gardens, *Wexford* 134 A3
☎ 051 388109 www.kilmokea.com
Many rare and tender trees and shrubs grow in these 2.8ha (7 acres) of frost free gardens. Divided into two parts, a formal walled garden and a woodland garden, there are features such as an Italian loggia and pool, topiary, herbaceous borders and woodland walks with a lake, rhododendrons, magnolias and the giant borage.

Kilrush Heritage Centre, *Clare* 122 A2
☎ 065 905 1047 / 1577
The effects of the Great Famine and the evictions of 1888 are examined along with the history of the area.

Kiltartan Gregory Museum, *Galway* 119 C3
☎ 091 632346
www.gortonline.com/gregorymuseum
Containing rare manuscripts, first editions, photographs and memorabilia relating to dramatist Lady Augusta Gregory of Coole Park and the Irish Literary Revival, the museum is housed in a former schoolhouse built by the Gregory family in 1892. The second of the two rooms has been recreated as an early 20th century schoolroom with desks, blackboard, maps, paintings and charts.

Kiltartan Gregory Museum Photo © Ireland West

Kiltimagh Town Museum, *Mayo* 110 B3
☎ 094 938 1132
Located in the restored old railway station office and two railway carriages dating back to 1894, the museum has a collection of many interesting artefacts which illustrate the history and folklore of the area. The old station master's house is now an art exhibition centre displaying national and international artists, while the whole of the restored station complex is set within a sculpture park.

King House, *Roscommon* 103 C4
☎ 071 966 3242 www.kinghouse.ie
Built around 1730 for Sir Henry King, the house is a splendid Georgian mansion which has been beautifully restored and overlooks the River Boyle. Between 1788 and 1922 King House became a military barracks for the Connaught Rangers, a British army regiment, and more recently has housed the Irish army. Lively interactive exhibitions using life size models and special effects tell the story of the house and those who lived in it and give impressions of the town and surrounding area from the time of the Kingdom of Connaught.

King House Photo © Ireland West

King John's Castle, *Limerick* 157 B1
☎ 061 360788
www.shannonheritage.com/KJC.htm

In the old town of Limerick on an island formed by the River Shannon and the River Abbey, the 13th century castle is a fine example of Norman fortified architecture. An exhibition tells of the origin and development of the city and the castle's role in Limerick's dramatic history; life sized wooden sculptures represent the people who inhabited the castle at various times in its history. Costumed animators illustrate the life and trades of 13th century Limerick and there is a display of battering rams and catapults.

King John's Castle, *Louth* 106 A4
☎ 042 933 5484

The castle remains date back to the late 12th century, are strategically located to command the quay. Overlooking Carlingford Lough it played host to King John who stayed here on his way to attack Hugh de Lacy, at Carrickfergus. It has an unusual D-shape while the west gateway was designed to allow the entry of only one horseman at a time. The remains of an earlier castle include the southwest tower and the west wall.

Kinturk Cultural Centre, *Cookstown* 105 D1
☎ 028 8673 6512

The centre tells the story of the fishermen of Lough Neagh and the eel industry with displays of traditional boats and equipment and an audiovisual show. There are boat trips and walks from the centre, situated on the west side of Lough Neagh.

Kirkistown Race Circuit, *Ards* 107 D2
☎ 028 4277 1325   www.kirkistowncircuit.com

This 2.5km (1.6 mile) track hosts a variety of motorsport including car, rallycross, motorcycle and kart racing and is the only RAC approved circuit in Northern Ireland. Built on an old wartime airfield, it was opened in 1951 by the 500 Motor Racing Club of Ireland.

Knappogue Castle, *Clare* 123 C1
☎ 061 360788
www.shannonheritage.com/Knappogue_Day.htm

The central tower was originally built by the MacNamaras in 1467 and has been added to over the years, mainly in a neo-Gothic style. The grounds are in the process of being restored.

Knock Basilica & Shrine   Photo © Mayo Naturally

Knock Basilica & Shrine, *Mayo* 110 B3
☎ 094 938 8100   www.knock-shrine.ie

One of the great Marian shrines of the world, Our Lady's Shrine at Knock attracts over 1.5 million visitors each year. An apparition of the Virgin Mary, St Joseph and St John on 21 August 1879 was witnessed by 15 local people on the south gable of the parish church of St John the Baptist. Ever since, Knock has been a place of pilgrimage. The focal point of the shrine is the gable of the apparition and the shrine Oratory. Nearby is the Basilica of Our Lady built in 1976 to accommodate the flow of pilgrims. It is the largest church in Ireland with room for up to 20,000 people. Pope John Paul II visited Knock on his tour of Ireland in September 1979.

Knock Folk Museum, *Mayo* 110 B3
☎ 094 938 8100

In addition to the 1879 Apparition, the museum and also depicts the customs and lifestyle of people in rural Ireland at the time and in the century following. Displays include fishing, farming, crafts, education, housing and clothing. The museum also has a section about Monsignor James Horan, the parish priest responsible for the building of the Basilica at Knock and who initiated the invitation to Pope John Paul II to visit Ireland. Horan's dogged determination was also responsible for the construction of Knock airport.

Knockabbey Castle & Gardens, *Louth* 114 B1
☎ 01 677 8816   www.knockabbeycastle.com

Originally built in 1399 when it comprised just the tower house, which now houses the interpretative centre. It was taken from Roger Bellew by King William III after the Battle of the Boyne in 1690 as punishment for the support he gave to the deposed Catholic King James II. The 12ha (30 acre) grounds include a fern house, herbaceous border, Victorian flower gardens and some of the finest water gardens in Ireland, which have their origins in the 11th century. There is also a rare 17th century Tulip tree.

Knockmany Passage Grave, *Dungannon* 104 B2
☎ 028 6632 3110

These 1-2m (3-6ft) high stones are now enclosed in cairn to protect the remarkable carvings of unknown date but are probably Neolithic or Bronze Age. There is a pleasant walk leading from the lower car park, passing a lake, through a forest and up the hill to the tomb. The stones can be seen but if closer inspection is required the Department of the Environment should be contacted in advance.

Kylemore Abbey & Garden, *Galway* 116 B2
☎ 095 41146 / 41437   www.kylemoreabbey.com

Built in 1868 by a wealthy Manchester merchant, the neo Gothic house is now a monastic home and international school for girls in a picturesque lakeside setting at the foot of Duchruach Mountain. Kylemore has a restored Gothic church and a Victorian garden of more than 2ha (5 acres) surrounded by a wall 800m (1600ft) long. The garden features the original formal flower garden and kitchen garden and a vast complex of Victorian glasshouses which were used to grow exotic plants and fruit.

Lackagh Museum & Heritage Park, *Galway* 119 C2
☎ 091 797444

A restored 19th century traditional Irish thatched cottage with open hearth and an

Kylemore Abbey   Photo © Ireland West

open dresser displaying crockery, reflecting a way of life which has almost gone. Rural artefacts on display include a spinning wheel and butter churns. Outside the cottage there is an impressive display of farm machinery.

Lagan Lookout Centre, *Belfast* 139 B1
☎ 028 9031 5444   www.laganside.com
Multimedia and audiovisual displays explain the history of the £14m weir and the industrial and cultural history of Belfast.

Lahinch Seaworld, *Clare* 118 A4
☎ 065 708 1900   www.iol.ie/~seaworld
The aquarium uncovers the diversity of life at the Clare coastline and of the Atlantic Ocean. Features a 'blow hole' as found in Doolin, a magnificent section of the rugged Clare coastline.

Larchill Arcadian Gardens, *Kildare* 114 B3
☎ 01 628 7354   www.larchill.ie
This mid 18th century garden is unique in being the only surviving example of an Arcadian (ornamental farm) garden in Ireland or Europe. In the 26ha (64 acres) of parkland there are 10 follies situated around a 40 minute circular walk. There are also gazebos and a walled garden plus a 3ha (7.4 acres) lake with a Greek temple. The parkland is stocked with the largest number of rare breeds in Ireland.

Layde Church, *Moyle* 100 B2
☎ 028 2076 2024
These ruins sit in a quiet valley and date from around 1638 though the site may have existed in the early days of Christianity. There are two high crosses, the older being unusual as it has a hole in its head. At the entrance to the graveyard are buried the bodies of two young lovers who took their own lives after she became pregnant..

Laytown Racecourse, *Meath* 115 C2
☎ 041 984 2111
An annual three day meeting on the 5km (3 mile) strand at Laytown is the only event of its kind in Europe which is governed by the rules

of racing. The strand is closed from early morning on race day and by the time the first race is ready to start the tide has gone out, and racing can begin. The grandstand steps are cut into the sand dunes. The event has had changed little since it began in 1876.

Leap Castle, *Offaly* 124 B2
☎ 057 913 1115   www.leapcastle.com
Built in 1250 by the Princes of Ely, the O'Carrolls, to guard the pass from the Slieve Bloom mountains to Munster, this is supposedly the most haunted castle in Ireland. It harbours a ghost with an obnoxious smell! During the civil unrest of 1922 it was badly burnt but the remains are still standing.

Leenane Sheep & Wool Centre, *Galway* 117 C1
☎ 095 42323   www.sheepandwoolcentre.com
An interpretative centre tracing the history of sheep and illustrating the importance of wool in north Connemara and in Ireland. Several breeds of sheep, some of them ancient western European breeds, can be seen grazing at the centre and, as well as a display of artefacts, there are demonstrations of carding, spinning, weaving, felting and dyeing with natural dyes. Local places of interest and history are featured on an audiovisual display.

Leenane Sheep & Wool Centre   Photo © Ireland West

Lismore Castle Gardens

Leisureland, Donegal 98 B2
☎ 074 938 2306   www.leisurelandredcastle.ie
An indoor heated fun park with attractions including pirate boat rides, remote control boats, safari train, dodgems, small cars, mega trucks, ball pool, shooting gallery and pool tables.

Leopardstown Racecourse, Dún Laoghaire-Rathdown 115 D4
☎ 01 289 0500   www.leopardstown.com
One of the top European racetracks, Leopardstown is 10kms (6 miles) from Dublin. It hosts 22 race meetings per year of both Flat and National Hunt Racing.

Leslie Hill Open Farm & Gardens, Ballymoney 99 D2
☎ 028 2766 6803   www.lesliehillopenfarm.co.uk
18th century landscaped estate with walled garden and lakes; nature trails and horse-trap rides through the grounds. Working farm and blacksmith's forge along with farm animals, poultry and pets.

Limerick City Gallery of Art, Limerick 157 B3
☎ 061 310633   www.limerickcity.ie/LCGA
Features a permanent collection of works of art by acclaimed Irish artists from the 18th, 19th and 20th centuries and an extensive programme of temporary exhibitions.

Limerick City Museum, Limerick 157 B1
☎ 061 417826
Adjacent to King John's Castle, the award winning museum presents Limerick's long and varied history. The collection includes artefacts from prehistoric and medieval times including currency circulating at the time of the Vikings. Among the museum's treasures are the city charters of Charles I and the Civic Sword and City Maces. There are displays of local crafts, notably Limerick lace, and exhibits relating to trades history.

Limerick Racecourse, Limerick 123 C2
☎ 061 320000   www.limerick-racecourse.com
A 2km (1.25 mile) National Hunt and Flat racing course which opened in 2001, 9kms (6 miles) SW of Limerick City.

Linen Hall Library, Belfast 139 B2
☎ 028 9032 1707   www.linenhall.com
Belfast's oldest library and Ireland's last subscription library, founded in 1788 and is the leading centre for Irish and local studies in Northern Ireland. Specialising in Irish culture and politics, the library also has a unique collection of Belfast and Ulster early printed books. The Northern Ireland Political Collection is the definitive archive of the Troubles. The reference service is free and open to the general public.

Linen Mill Museum, Mayo 109 C4
☎ 098 25411
The Westport textile industry grew up in the 18th century and this museum tells the story through a collection of photographs, books and displays connected with all aspects of the industry.

Liscarroll Castle, Cork 123 C4
☎ 021 425 5100
Built at the end of the 13th century, the ruins include a large Keep with four huge towers at each corner, a heavily fortified main gate and a strong curtain wall.

Lismore Castle Gardens, Waterford 132 B3
☎ 058 54424   www.lismorecastle.com
Situated above the River Blackwater, the castle was built in the 19th century by Joseph Paxton, architect of the Crystal Palace in London, for the 6th Duke of Devonshire, incorporating the remains of the medieval castle erected by Prince John of England in 1185. The castle is partially surrounded by delightful walled gardens, with areas of woodland, shrubberies, and a yew walk. In early spring the gardens are at their best when the camellias and magnolias are in flower. The Elizabethan poet Edmund Spencer is said to have composed part of the Faerie Queene in the grounds. Lismore is still the Irish home of the Duke of Devonshire and the castle itself is not open to the public.

Lismore Heritage Centre, Waterford 132 B3
☎ 058 54975   www.discoverlismore.com
Housed in the former courthouse, the heritage centre traces the history of Lismore from its foundation in 636. An multimedia presentation takes up the themes of monastic Lismore, the Vikings, the Normans, Walter Raleigh, and Lismore Castle, Cathedral and Church.

Lissadell House, Sligo 102 B2
☎ 071 916 3150   www.lissadellhouse.com
Situated in conifer covered parkland overlooking Drumcliffe Bay, Lissadell House was built in Classical style in the 1830s for the

patriotic Gore-Booth family. The Arctic explorer Sir Henry Gore-Booth was born here, as were his daughters Eva and Constance, who became the first female member of the British House of Commons, but who chose to sit instead in the revolutionary Dail Eireann. Constance was condemned to death for her part in the 1916 Easter Rising.

Lisselan Gardens, *Cork* 130 B3
☎ 023 33249 www.lisselan.com
Laid out in the valley of the Argideen River in the 1850s, the 12ha (30 acre) gardens include an azalea garden, water and rock gardens, shrubbery and orchard and woodland walks. Gum Trees, Handkerchief Trees and Japanese Maples are amongst the wide variety of species from all over the world.

Listowel Racecourse, *Kerry* 121 D3
☎ 068 21144 www.listowelraces.ie
A rectangular National Hunt and Flat racing course with nine race days a year.

Locke's Distillery Museum, *Westmeath* 113 C4
☎ 057 933 2134
www.lockesdistillerymuseum.com
The original distillery closed in 1957, after 200 years of production. In 1982 restoration of the buildings commenced, and they now house the last working example of a small pot still distillery in Ireland. The whole process of making the whiskey can be seen and working conditions in the 19th century appreciated. At the end of the tour, there is a complimentary tasting of the product and home made food can be sampled in the restaurant.

Lodge Park Walled Garden & Steam Museum, *Kildare* 114 B4
☎ 01 627 3155 www.steam-museum.ie
A restored 18th century walled garden featuring a superb south facing shrub and perennial border edged with clipped box and topiaried yews running the length of the garden. The orchard is entered through a beautiful rosarie. The steam museum houses engines used in the brewing and distilling industry as well as models of steam locomotives used in the 19th century.

Lory Meagher Heritage Centre, *Kilkenny* 125 C4
☎ 056 776 9202
This is the home of the Kilkenny Gaelic Athletic Association (GAA) Museum. The two storey 17th century thatched mansion was the home of the 1920s hurling hero, Lory Meagher. It has been beautifully restored and shows the lifestyle of a well-to-do Irish farming family of the time. The museum is housed in an adjoining restored stone building and contains all kinds of hurling mementos, trophies, reports and a section for clubs.

Lough Gur Visitor Centre, *Limerick* 123 D2
☎ 061 360788
Archaeological excavation and survey has shown this to be the most important Stone age site in Ireland, with evidence of Neolithic farming, dwellings and ritual and burial sites dating back 5000 years. The lough side visitor centre in a re-constructed Neolithic house has an audiovisual show illustrating the site's history and there are many artefacts on display. Walking tours cover many of the archaeological features of the site.

Lough Key Forest Park, *Roscommon* 103 C4
☎ 071 966 2363
Lough Key is a beautiful lough with several wooded islands and is linked to the Shannon River system. Formerly part of the Rockingham estate and comprising 350ha (864 acres) of mixed woodland and open parkland, the forest park has a wide range of habitats which encourages a diversity of wildlife. Numerous features of archaeological and historical interest are found within the park including an observation tower built on the site of Rockingham House which was destroyed by fire, an icehouse, and underground tunnels used by servants.

Lough-na-Crannagh, *Moyle* 100 A1
☎ 028 2076 2024
A remarkably well-preserved crannóg (lake dwelling) likely to date from around AD600. The circular stone walls are 30m x 26m (100ft x 85ft) in diameter and rise 1–1.5m (3–4ft) above the lake surface. It is likely to have been built with a view to being easy to defend.

Lough Navar Forest, *Fermanagh* 103 D2
☎ 028 6634 3032 www.forestserviceni.gov.uk
Red deer and wild goats inhabit Lough Navar Forest, through which there is an 11km (7 mile) scenic drive to a spectacular viewpoint over Lower Lough Erne, Donegal Bay and the Sperrin Mountains and several way-marked walking trails. The forest is managed to enhance the landscape and for the benefit of wildlife by planting more broadleaved trees such as oak, beech and birch amongst the conifers and by clear felling other areas. Several small loughs and rocky crags are also a feature of the forest scenery.

Lough Neagh Discovery Centre, *Craigavon* 106 A1
☎ 028 3832 2205 www.oxfordisland.com
Set within the Oxford Island National Nature Reserve, the centre has an award winning interactive exhibition which illustrates the wildlife, management and history of Lough Neagh. A programme of events takes place throughout the year including guided nature walks, pond-dipping and bird watching.

Lough Neagh Discovery Centre Photo © Northern Ireland Tourist Board

Lough Rynn Castle Estate, *Leitrim* 112 B1
☎ 071 963 2700 www.loughrynn.ie
Set on the shores of Lough Rynn, the estate dates back to 1859 and includes nature trails and woodland walks. A turreted summerhouse affords beautiful views over Lough Rynn. Lough Rynn house, built in 1832, was the former home of the Earls of Leitrim, the Clement's family. A Nick Faldo designed championship course is a recent addition to the estate.

Loughcrew Cairns, *Meath* 113 D2
☎ 049 854 2009
www.knowth.com/loughcrew.htm
There are many cairns on the hills in this area, known as the Hills of the Witch. The main concentrations are on three peaks, Cairnbane, Sliabh na Cailli and Patrickstown and comprise of Neolithic passage tombs about 5000 years old. One of the largest is Cairn T on Cairnbane, which contains a cruciform chamber and some wonderful Neolithic art.

Loughcrew Gardens, *Meath* 113 D2
☎ 049 854 1922   www.loughcrew.com
Started in 1660, the Naper family have continuously developed these gardens whilst retaining their historical setting. They include a medieval motte and St Oliver Plunkett's Family Church and Tower House; from the 17th century, there is a magnificent yew walk. The gardens have been carefully redeveloped in the 19th and 20th centuries to include rockeries, follies, watergardens, woodland walks, watermill, vistas with hidden fairies, giant bugs and spiders in trees!

Louth County Museum, *Louth* 106 A4
☎ 042 932 7056
The role of the County Museum is to show the social, natural and archaeological history of the County from prehistoric times to today. It achieves this through a series of changing exhibitions using local artefacts, models and interactive displays. The ground floor houses the only permanent display showing the industrial and agricultural history of Louth. This beautifully restored 18th century warehouse also has a 72 seat theatre. There are many artistic events, lectures and workshops throughout the year.

Lullymore Heritage & Discovery Park, *Kildare* 114 A4
☎ 045 870238   www.lullymorepark.com
Designed to tell the story of the Irish people and boglands, this heritage park is located on a mineral island in the Bog of Allen, the largest bogland in Ireland. There is a reconstruction of a neolithic farmstead, a replica of Newgrange and visitor centre. Other features include theme gardens, a fairy bower, exhibitions of the 1798 rebellion and the Famine, an adventure park, crazy golf, tea rooms and a craft/souvenir shop.

Lusitania Memorial, *Cork* 131 D3
☎ 021 477 2234   www.lusitania.net
The RMS Lusitania was struck and sunk by German torpedoes 22kms (14 miles) off the Old Head of Kinsale in 1915 which was an important factor in bringing America into the war as 128 of those who died were Americans. 1,201 of the 1,965 on board lost their lives in the disaster and there are memorials on the Old Head of Kinsale and also in Cobh where many of the dead and survivors were taken.

Lusitania Memorial, Cobh

Lusk Heritage Centre, *Fingal* 115 D3
☎ 01 647 2461   www.heritageireland.ie
This centre comprises a church built in the 19th century, with an older round tower and a medieval belfry. An exhibition about medieval churches in North County Dublin is housed in the belfry, along with the 16th century effigy tomb of Sir Christopher Barnewall and Marion Sharl, his wife.

Maebh's Cairn, *Sligo* 101 D3
☎ 071 916 1201
Legend has it that the remains of Maebh, warrior queen of Connaught, are buried in this cairn which is around 6000 years old. It consists of a passage and several chambers and is 11m (35ft) high and 61m (200ft) across. She is famous for the 'Cattle Raid of Cooley' in which she took by force, the Brown Bull belonging to the Daire of Cooley in the province of Ulster.

Maghera Caves, *Donegal* 96 B4
☎ 074 972 1148   www.magherabeach.com
Several sea caves accessible at low tide by a short walk across the wide, sandy Maghera Beach.

Maghery Country Park, *Craigavon* 105 D1
☎ 028 3832 2205   www.oxfordisland.com
A place for birdwatching and woodland nature walks on the shores of Lough Neagh. Fishing is also popular at Maghery canal. Coney Island lies 1km (0.6 mile) offshore and is the only inhabited island in Lough Neagh; boat trips to the island are sometimes available from the park.

Malahide Castle, *Fingal* 115 D3
☎ 01 846 2184   www.malahidecastle.com
Originally built in 1185, Malahide Castle was the seat of the Talbot family until 1973 when the last Lord Talbot died; the history of the family is detailed in the Great Hall alongside many family portraits. Malahide also has a large collection of Irish portrait paintings, mainly from the National Gallery, and is furnished with fine period furniture. Within the 100ha (250 acres) of parkland surrounding the castle is the Talbot Botanic Gardens, largely created by Lord Milo Talbot between 1948 and 1973.

Mannan Castle, *Monaghan* 105 D4
☎ 047 81122
The stone ruins of the castle are situated on a motte and inner bailey with causeway. It is situated on a south facing slope with wonderful panoramic views of the Carrickmacross countryside.

Marble Arch Caves, *Fermanagh* 103 D3
☎ 028 6634 8855   www.marblearchcaves.net
This system of caves with rivers, waterfalls, winding passageways and huge chambers has been formed by the action of three streams on a bed of limestone on Mount Cuilcagh. Underground they converge to form a single river, the Cladagh, which flows via the 9m (30ft) limestone Marble Arch into Lough Macnean. The tour of these spectacular show caves includes a boat ride and the presentation of an array of illuminated and named rock formations including stalactites and stalagmites. There is also an exhibition area and audio-visual theatre.

Maynooth Castle, *Kildare* 114 B4
☎ 01 628 6744

Built in 1175, the home of the Earls of Kildare, much of the original building still stands, including the keep which is one of the largest of its type in Ireland. In the 15th century it was the stronghold of the Great Earl of Kildare, Garret Mór Fitzgerald. It had fallen into disrepair by the early 17th century but was renovated by the Earl of Cork. The ruined keep and gatehouse survive which forms an impressive entrance to Maynooth College, founded in the late 18th century.

Mayo North Family Heritage Centre, *Mayo* 109 D3
☎ 096 31809   www.mayo.irishroots.net

Located in the grounds of Enniscoe Estate near Crossmolina, the centre offers assistance to those wishing to trace their Mayo ancestry and, with the aim of developing the skills of traditional crafts, the heritage centre also provides forge and craft training. Historic local agricultural tools and household artefacts are on display in the heritage museum and forge.

Meeting of the Waters, *Wicklow* 127 C2
☎ 0404 69117

The Rivers Avonmore and Avonbeg meet about 4km (2.5 miles) north of the village of Avoca to form the River Avoca. At this meeting point, the poet Thomas Moore is said to have sat on the root of a tree in the form of a 'rustic' seat and written the words to the Irish melody Sweet Vale of Avoca.

Mellifont Abbey, *Louth* 115 C2
☎ 041 982 6103   www.mellifontabbey.ie

Mellifont was Ireland's first Cistercian abbey. Founded in 1140 by the King of Uriel, at the instigation of St Malachy, who had been inspired by St Bernard's work at Clairvaux, the abbey became the home of the Moore family after its suppression in 1539. Though scattered, the remains are of great interest and include portions of the Romanesque cloister arcade, the 13th century chapter house extension, and the octagonal washroom.

Metal Man Tower, *Waterford* 133 D3
☎ 051 381572

A large cast-metal figure sitting on top of one of three huge pillars erected in 1823 to warn boats of dangerous shallow waters. Local folklore says that if a woman hops bare-footed three times around the centre pillar, she will be married within the year.

Michael Collins Centre, *Cork* 131 C3
☎ 023 46107   www.michaelcollinscentre.com

The only centre in Ireland dedicated to the life and times of the famous leader using video, displays and a guided tour of an exhibition of memorabilia. There are also tours by appointment around the area to places closely associated with Michael Collins including his birthplace at Woodfield and the monument at Béal na mBláth where he died in an ambush.

Michael Davitt Museum, *Mayo* 110 B3
☎ 090 903 1022

The museum contains an extensive collection of documents, Land Acts, photographs and memorabilia relating to Michael Davitt (1846–1906) who was founder of the Land League, a mass movement which was to bring about land reform for Irish tenant farmers. He was also a Member of Parliament for South Mayo, author and journalist and a founding patron of the Gaelic Athletic Association (GAA). Davitt's grave is in the grounds of nearby Straide Abbey.

Millmount Museum, *Louth* 115 C2
☎ 041 983 3097 / 6391   www.millmount.net

The museum is housed in a former military complex, built in the early 19th century. The main attraction here is an exhibition of trade banners painted in the 1700s to mid 1800s; those depicting the broguemakers, carpenters and weavers are the only Guild banners left in Ireland. Other historical artefacts from the area are also on display here. The Martello Tower was built by the British army in the 18th century, as a defence in the Napoleonic wars. It was damaged in the Irish Civil War in 1922 but has been restored to house a military museum.

Millstreet Country Park, *Cork* 130 B1
☎ 029 70810   www.millstreetcountrypark.com

A 200ha (500 acre) park which includes a visitor centre, themed gardens containing rare shrubs, flowers, bogland and an ornamental lake. Wildlife includes red deer, stoats, otters and brown trout. Of archaeological interest are a 4 – 5000 year old stone circle and a Fullacht Fiadh – a bronze age cooking site.

Mitchelstown Cave, *South Tipperary* 132 A2
☎ 052 67246

A 1km tour through the cave system takes in spectacular stalagtites, stalagmites and calcite columns. The Earl of Desmond hid from the English in 1601 in the old cave, which is not open to the public, and it was not until 1833 that the current caves were discovered.

Mizen Head Signal Station (*see page 66*)

Photo © Fáilte Ireland

Mizen Head Signal Station, *Cork* 129 C4
☎ 028 35115 / 35225　　　www.mizenhead.ie
Ireland's most south westerly point, the visitor centre is linked to the offshore island on which the lighthouse is situated by 99 steps and a spectacular arched bridge. The lighthouse keeper's house has been converted to contain an audiovisual display, maps and archives, the Fastnet Lighthouse room and a room dedicated to the underwater life and the dozens of wrecks lying around the Mizen.

Model Arts & Niland Gallery, *Sligo* 102 B3
☎ 071 914 1405　　　www.modelart.ie
Housed in a renovated 100 year old model school, the Niland Art Collection includes works by John and Jack B. Yeats, Estella Solomons, Paul Henry and Louis le Broquy. There is also a cinema and performances of jazz, contemporary, classical and traditional music.

Monaghan County Museum, *Monaghan* 105 C3
☎ 047 82928　　　www.monaghan.ie/museum
With archaeology, folklife, craft, transport, coin and industrial collections, this award winning museum displays the history of Monaghan since earliest times. The unique 14th century Cross of Clogher is one of the treasures of the museum and there is a fine collection of artefacts from early medieval crannog settlements.

Monaincha Abbey, *North Tipperary* 124 B2
☎ 057 912 0110
Once on an island in a lake, the abbey has a richly decorated Romanesque west doorway and chancel arch and also a high cross. It was an important place of pilgrimage in the Middle Ages. The lake was drained in the 19th century but the land on which the abbey stands is still known as Holy Island.

Monasterboice, *Louth* 115 C1
☎ 041 982 2813
Just north of Drogheda is the early 6th century ruin of Monasterboice (meaning 'Buite's monastery'). Although a small site, there is a Round Tower in excellent condition and two of the finest 10th century High Crosses in Ireland. The Cross of Muirdach is 5.2m (17ft) high and although not the tallest, the carvings on it are remarkably clear.

Monasterboice　　　Photo © Fáilte Ireland

Mondello Park Race Circuit, *Kildare* 114 B4
☎ 045 860200　　　www.mondellopark.ie
Ireland's premier racing circuit hosting many types of motor racing, both cars and motorbikes. It has now moved into motorsport entertainment and members of the public can experience driving performance cars on this superb track.

Monea Castle, *Fermanagh* 103 D2
☎ 028 6632 3110
Built in 1618 in Scottish Plantation style by the Rev. Malcolm Hamilton and burnt out in 1750. Monea is in a reasonable state of preservation; two imposing barrel shaped towers remain at the front capped with crow-stepped gables.

Moneen Church, *Clare* 121 C2
☎ 065 905 1577　　　www.kilbaha.net
Most famous for housing the 'Little Ark', a portable altar from which Mass could be taken. It was built in 1852 by local priest Father Michael Meehan, after his church had been closed down by the agent for the local landlord, Marcus Keane. Every Sunday it was taken down to the foreshore between high and low water where Mass was held and, as the foreshore is no-mans land, they were beyond the influence of the landowners. The Keane house is now in ruins and locals still have nothing to do with it.

Moone High Cross, *Kildare* 126 A2
☎ 045 521240
Located in Moone Abbey churchyard, on the site of an early Columban monastery, the 7th century Moone High Cross stands over 5m (16ft) high. It is made of granite and contains 51 sculptured panels. It was discovered in pieces in the late and mid 19th century and finally reconstructed in 1893.

Mount Juliet Golf Club, *Kilkenny* 125 D4
☎ 056 73000　　　www.mountjuliet.com
Designed by Jack Nicklaus and opened in 1992, the Irish Open was held here in 1993 – 95 and was extended to over 7000 yards in preparation for the World Golf Championship in 2002. It was also host to the 4th National Putting Championships in 2001.

Mount Stewart, *Ards* 107 C1
☎ 028 4278 8387 / 8487　　　www.ntni.org.uk
The 18th century former seat of the Marquess of Londonderry and childhood home of Lord Castlereagh, the 19th century Prime Minister. A severely Classical building, it sits amid 32ha (78 acres) of gardens planted in the 1920s which are renowned for the many rare and unusual plants which flourish in the mild climate. There are colourful parterres and displays of almost every style of gardening. The Temple of the Winds, also in the grounds and overlooking Strangford Lough, is an octagonal banqueting hall built in 1785. A National Trust property.

Mount Stewart　　　Photo courtesy of National Trust Northern Ireland

Moyne Abbey
Photo © Mayo Naturally

Mount Usher Gardens, *Wicklow* 127 D2
☎ 0404 40116   www.mount-usher-gardens.com
Charmingly located by the River Vartry, the gardens of Mount Usher are made up of 8ha (20 acres) planted with over 5000 species of flora. Including many sub-tropical plants, the naturalised gardens, laid out in 1868 by Edward Walpole, of a Dublin family of linen manufacturers, are famous for the Eucalyptus and Eucryphia collections and offer some fine woodland walks.

Moyne Abbey, *Mayo* 110 B1
☎ 096 70848
A Franciscan friary founded in 1460; the church is cruciform in shape and has a bell tower suspended over the chancel arch. Moyne is now a ruin, destroyed by the governor of Connaught in the late 16th century.

Muckross Friary, *Kerry* 129 D1
☎ 064 31440   www.heritageireland.ie
This well preserved friary was built in 1448 though the tower dates from the 17th century and is the only example of a Franciscan tower in Ireland that is as wide as the friary itself. The superbly preserved cloisters surround an old yew tree, probably as old as the friary. In the graveyard are the graves of ancient chieftains and the last King of Desmond.

Muckross House

Muckross House, *Kerry* 129 D1
☎ 064 31440   www.muckross-house.ie
A Victorian mansion built in 1843 in the Elizabethan style. The interior shows not only the lifestyle of the gentry of the period but also that of the servants. The grounds have water gardens, colourful displays of azaleas and rhododendrons in the spring and a limestone rock garden. There are also craft workers demonstrating weaving, bookbinding and pottery and the Killarney National Park Visitor Centre. Three working farms in the grounds use the traditional farming methods of the early 20th century.

Mullingar Cathedral, *Westmeath* 113 D3
☎ 044 934 8338 / 934 8402
This Roman Catholic cathedral, dedicated as Cathedral of Christ the King, was built in 'modernised Renaissance' style, with a dome and twin towers, just before World War II. Above the Sacristy is a museum of interesting ecclesiastical exhibits.

Murlough National Nature Reserve, *Down* 106 B3
☎ 028 4375 1467   www.ntni.org.uk
Ireland's first nature reserve, Murlough is an area of sand dunes (some of which were formed over 5000 years ago), heath, grassland and woodland surrounded by the estuary of the Carrigs River and the shore of Dundrum Bay. With the diversity of habitats there is a wide range of plants, birds and wildlife including badgers and stoats. The estuary attracts many species of wader, duck and geese, migration times being of particular interest. Common and grey seals are visitors to the beach. A National Trust property.

Na Seacht Teampaill (Seven Churches), *Galway* 117 C4
☎ 099 61263   www.visitaranislands.com
Located at the western end on Inis Mor, only two churches remain and these date from the 12th and the 15th centuries. Surrounding the churches are a community of ruined domestic buildings, which are now enclosed by a 19th century wall, and the remains of three 11th century high crosses. It is thought that around AD800 the church encouraged pilgrimages to remote parts of Ireland which may have resulted in this community being established.

National Botanic Gardens, Belfast

Photo © Northern Ireland Tourist Board

Naas Racecourse, *Kildare* 126 B1

☎ 045 897391   www.naasracecourse.com

This 2.4km (1.5 mile) racecourse is about 40km (25 miles) from Dublin City, in the heart of the thoroughbred county of Kildare. It hosts both National Hunt and Flat race meetings throughout the year.

National Botanic Gardens, *Belfast* 106 B1

☎ 028 9032 4902

One of Belfast's most popular parks with notable rose garden and herbaceous borders established in 1920. The Palm House was built in 1840 by Richard Turner of Dublin and is one of the earliest examples of a curved glass and wrought iron glasshouse. The Victorian tropical ravine, completed in 1889, has a raised balcony which overlooks the plants growing in a sunken glen including bromeliads, orchids, bananas, cinnamon and papyrus.

National Botanic Gardens, *Dublin City* 115 C4

☎ 01 804 0300

Established in 1795, these magnificent gardens occupy an area of 20ha (49 acres) and contain a fabulous collection of plants, shrubs and trees. Many of the plants come from tropical Africa and South America and are housed in large Victorian glasshouses. Features include a rose garden, rockery and wall plants, herbaceous borders, vegetable garden and arboretum.

National Concert Hall, *Dublin City* 147 B3

☎ 01 417 0077   www.nch.ie

Home of the National Symphony Orchestra of Ireland, but also a venue for international artists and orchestras, jazz, contemporary and traditional Irish music. The classical building was designed for the Great Exhibition of 1865, then became the centrepiece of University College Dublin before opening as Ireland's National Concert Hall in 1981.

National Famine Monument, *Mayo* 109 C4

☎ 098 64114

Situated at the foot of Croagh Patrick opposite the Information Centre stands a bronze monument to the Great Famine of the 1840s sculpted by John Behan depicting a 'coffin ship' with skeleton bodies in the rigging.

National Gallery of Ireland, *Dublin City* 147 C2

☎ 01 661 5133   www.nationalgallery.ie

Paintings by illustrious 20th century European artists such as Morrisot, Bonnard, Picasso and Monet hang in the National Gallery as well as the work of Old Masters including Titian, Caravaggio, Rembrandt and Vermeer. There is the National Collection of Irish art, a room dedicated to the work of Jack B. Yeats, English paintings, and over 250 sculptures. William Dargan organised the 1853 Dublin Exhibition on this site and used the proceeds to found the collection; his statue stands on the lawn.

National Garden Exhibition Centre, *Wicklow* 127 D1

☎ 01 281 9890   www.gardenexhibition.ie

Kilquade is the home of the National Garden Exhibition Centre. It started life as a nursery and now has 18 different gardens of all shapes, sizes and styles designed by some of the best garden designers and contractors in Ireland. Some of the gardens are permanent and include a herb knot garden, a gothic garden and a woodland and water garden. The Rose Garden forms the hub of the garden from which paths radiate off to the other gardens. Refreshments are available and there is a plant sales area.

National Library of Ireland, *Dublin City* 147 C2

☎ 01 603 0200   www.nli.ie

Offers over half a million books, a vast collection of maps, prints and manuscripts and an invaluable collection of Irish newspapers and periodicals. The impressive Victorian building has been home to the Library since

National Famine Monument

1890, and there is a large domed reading room.

National Maritime Museum, *Dublin City* 151 C2
☎ 01 280 0969

A former Mariner's Church is home to the museum which features a French Longboat sent to Bantry Bay in support of the United Irishmen in 1796. There are models of the Irish Fleet, a lifeboat display and an exhibit about Robert Halpin, captain of the Great Eastern steamship which laid the first transatlantic telegraph cable in 1866.

National Museum of Country Life, *Mayo* 110 B3
☎ 094 903 1773   www.museum.ie/countrylife/

The only branch of the National Museum of Ireland to be situated outside Dublin was officially opened in September 2001. Housed in modern purpose-built exhibition galleries, the collection portrays the social history of rural Ireland with the primary focus between 1850 and 1950. The lives of the Irish people are presented in the context of history, folklore and the natural environment. The new galleries are adjacent to the restored Victorian Gothic style house of Turlough Park and overlook the lake and formal gardens.

National Museum of Ireland (Archaeology & History), *Dublin City* 147 C2
☎ 01 677 7444

Houses a fabulous collection of national antiquities, including prehistoric gold ornaments, and outstanding examples of Celtic and medieval art. The 8th century Ardagh Chalice and Tara Brooch are amongst the treasures. The entire history of Ireland is reflected in the museum with 'The Road to Independence Exhibition' illustrating Irish history from 1916–1921. There is also an Ancient Egypt exhibition.

National Museum of Ireland (Decorative Art & History), *Dublin City* 146 A2
☎ 01 677 7444

Ireland's museum of decorative arts and economic, social, political and military history, based in the oldest military barracks in Europe. Major collections include Irish silver, Irish country furniture and costume jewellery and accessories. The work of museum restoration and conservation is explained and the Out of Storage gallery provides visitors with a view of artefacts in storage.

National Museum of Ireland (Natural History), *Dublin City* 147 C2
☎ 01 677 7444

First opened in 1857 and hardly changed since then, the museum houses a large collection of stuffed animals and the skeletons of mammals and birds from both Ireland and the rest of the world. The exhibits include three examples of the Irish Great Elk which became extinct over 10,000 years ago and the skeleton of a Basking Shark. Fascinating glass reproductions of marine specimens, known as the Blaschka Collection, are found on the upper gallery.

National Photographic Archive, *Dublin City* 147 B2
☎ 01 603 0371   www.nli.ie

Established in 1998, it has over a million photographs recording people, political events, and scenes of Irish cities, towns and countryside. Images from the collection are always on view. There is also a reading room and darkrooms.

National Sea Life Centre, *Wicklow* 127 D1
☎ 01 286 6939

Features marine life from the seas around Ireland including stingrays, conger eels, and sharks; also freshwater fish from Irish rivers and streams. A touch pool gives children the opportunity to pick up small creatures such as starfish, crabs and sea anemones. By way of contrast is the fascinating 'Danger in the Depths' tank with many sea creatures from around the world which have proved harmful or fatal to humans.

National 1798 Rebellion Centre, *Wexford* 134 B2
☎ 053 923 7596

The centre tells the story of the 1798 rebellion and gives an insight into the beginnings of modern democracy in Ireland. The latest technology is employed to provide interactive displays and audiovisual information and visitors can choose their own pace to travel through the unfolding story.

National Transport Museum, *Fingal* 115 D4
☎ 01 832 0427 / 847 5623
www.nationaltransportmuseum.org

A collection of buses, trams, trucks, tractors and fire engines, some dating back to 1880, along with other memorabilia from the transport industry.

National Wax Museum, *Dublin City* 146 A2
☎ 01 872 6340

Over 300 life-size wax figures of well-known people and personalities from the past and present ranging from Eamon De Valera to Elvis Presley. There is also the Hall of Megastars, the Children's World of Fairytale and Fantasy and the dimly lit Chamber of Horrors.

National Museum of Ireland (Natural History)

Navan Fort

Navan Fort, *Armagh* 105 D2
☎ 028 3752 1800 / 1801   www.ehsni.gov.uk
Once known as Emain Macha, the earthworks
at Navan are of a 7ha (17 acre) hill fort,
crowned by a ceremonial tumulus, which
together form the remains of the seat of the
Ulster kings until AD332. The visitor centre
has exhibitions and audiovisuals to interpret
the myths and legends of the area.

Navan Racecourse, *Meath* 114 B2
☎ 046 902 1350   www.navanracecourse.ie
48kms (30 miles) north of Dublin, Navan was
founded in the 1920s. It hosts top class racing
and many famous National Hunt horses have
competed here, including Arkle. It now
includes an 18 hole golf course.

Nenagh Castle, *North Tipperary* 124 A3
☎ 067 31610
Built in 1200 though the castellations were
not added until 1858. The walls are 6m (20ft)
thick and it is five storeys and 30m (100ft)
high. It was originally one of five towers that
linked the curtain wall of the original castle.

Nenagh Heritage Centre, *North Tipperary* 124 A3
☎ 067 33850
Housed in the Governor's House of the former
gaol, the history of which is a feature of the
Centre. There are also details of the seventeen
men who were hanged here in the mid 19th
century.

Nendrum Monastic Site, *Ards* 107 C1
☎ 028 9182 6846   www.ehsni.gov.uk
Three concentric stone wall enclosures are the
remains of a pre-Norman monastery
associated with St Mochaoi. Also found on the
site are the base of a round tower, a sundial
and cross slabs from the 12th century.
Situated on Mahee Island in Strangford Lough,
Nendrum is reached by causeway and has a
small museum with displays about monastic
life and St Mochaoi.

Ness Wood Country Park, *Londonderry* 98 B3
☎ 028 7772 2074   www.ehsni.gov.uk
19ha (47 acres) of woodland, originally
dominated by oak trees but many other
species were added from the 17th century.
The highlight is Ulster's highest waterfall, a
spectacular 9m (30ft) drop in the River
Burntollet, which has also created a series of
gorges and rapids.

Newbridge House & Farm, *Fingal* 115 D3
☎ 01 843 6534
Built in 1737 for Archbishop Charles Cobbe,
and still the residence of his descendants,
Newbridge has one of the most beautiful
period manor house interiors in Ireland and is
set within 142ha (350 acres) of parkland. A
fully restored 18th century farm lies on the
estate together with dairy, forge, tack room,
and estate worker's house.

Newbridge Silverware, *Kildare* 126 B1
☎ 045 431301   www.newbridgesilverware.com
Since 1934, silverware has been produced here
by craftsmen using traditional skills. Today,
the range includes cutlery, jewellery,
kitchenware giftware and executive giftware.

Newman House, *Dublin City* 147 B3
☎ 01 716 7422
Newman House is made up of two splendid
18th century Georgian mansions, which were
once part of the buildings of the Catholic
University of Ireland and named after Cardinal
Newman, the first rector of the university.
There is a classroom furnished as it would
have been when James Joyce was a pupil here
from 1899–1902. A guided tour explains the
history and heritage of the house and how it
was restored.

Newmills Corn & Flax Mills, *Donegal* 97 D3
☎ 074 912 5115   www.heritageireland.ie
A group of buildings, the oldest of which is
said to be 400 years old, including both a corn
and a flax mill which were powered by the
River Swilly. The corn mill, once used for
grinding oats and barley, has one of the
largest remaining working waterwheels in
Ireland, made by the Stevenson Foundry of
Strabane in 1867.

Newry & Mourne Museum, *Newry & Mourne* 106 A3
☎ 028 3031 3138
Situated in Newry's oldest building, Bagenal's
Castle which is undergoing major restoration
after being rediscovered in 1996. "A Border
Town's Experience of the 20th Century" looks
at the development of the region.

Newry Cathedral, *Newry & Mourne* 106 A3
☎ 028 3026 2586
Designed by Local architect Thomas Duff and
completed in 1829 costing £8,000, it was the
first Catholic Cathedral opened after the

granting of Catholic Emancipation. Later additions include the tower and transept in 1888 and an extension to the nave in 1904. Much of the interior marble and mosaics is the work of Italian craftsmen brought over specifically to carry out the work.

Newtown Castle, *Clare* 118 B3
☎ 065 707 7200   www.burrencollege.ie
A 16th century towerhouse with unique architectural features which was restored in 1994. A nature trail just over 1km in length runs from the castle which is part of Burren College of Art.

Newtownbarry House, *Wexford* 126 B4
☎ 053 9377340   www.newtownbarryhouse.com
This late 19th century country house is one of the last to be designed by Charles Lanyon (1813–1889). There is fine woodworking on the staircase, in the drawing room and in the library which houses the Ros Tapestry, the largest tapestry in Europe. The River Slaney flows through the estate which includes a lake and waterfall, rose garden on the site of the former tennis court and sunken garden which has its origins in the 18th century. There is also an art gallery which exhibits local and internationally acclaimed artists.

North Down Heritage Centre, *North Down* 136 A3
☎ 028 9127 1200
www.north-down.gov.uk/heritage/
Set in woodland at the rear of Bangor Castle with permanent and temporary exhibitions illustrating the area's history, archaeology and wildlife. Treasures include the Ballycroghan Swords dating from 500BC, a bronze 9th century monastic handbell found near Bangor and a collection of antique objects d'art from the Far East; also railway and toy collections and exhibits showing how Bangor developed as a holiday resort.

Number Twenty Nine, *Dublin City* 147 C3
☎ 01 702 6165
This elegant four-storey house has been restored and furnished exactly as it would have been between 1790–1820 by any well-to-do middle class family. Everything in the house is authentic with period items from the National Museum. The wallpaper was hand-made for Number 29 using 18th century techniques. Among the rooms in the house are a kitchen, pantry, governess' room, nursery and boudoir.

Ocean & Country Visitor Centre, *Galway* 116 B2
☎ 095 43473
A sealife centre with exhibitions of local maritime history, Ireland's only glass bottomed boat tours and a nature trail along the seashore. The adjacent park has a pets' corner and children's play area. Sea angling trips are available most evenings.

Oceanworld, *Kerry* 120 B4
☎ 066 9152111   www.dingle-oceanworld.ie
The shark tank is the first of its kind in Ireland, the 9m (30ft) long Ocean Tunnel allows fish to swim overhead and the Touch Pool allows interaction with the fish. There are also displays relating to the wrecks in Blasket Sound and the voyages of Brendan the Navigator.

Odyssey, The, *Belfast* 139 C1
☎ 028 9045 1055
www.theodyssey.co.uk   www.w5online.co.uk
A multi-functional entertainment centre comprising a 10,000 seat arena, W5; an interactive discovery centre run by the Museums and Galleries of Northern Ireland and a cinema and leisure complex.

Oideas Gael (Ulster Cultural Insitute), *Donegal* 96 A4
☎ 074 973 0248   www.oideas-gael.com
An Irish language and cultural centre which offers courses and cultural activity holidays for adults which include painting, music, dancing, archaeology and hill walking, as well as the Irish language.

Old Barracks Heritage Centre, The, *Kerry* 128 B2
☎ 066 947 2777
Housed in the unusual conical tower of the Royal Irish Constabulary Barracks constructed in the 1870s. The building would not be out of place in India and it has been said that an Irish Police Station stands on the Indian North West frontier after the plans were accidentally switched! A variety of exhibits show the history of the town and of the building.

Old Bushmills Distillery, *Moyle* 99 D1
☎ 028 2073 1521   www.bushmills.com
Established in 1608, this is the world's oldest licensed whiskey distillery and offers tours of the Irish single malt distilling process.

Old Bushmills Distillery   Photo © Northern Ireland Tourist Board

Old Jameson Distillery, *Dublin City* 146 A2
☎ 01 807 2355   www.whiskeytours.ie
The art of Irish Whiskey making shown through an audiovisual presentation, working models of the distilling process and guided tour of the old distillery which was in use between 1780–1971.

Ormond Manor House, *South Tipperary* 133 D1
☎ 051 640787 / 056 772 4623 (Winter)
www.heritageireland.ie
A combination of the original 15th century fortress and the Elizabethan Mansion House built by Thomas Butler, the 10th Earl of Ormond, a century later. It is Ireland's most impressive example of an unfortified manor house of the period. The Long Gallery is a most impressive room having a decorative plasterwork ceiling and two ornate fireplaces.

Ossian's Grave, *Moyle* 100 B2
☎ 028 2076 2024
A court tomb about 5000 years old on the lower slopes of Glenaan, one of the seven Glens of Antrim. Despite its name it dates from well before the time of the legendary poet and warrior Ossian.

Our Lady's Well, *Kerry* 129 D2
☎ 064 41233
One of a number of historic sites in Kenmare including a large Stone Circle and St Finians Church.

Oxford Island National Nature Reserve, *Craigavon* 106 A1
☎ 028 3832 2205
The 109ha (269 acre) reserve comprises woodlands, ponds and wildflower meadows on the south shores of Lough Neagh, the largest lake in the British Isles. Oxford Island is now a peninsula but was an island prior to the lowering of Lough Neagh in the 1850s. Access for visitors includes 8km (5 miles) of walks and nature trails and the facility of five bird watching hides. The Lough Neagh Discovery Centre lies within the Reserve and has conference facilities, café and shop.

Palace Stables Heritage Centre, *Armagh* 105 D2
☎ 028 3752 1801
Characters in period costume recreate many aspects of life during the Georgian period in Armagh in the restored stable and courtyard of the former palace of the archbishop and primate of the Church of Ireland, built in 1770. A guided tour includes the primate's chapel, the ice house, ornamental gardens and a 'garden of the senses'. Near the entrance are the ruins of the Franciscan friary church founded by Archbishop Patrick O'Scanail in 1263; at 50m (163ft) it is the longest friary church in Ireland.

Parkanaur Forest Park, *Dungannon* 105 C1
☎ 028 8776 7432   www.forestserviceni.gov.uk
Home to a herd of white fallow deer and full of colour in spring with daffodils and rhododendrons. There are nature walks through beech and oak woodland and a Victorian garden and wishing well. Formerly part of the Burgess Estate.

Parke's Castle, *Leitrim* 102 B3
☎ 071 916 4149   www.heritageireland.ie
An early 17th century fortified manor that was built by Robert Parke on the shore of Lough Gill and recently restored. Fortified with picturesque towers and gatehouses, the castle played a key role in the war of 1641–1652. There is an audiovisual presentation within the castle, a traditional 17th century style blacksmith's forge and models of the Parke family dressed in period costume. The courtyard shows evidence of an earlier 16th century tower house.

Patrick Kavanagh Centre, *Monaghan* 105 D4
☎ 042 937 8560
www.patrickkavanaghcountry.com
Housed in the former St Mary's church, the centre commemorates the poet and novelist Patrick Kavanagh who was born in Inniskeen. Paintings and models illustrate his poems 'The Great Hunger' and 'A Christmas Childhood' and the poet's death mask is on display. A unique feature of the centre is the performance tour of 'Kavanagh Country' which takes in many sites associated with the poet and concludes with a one-man show by a local actor. The centre also stages local history exhibitions includes an audiovisual theatre and research library.

Patterson's Spade Mill, *Newtownabbey* 100 B4
☎ 028 9443 3619   www.ntni.org.uk
A working water-driven spade-making mill, the last surviving one in Ireland. Demonstrations of how garden and turf spades are made with the original hammers, turbines and a press installed in 1919. A National Trust property.

Pearse Museum, *South Dublin* 115 C4
☎ 01 493 4208   www.heritageireland.ie
Housed in the former school run by nationalist Patrick Pearse from 1910–1916, it includes an audiovisual presentation and a nature study room with displays on Irish flora and fauna. Pearse was executed in 1916 for his part in the Easter Rising.

Peatlands Park, *Dungannon* 105 D1
☎ 028 3885 1102   www.ehsni.gov.uk
Bogs and deciduous woodland make up this park which is crossed by a network of way-marked paths and boardwalks. A visitor centre gives an insight into the increasingly threatened habitat of the peatlands. Commercial turf cutting was carried out here until the 1960s and the narrow gauge railway used in the operation has been reconstructed for use by visitors, who may also experience turf cutting at an outdoor turbary site. The area has a rich variety of flora and fauna and a bog garden enables visitors to see many of the plants and insects in close-up.

Phoenix Park Visitor Centre, *Dublin City* 115 C4
☎ 01 677 0095   www.heritageireland.ie
The visitor centre illustrates the history and wildlife of the park with an audiovisual display, a variety of fascinating exhibits and temporary exhibitions. Adjoining the centre is a restored medieval tower house, Ashtown Castle. On Saturdays there are free guided tours to the Irish President's House which is situated in the Park.

Pickie Family Fun Park, *North Down* 136 A2
☎ 028 9185 7030
Entertainment park including a miniature railway, go-karts, adventure playground, paddling pool and swan pedal boats.

Portglenone Forest Park, *Ballymena* 99 D3
☎ 028 2955 6000   www.forestserviceni.gov.uk
With beech and oak woods and renowned for bluebells in spring, Portglenone has riverside walks and nature trails along the banks of the River Bann.

Portmarnock Golf Club, *Fingal* 115 D3
☎ 01 846 2968   www.portmarnockgolfclub.ie
One of the oldest and finest links courses in Ireland and host to several Irish Opens as well as the 1992 Walker Cup and 2006 Amateur Championship.

Portrush Countryside Centre, *Coleraine* 99 D1
☎ 028 7082 3600   www.ehsni.gov.uk
Illustrating the geology, seascapes and wildlife of the area, the centre features an indoor rock pool and rock and fossil exhibition; adjacent is a nature reserve where visitors can search for ammonites.

Portrush Puffer, *Coleraine* 99 D1
☎ 028 7032 5400   www.translink.co.uk
A road train running around Portrush popular
with both locals and tourists especially
children. Runs in July and August every 30
minutes.

**Portumna Castle & Gardens, *Galway*
124 A1**
☎ 090 974 1658   www.heritageireland.ie
This early 17th century Jacobean semi-
fortified house overlooking Lough Derg was
built by Richard de Burgo, 4th Earl of
Clanrickarde, and remained in the de Burgo
family until it was gutted by fire in 1826.
Although influenced by English and
Renaissance houses, Portumna still has a
distinctive Irish appearance. There are
exhibitions in the gatehouse and in the castle,
where the ground floor is open to the public.

Portumna Forest Park, *Galway* 124 A1
☎ 057 912 0110
Situated on the north shores of Lough Derg,
the forest park comprises almost 600ha (1482
acres) with a wide variety of habitat including
marsh, lake, grassland, coniferous forest and
mixed woodland making it rich in bird and
wildlife; fallow deer, pine martens, otters, mute
swans and goldcrests are among the resident
mammals and birds. Facilities include forest
and lakeside walks with observation points,
and a viewing tower on the nature trail.

Poulnabrone Megalithic Tomb, *Clare* 118 B3
☎ 065 6828366
The distinctive Poulnabrone dolmen is known
the world over and is a single chambered tomb
dating from 2500BC that would originally
have been earth covered.

Powerscourt, *Wicklow* 127 D1
☎ 01 204 6000   www.powerscourt.ie
A disastrous fire in the 1970s has left only the
shell of Powerscourt House, built in 1730 for
Viscount Powerscourt by the Huguenot
architect Richard Cassels and then enlarged
and altered in the 19th century. Its mountain
setting is magnificent, however, as are the
gardens with their handsome 19th century
terraces, Monkey Puzzle Avenue, and Japanese
Garden, added in 1908. In the grounds, and
approachable by a separate car entrance, is a
spectacular 120m (400ft) waterfall.

**Prince August Toy Soldier Factory &
Visitor Centre, *Cork* 130 B2**
☎ 026 40222   www.princeaugust.ie
Visitor centre and factory shop which also
offers painting classes for which pre-booking is
essential. The visitor can see the production of
the moulds, casting of the toys and painting
of the figures. The shop offers not only the
figures for sale but also chess sets and
moulds.

Proleek Dolmen, *Louth* 106 A4
☎ 042 933 5484
Proleek is the site of the so called 'Giant's
Load', a tomb that is the legendary grave of
Para Bui Mor Mhac Seoidin, the Scottish giant
who challenged Finn MacCool. A trio of smaller
upright stones supporting a larger capstone,
the tomb dates back to 3000BC. It is thought
that the capstone was hauled into position by
means of a vanished earthen ramp.

Punchestown Racecourse, *Kildare* 126 B1
☎ 045 897704   www.punchestown.com
This 3.2km (2 mile) course was founded in
1793 and is regarded as the home of National
Hunt racing. It is renowned for its double bank
and stone walls but now includes bush fences
and hurdles, with Flat Racing also taking
place. The largest race is the four day National
Hunt Festival, run every April.

Queen's Visitor Centre, *Belfast* 138 B3
☎ 028 9033 5252   www.qub.ac.uk/vcentre
Established in 1845 as one of three Queen's
colleges in Ireland, Queen's became a
university in 1908. The visitor centre provides
information about the university and presents
a varied programme of exhibitions. Located at
the heart of the campus in the Lanyon Room,
the centre is named after Charles Lanyon who
was the architect of the main Queen's
university building and many other public
buildings in Ireland.

Queenstown Story, The, *Cork* 131 D2
☎ 021 481 3591   www.cobhheritage.com
Housed at one end of the railway station, the
maritime history of Cobh is told covering Irish
emigration, transportation of convicts and the
loss of the Lusitania. The town reverted to its
original name, Cobh, in 1921 after being
renamed Queenstown in 1849 after a visit by
Queen Victoria.

Queen's University   Photo © Northern Ireland Tourist Board

Quiet Man Heritage Cottage, *Mayo* 117 D2
☎ 094 954 6089
The Quiet Man, the 1951 film staring John Wayne and Maureen O'Hara was set in the west of Ireland and filmed around Cong. The ground floor of the thatched cottage has been designed as a replica of the film's 'White-o-Mornin' Cottage' with artefacts and furnishings representing a typical Irish cottage of the 1920s. The upstairs of the cottage houses a historical and archaeological exhibition relating to Cong and the surrounding area.

Quin Abbey, *Clare* 123 C1
☎ 065 682 8366
The village of Quin is noted for a Franciscan friary founded in the early 15th century, the first Observantine house in Ireland. The ruins, incorporating an earlier castle, are sufficiently well preserved to clearly demonstrate the layout of a medieval friary.

Quoile Countryside Centre, *Down* 107 C2
☎ 028 4461 5520   www.ehsni.gov.uk
Situated beside the ruins of 16th century Quoile Castle, the centre has displays on the wildlife of the Quoile Pondage Nature Reserve.

Quoile Pondage, *Down* 107 C2
☎ 028 4461 5520   www.ehsni.gov.uk
Once a saltwater estuary before a tidal barrage was built in 1957, Quoile Pondage is now freshwater and the wetland reserve is fringed with natural woodland. Paths wend their way along the river and there is an abundance of birds, insects and wildflowers.

Rahan Monastic Site, *Offaly* 113 C4
☎ 057 935 2617
The site dates back to the 6th century and was founded by St Carthach with the main church now part of the Church of Ireland parish church. There is also a well preserved church with intricate Romanesque doorway and a strong Mediterranean influence.

Rathfarnham Castle, *South Dublin* 115 C4
☎ 01 493 9462   www.heritageireland.ie
Dating from around 1583, this castle has 18th century interiors by Sir William Chambers and James Stuart and is presented to visitors as a castle undergoing conservation.

Rathmacknee Castle, *Wexford* 135 C3
☎ 053 912 3111
This late medieval castle was probably built by John Rosseter, Seneschal of the Liberties of Wexford in 1451. Although now lacking a roof and floors, this is still a remarkably well preserved building. The five storey tower stands at the south east corner of the five sided bawn, the wall of which is 1.2m (4 ft) thick and 7m (24ft) high. There is a round turret on the north east corner and a smaller square one on the north west corner, making this castle almost complete.

Rattoo Round Tower, *Kerry* 121 D3
☎ 066 712 1288
This mid 19th century, 27m (88ft) high tower still has its original conical stone roof. Originally it sat on an earth causeway in a swamp which was then drained and the causeway removed so that the surrounding fields could be cultivated. The fields are still ploughed to within a couple of feet of the tower. The monastic site was founded in the 6th century by Bishop Lughach, although the present church ruin is from a later date.

Redburn Country Park, *Belfast* 106 B1
☎ 028 9181 1491   www.ehsni.gov.uk
Redburn provides over 30ha (74 acres) of parkland and woodland with displays of bluebells in spring. From the escarpment in the park there are magnificent views over Belfast Lough, the city and the south Antrim Hills.

Reginald's Tower, *Waterford* 134 A3
☎ 051 304220   www.heritageireland.ie
For more than 1000 years a defensive tower has stood on this site to protect the quays of Waterford. The present circular structure dates back to the early part of the 13th century but has 15th century additions and, besides its defensive role, has also been used as a mint, prison and military store. Recently restored to its medieval appearance, there is now a collection of civic regalia and decorated civil charters in the tower and an exhibition of Viking and medieval artefacts.

Reginald's Tower

Ring of Kerry, *Kerry* 129 C2
☎ 064 31633
The Ring of Kerry is a famous circular scenic route of about 185kms (115 miles) around the Iveragh Peninsula. Killarney is generally considered the gateway to the peninsula, though the best section lies between Kenmare and Killorglin. The principal route follows the coast and encircles Irelands highest mountains, Macgillykuddy's Reeks, although some of the finest scenery is to be found along the unmarked roads running through the interior of the peninsula.

Riverstown House, *Cork* 131 D2
☎ 021 482 1205   www.castlesireland.com
To the east of Cork city is Riverstown House, originally dating from 1602 though it was extensively remodelled and extended in 1745 by Jemmett Browne, later to become Bishop of Cork. There is marvellous ceiling and wall stuccowork by the Lafrancini brothers, a carved wooden fireplace in the Green Drawing Room, original Barry engravings and a marble carving.

Rock of Cashel, *South Tipperary* 124 B4
☎ 062 61437   www.heritageireland.ie
One of the most spectacular sights in Ireland, the Rock of Cashel is a steep limestone outcrop surmounted by the ruins of the ancient capital of the Kings of Munster. According to legend, St Patrick baptised Corc the Third here; and Brian Boru, High King of Ireland, was crowned here in 977. In 1101 King Murtagh O'Brien donated the rock to the

church after which it became the See of the Archbishopric of Munster. The ruins are extensive and fascinating. Cormac's Chapel, built in the 1130s contains a magnificent carved 11th century sarcophagus; whilst the carved Cross of St Patrick is set into the coronation stone of the Kings of Munster. The main cathedral is essentially 13th century and although it has suffered pillage and neglect, it remains a fine example of Irish Gothic architecture.

Rock of Cashel   Photo © Fáilte Ireland

Rock of Dunamase, *Laois* 125 D2

☎ 057 862 1178

Close to Portlaoise, on the Stradbally road, a large ruined castle sits on top of this 46m (150ft) rock, all that remains of what was a considerable fortress, destroyed in the Cromwellian wars. Through the marriage of the daughter of the King of Leinster, it had moved into Anglo Norman hands in the late 12th century, and was twice rebuilt, in 1250 and at the end of the 15th century. There are fine views to be had from the summit of the rock where the remains of the gatehouse, walls and 13th century keep are still in evidence.

Roe Valley Country Park, *Limavady* 99 C2

☎ 028 7772 2074   www.ehsni.gov.uk

Ulster's first domestic water powered electricity generating station, built in 1896, is to be found in the wooded valley as well as ruined water mills which were once used to produce linen. A visitor centre presents the history of the valley and there is a countryside museum and numerous riverside walks. In spring the woodland floor is carpeted with flowers and wildlife includes otters, foxes, badgers, rare butterflies and sparrowhawks. Opportunities exist for canoeing, rock-climbing and fishing.

Rogerstown Estuary Nature Reserve, *Fingal* 115 D3

☎ 01 281 9878   www.birdwatchireland.ie

Covers an area of 363ha (900acres) and is divided by the main Dublin to Belfast railway line. The outer estuary is accessible by public roads on both the northern and southern sides of the estuary. A hide on the inner estuary is accessible by a short walk from the car park. Over wintering birds include Brent Geese, Teal, Shelduck, Wigeon, Lapwing, Ringed Plover, Golden Plover, Grey Plover, Curlew, Knot, Dunlin, Redshank, Black-tailed Godwit and Oystercatcher.

Roscommon Castle, *Roscommon* 112 A2

☎ 090 662 6342

The substantial ruins of the castle built in 1269 by Robert de Ufford has a chequered history, taken alternatively by the English and Irish until 1690 when it was burned down and fell into ruin. The three storey castle has a quadrangular plan, twin towers at the entrance gateway and is surrounded at some distance from the curtain wall by a moat.

Roscommon Heritage & Genealogy Centre, *Roscommon* 112 A1

☎ 071 963 3380   www.roscommonroots.com

Offering a family research service for people whose ancestors came from County Roscommon, the centre has a comprehensive database which includes census, land, church and civil records. It is housed in a former church built in 1819 with a unique octagonal nave.

Roscommon Castle   Photo © Ireland West

Ross Castle

Roscommon Racecourse, *Roscommon* 112 A2
☎ 090 666 3494 www.air.ie
National Hunt and Flat racing course with eight race days a year including five evening meetings.

Roscrea Castle & Damer House, *North Tipperary* 124 B2
☎ 0505 21850 www.heritageireland.ie
The Castle includes a gatehouse, curtain walls and twin corner towers dating from the 1280s. In the courtyard stands Damer House which was on the verge of being demolished in the 1970s but was saved by the Irish Georgian Society. Restoration since then has included the magnificent carved wooden staircase and an elegant carved stone doorway.

Ross Castle, *Kerry* 129 D1
☎ 064 35851 / 2 www.heritageireland.ie
Recently restored 14th or 15th century castle which stands at the entrance to a peninsula extending into Lough Leane in the Killarney National Park. It was the last stronghold in Munster to fall to Cromwell's army in 1652. Two of the four corner towers were removed in 1688 to allow room for expansion though the remaining two still survive.

Rosserk Friary, *Mayo* 110 B1
☎ 096 70848
The remains of a friary dating from 1441, one of the best preserved in the country, which was destroyed by the governor of Connaught in the late 16th century.

Rossmore Forest Park, *Monaghan* 105 C3
☎ 047 81968 www.coillte.ie
Situated to the SW of Monaghan Town, the forest comprises a mixture of broadleaved and coniferous trees, many of which, including cedars and monkey puzzle trees, are the originals planted in the estate of the 19th century Rossmore Castle, now a ruin. The former walled garden has notable yew hedges and there are two prehistoric tombs. In early summer there is a spectacular display of rhododendrons and azaleas.

Rostrevor Oakwood Nature Reserve, *Newry & Mourne* 106 A4
☎ 028 4372 2222 www.ehsni.gov.uk
Within Kilbroney Forest Park, the reserve is a mature oak wood on a steep slope overlooking Carlingford Lough, possibly dating back 1000 years. Rich in woodland birdlife and with a trail through the reserve.

Rothe House, *Kilkenny* 125 D4
☎ 056 772 2893 www.rothehouse.com
Built in the late 16th century by a wealthy merchant, John Rothe, this is a typical Tudor middle class house. The three stone buildings are now owned by the Kilkenny Archaeological Society and contain a collection of period costumes, the city and county museum, a genealogical research centre and some impressive oak furniture and pictures. The third building has been recently restored and houses the brewhouse, bakery and great kitchen.

Rowallane Garden, *Down* 107 C2
☎ 028 9751 0131 www.ntni.org.uk
First established in the 1860s by the Rev. John Moore, this natural-looking garden is planted with many rare trees, shrubs and plants from all round the world. Rowallane is memorable in spring with flowering bulbs, trees and shrubs including rhododendrons and azaleas. In summer, orchids flower in the meadows. Fuchsias and shrub roses flourish in a walled garden where there is also a national collection of penstemon; the rock garden is planted with primulas and heathers. A National Trust property.

Royal Irish Fusiliers Museum, *Armagh* 105 D2
☎ 028 9052 2911
www.rirfus-museum.freeserve.co.uk
Artefacts on display, including uniforms and medals, illustrate the history of the regiment from its inauguration in 1793 in response to the Napoleonic threat. The regiment was amalgamated with the Iniskilling Fusiliers and Ulster Rifles in 1968. Located in the 18th century former residence of the 'Sovereign' or

Mayor of Armagh, the museum also has militaria from the militias of Armagh, Cavan and Monaghan on display.

Russborough House, *Wicklow* 126 B1
☎ 045 865239

One of Ireland's foremost Palladian houses was built for a Dublin brewer, Joseph Leeson, 1st Earl of Milltown, by Richard Cassels and Francis Bindon in the 1740s. A granite exterior conceals an interior coated in extravagant stucco work and bearing a fine painting collection.

St Aidan's Cathedral, *Wexford* 126 B4
☎ 053 923 5777   www.puginireland.com

Recently restored, this cathedral was originally designed by A.W. Pugin. It was dedicated in 1860 but the spire was not completed until 1873. The paints used in the restoration of the decorative stencilling, are replicas of the original paintwork, reproduced from paint samples found in the cathedral.

St Anne's Cathedral, *Belfast* 139 B1
☎ 028 9032 8332   www.belfastcathedral.org

Built on the site of the former parish church, the Hiberno-Romanesque Cathedral Church of St Anne was consecrated in 1904 but not finally completed until 1981. Architect W.H. Lynn created an awe inspiring baptistry in 1928 with over 15,000 pieces of coloured glass depicting the Creation. There is fine stained glass, notably in the Great West Window, and mosaics by Gertrude Stein. Lord Carson, leader of the opposition to Home Rule who died in 1935, is buried here in the south aisle.

St Brendan's Cathedral, *Galway* 119 D3
☎ 091 841212

Stained glass windows, sculpture, metalwork, woodcarving and textiles were created by some of Ireland's greatest craftspeople in the early 20th century, making this a treasure house of the art of the Celtic Renaissance. The architect, W.A. Scott designed the chalice, candelabra, metal work lamps and the benches. The corbels, baptismal font and nave capitals are by Michael Shorthall and the stations of the cross by E. Rhinds.

St Brigid's Cathedral & Round Tower, *Kildare* 126 A1
☎ 045 521229

This 13th century protestant cathedral, restored by the Victorians, is built on the 5th century site of a religious centre founded by the patron Saint of Ireland, St Brigid. The centre then housed both monks and nuns. In the grounds a restored fire pit is visible. This pagan feature used to contain a perpetually burning fire, tended by virgins, until the dissolution of the monasteries in the 16th century. The cathedral contains the tomb of the 16th century Bishop of Kildare, Walter Kellesley and in the graveyard are the earls and dukes of Kildare. The Round Tower, built near the cathedral, is 12th century.

St Canice's Cathedral, *Kilkenny* 125 D4
☎ 056 776 4971

The city actually takes its name from St Canice who founded a monastery here in the 6th century, upon the site of which stands the current cathedral. Much restored in the 19th century, it is the second largest medieval cathedral in Ireland. Inside is the finest display of burial monuments in the country whilst the high round tower adjacent to the cathedral is the only substantial relic from the monastery. The building is essentially 13th century and the oldest tomb is also from this period, although the oldest decipherable slab is that of Jose Kyteler, the father of Alice Kyteler, tried for witchcraft in 1323.

St Columb's Cathedral, *Londonderry* 160 A2 (see page 78)
☎ 028 7126 7313   www.stcolumbscathedral.org

Built in 1633, the cathedral is the oldest building in the City of Londonderry. It stands within the Walls of Derry and is dedicated to St Columba who established the Christian settlement here in the 6th century. Stained glass depicts famous people who have been connected with the cathedral, including the governor of the city during the 105 day Jacobite siege of 1688-1689. Even though it has suffered at the hands of terrorist bombings during the 20th century, the cathedral is now the second most popular attraction in Northern Ireland.

St Anne's Cathedral

Photo © Northern Ireland Tourist Board

St Columb's Cathedral   Photo © Northern Ireland Tourist Board

St Connell's Museum, *Donegal* 97 C4
☎ 074 955 1277
The museum illustrates the history, traditions and heritage of the Glenties area and includes a wildlife exhibition, local writers' corner, Donegal railways collection and a display about the Great Famine of 1845–1847.

St Edan's Cathedral, *Wexford* 127 C4
☎ 053 936 6124
The original cathedral was built here in the early 13th century, although a church had stood here since the 8th century. The medieval building was burnt down in the reign of Elizabeth the First and little remains. It was not until the 19th century that it was rebuilt again.

St Feidhlimidh Cathedral, *Cavan* 104 A4
☎ 049 433 1942
Completed in 1860 to a design by English architect William Slater of which the well-travelled 12th century Romanesque doorway is probably its finest feature. In the graveyard is the tomb of William Bedell (1571–1642), Bishop of Kilmore, who carried out the first translation of the Old Testament into Irish. The old cathedral is now used as the parish hall adjacent to which are the ruins of the bishop's palace.

St Fin Barre's Cathedral, *Cork* 142 B2
☎ 021 496 3387   cathedral.cork.anglican.org
Cork's triple spired Church of Ireland Cathedral was founded in 1870 on the site of St Fin Barre's 7th century monastic school and replaced the medieval cathedral which was badly damaged during the siege of Cork in 1690. Built in the Gothic style by William Burges the cathedral is relatively small though the design gives a spacious feel. There are more than 1200 sculptures built into the structure and several relics from the old cathedral have been preserved including two doorways which have been built into the south wall of the grounds.

St John's Cathedral, *Limerick* 157 C2
☎ 061 317522
Legend has it that Donal O'Brien, the King of Thomond, donated his palace as the site for a Cathedral in the latter half of the 12th century although the present St John's Cathedral was not completed until 1861. The design is Victorian Gothic and it has the highest spire in Ireland at 94m (308 ft) from the base of the tower to the top of the iron cross. It officially became a Cathedral in 1912 in a decree by Pope Pius X and a new copper roof was added during renovations in the early 1950s.

St John's Theatre & Arts Centre, *Kerry* 121 D3
☎ 068 22566   www.stjohnstheatrelistowel.com
The transformation of the old Church of Ireland into the St John's Theatre & Arts Centre started in 1988 and took two years. It is now host to numerous local and national theatrical productions and arts, dance and musical events. It is also the site of the Tourist Information office.

St Kilian's Heritage Centre, *Cavan* 114 A1
☎ 046 924 2433
St Kilian was born in Mullagh in AD640 and became a missionary at the age of 46 in Wurzburg, Germany, where he was martyred three years later. The heritage centre gives an insight into his life and work, including the cult which developed after his martyrdom and the work of Irish missionaries in Europe in the 6th and 7th centuries. Maps, facsimiles, sculpture and art reproductions are displayed and there is an audiovisual presentation. Also of interest

St Fin Barre's Cathedral   Photo © Fáilte Ireland

is an exhibition which explains the development of Gaelic script from the Ogham writing of the 4th–7th centuries and the earliest examples of written Irish in the mid 8th century to the illuminated script of the Book of Kells.

St Louis Convent Heritage Centre, *Monaghan* 105 C3
☎ 047 83529

Through documents, memorabilia, artefacts, models and commemorative albums, the centre traces the history of the order of the Sisters of St Louis back to their origins in 17th century Turkenstein. An Institute was later established in France in 1842 and the order spread to Ireland in 1859 and then to England, West Africa and the Americas. Particular emphasis is given to the Sisters' work in health care and educational development in Nigeria and Ghana. The heritage centre also displays their traditional crafts.

St Macartan Catholic Cathedral, *Monaghan* 105 C3
☎ 047 81122

Constructed in the gothic revival style between 1861 and 1891 and is widely thought to be the best work of J.J. McCarthy. It has a slender spire and three large rose windows. The interior was renovated in the 1980s though the magnificent wooden hammerbeam roof is part of the original design.

St Mary's Cathedral, *Dublin City* 147 B2
☎ 01 874 5441   www.procathedral.ie

A Greek Doric style building designed by John Sweetman and built between 1815 and 1825, with the interior modelled on the Church of St Philippe de Roule in Paris. St Mary's is Dublin's most important Catholic Church and is used on State occasions. Tenor John McCormack was once a member of the Palestrina choir that sings a Latin mass every Sunday.

St Mary's Cathedral, *Limerick* 157 B1
☎ 061 310293
www.cathedral.limerick.anglican.org

Founded in 1168 by Donal Mor O'Brien, King of Munster, this Anglican cathedral has many notable architectural features and furnishings; a pre-Reformation stone altar, the Reardos of the High Altar carved by the father of Patrick Pearse, and the renowned Misericords, a collection of 23 carved oak seats used by the clergy which date back 450 years. The cathedral was built on the site of O'Brien's home and the door is reputed to be the original door of his house.

St Mary's Church, *South Tipperary* 132 B1
☎ 052 22960

The medieval town walls bound the grounds of this church which has an unusual octagonal tower and was built on the site of an earlier 14th century church.

St Mel's Cathedral, *Longford* 112 B2
☎ 043 46566

Built of grey limestone, in the Renaissance style, St Mel's Cathedral dates from the 1840s. 24 columns of local stone support the roof and the tall dome is visible from outside the town. The museum at the rear of the building contains the 10th century St Mel's Crozier.

St Mochta's Church, *Louth* 105 D4
☎ 042 933 5484

Impressive remains of 15th century church. It is surrounded by a wall to offer protection from the cows grazing in the surrounding fields. The arched roof is the main feature of the interior which has just one window. The ruins of St Mary's Priory are adjacent.

St Muredach's Cathedral, *Mayo* 110 B2
☎ 096 70848

Standing tall on the banks of the River Nore, work on the Cathedral began in 1827 with the huge spire completed in 1855. It can now accommodate 1200 people.

St Patrick's Cathedral, *Dublin City* 147 B3
☎ 01 453 9472   www.stpatrickscathedral.ie

The National Cathedral of the Church of Ireland, it was built in the late 12th century on the site of the pre-Norman parish church of St Patrick. Architect John Semple added a spire in 1749 and St Patrick's was fully restored in the 19th century with finance from the Guinness family. The massive west tower houses the largest ringing peel of bells in Ireland. The cathedral is full of memorial brasses, busts and monuments to famous Irishmen.

St Patrick's Cathedral, *Dublin City*   Photo © Fáilte Ireland

St Patrick's Cathedral, *Louth* 106 A4
☎ 042 933 4648 www.stpatricksparishdundalk.org

Built after Catholic emancipation in 1828 when it was decided a more suitable place of worship should be made available. The noted architect John Duff was commissioned and his design was based on King's College Chapel in Cambridge. The tower was added later and modelled on Gloucester Cathedral. The interior features a beautifully carved altar, impressive mosaic walls, groined vaulting and stained glass windows though the light, airy feel is a product of the several clear windows. There have been many refurbishments over the years, the latest was in 2004 after a fire although major structural damage was fortunately avoided.

St Patrick's Cathedral (C. of I.), *Armagh* 105 D2

☎ 028 3752 3142   www.stpatricks-cathedral.org
A church has stood on this site for over 1500 years, being destroyed and rebuilt many times. The present cathedral was largely built by Archbishop O'Scanail in medieval times but the present fabric of the building reflects the restoration work which took place between 1834 and 1840 under the direction of Archbishop John George Beresford. Stained glass depicts St Patrick who came to establish his church here in AD444. There are a number of carved figures, possibly prehistoric, and the remains of high crosses from the 9th or 10th century. Brian Ború, High King of Ireland was killed at the Battle of Clontarf in 1014 and is buried in the cathedral grounds.

St Patrick's Cathedral (R.C.), *Armagh* 105 D2

☎ 028 3752 2802   www.armagharchdiocese.org
Construction started on St Patrick's Day in 1840 and was not completed until 24 July 1903 partly due to the disruption caused by the Great Famine. Sited on a hill top, the twin spires are visible from almost anywhere in the city. The interior contains red Armagh marble and was renovated in 1981 with brilliantly coloured frescos, mosaics and stained glass windows.

St Patrick's Cross, *Donegal* 98 B1

☎ 074 912 1160
Located by the roadside and next to the graveyard of the church at Cardonagh, St Patrick's Cross (which is also known as the Donagh Cross) is believed to be one of the oldest high crosses in Ireland, probably dating back to the 7th century. Cut from red sandstone with low relief carving, the cross is 3.5m (11.6ft) tall and has two short pillar stones on either side.

St Patrick's Purgatory, *Donegal* 103 D1

☎ 074 972 1148   www.loughderg.org
Also known as Station Island or simply Lough Derg and has been a place of pilgrimage for over 1000 years from June to 15 August. During this period the island is for the use of pilgrims only and neither tourists nor the unwell or old are welcome – "The nature of the penances excludes anyone under doctor's care and the very old".

St Patrick's Trian Visitor Complex, *Armagh* 105 D2

☎ 028 3752 1801   www.saintpatrickstrian.com
A dramatic and entertaining exhibition centre which touches on history, culture, genealogy and arts and crafts. The legacy of St Patrick and the story of Armagh are brought to life and there is an adaptation of Jonathan Swift's Gulliver's Travels. Writer and clergyman Swift was often a visitor to the area. The visitor complex takes its name from the ancient division of the city of Armagh into three districts or 'trians'.

St Patrick's Well, *Dungannon* 105 C2

☎ 028 8776 7259
A huge stone in the shape of a chair from which, legend has it, St Patrick preached to the locals and then ordered water to appear from a nearby rock in order to baptize the locals – St Patrick's Well.

St Peter the Rock Cathedral, *South Tipperary* 124 B4

☎ 062 61232   www.cashel.anglican.org
The present Cathedral was completed in 1784 and is famous for its Samuel Green organ which was completed in 1786. The nearby perimeter walls date back to the 13th century while parts of the graveyard may even pre-date this. In the grounds of the Cathedral is the Bolton GPA Library.

St Peter's Cathedral, *Belfast* 138 A2

☎ 028 9032 7573
www.stpeterscathedralbelfast.com
Built to fulfil the requirements of the influx of thousands of workers into Belfast in the 1800s. The cathedral was designed by Father Jeremiah McAuley and John O'Neill, both local architects. The distinctive twin spires were not added until 1885. It was virtually unchanged until after WWII when substantial renovation included replacing the side porches to incorporate a mortuary chapel and a baptistery.

SS Peter and Paul Cathedral, *Meath* 114 B3

☎ 046 943 7111
Founded by the Norman bishop Simon de Rochfort in 1206, this was once the largest Gothic church in Ireland. Parts of the nave and chancel are original and a priory, which was built in order to help maintain the cathedral, survives, though in ruins.

Salthill Gardens, *Donegal* 103 C1

☎ 074 973 5387   www.donegalgardens.com
The garden walls are over 100 years old although this contemporary garden is continually evolving. Features a good selection of perennials, shrubs and vegetables along with gravel paths, a greenhouse and a summer-house.

Scarva Visitor Centre, *Banbridge* 106 A2

☎ 028 3883 2163
The centre is situated at a basin on the Newry canal where coal used to be unloaded for the linen industry; the canal was built in 1742 and is the oldest summit-level canal in Britain, linking the old seaport of Newry with Lough Neagh. The centre describes the building of the canal and the associated development of Scarva as well as illustrating the history of Irish canals.

Scattery Island Centre, *Clare* 121 D2

☎ 065 905 2139   www.heritageireland.ie
Scattery Island (Inis Cathaig in Irish) in the Shannon Estuary is named after the mythical monster, 'Cathach', which St Senan drove out in the 6th century before founding one of the earliest Christian settlements. Amongst these remains is a 10th century round tower which unusually has its entrance at ground level. Though last inhabited in 1979, the island is easily accessible from Kilrush, where the Scattery Island Centre can be found, which tells the story of the island.

Schull Planetarium, *Cork* 129 D4

☎ 028 28315 / 28552
Situated in the grounds of the community college, this is the only planetarium in the Republic of Ireland. It includes recreations of the night sky – there are three different star shows each week which are unsuitable for young children, each one taking about 45 minutes.

Scrabo Country Park, *Ards* 107 C1
☎ 028 9182 0695   www.ehsni.gov.uk
The landscape around Scrabo is dominated by Scrabo Hill which is crowned by Scrabo Tower, erected in 1857 in memory of the third Marquess of Londonderry. The tower, with magnificent views across Strangford Lough, now houses a museum about its history and surrounding countryside. Impressive disused sandstone quarries with volcanic features are to be seen in the park and there are woodland walks through beech and mixed woodland and an iron age hill fort.

Scrabo Country Park

Seaforde Butterfly House & Gardens, *Down* 107 C2
☎ 028 4481 1225   www.seafordegardens.com
This tropical butterfly house has hundreds of free-flying exotic butterflies and is also home to insects, reptiles, amphibians and parrots. A new moghul style observation tower overlooks an 18th century walled garden which features a hornbeam maze and mixed tree and shrub borders. Seaforde has the national collection of eucryphia, an evergreen shrub family from the southern hemisphere. There is an adjoining tree and shrub nursery.

Seanchaí - Kerry Literary & Cultural Centre, *Kerry* 121 D3
☎ 068 22212   www.seanchai-klcc.com
North Kerry is well known for the richness of its literary heritage. Indeed Listowel has been described as the 'Literary Capital of Ireland'. Over 80 famous writers are remembered at Seanchaí (the Irish for 'storyteller'). There are also children's creative writing classes, a library and reading room, café and restaurant, film club and a book and gift shop.

Seat of Power Visitor Centre, *Donegal* 98 A4
☎ 074 914 1733   www.infowing.ie/seatofpower
Housed in the restored 18th century courthouse, the centre gives an insight into the history of Lifford and the important role the town played as a seat of power in Donegal. Once an O'Donnell stronghold, Lifford was to become an important administrative centre during the Plantation of Ulster and then the county's legal centre until the courthouse closed in 1938. Cells beneath the courthouse where prisoners awaited trial can be visited and an audiovisual show presents famous trials in which local people were tried and sentenced either to hanging or to deportation to Australia.

Selskar Abbey, *Wexford* 135 C2
☎ 053 914 6506
The 12th century Selskar Abbey was founded by Alexander de la Roche and is built on what is thought to be the oldest place of worship in the County, a pre-Christian temple dedicated to Odin. It is said that Henry II did penance here for the murder of Thomas a' Becket. The Abbey was largely ruined during the Cromwellian wars.

Shaw Birthplace, *Dublin City* 147 B3
☎ 01 475 0854
This delightful Victorian terrace home was the birthplace of one of Ireland's four Nobel prize-winners for literature, George Bernard Shaw. Restored to give the feeling that the Shaw family is still in residence, the home provides an insight into the domestic life of Victorian Dubliners.

Shean Garden, *Carlow* 126 A4
☎ 059 915 7652
A one acre farmhouse garden in the foothills of Mount Leinster which has been the home of the Smyth family since the farmhouse was built 400 years ago. There is a wide variety of rare plants, shrubs and trees in six separate gardens with helpful advice on garden plans and ideas available.

Silent Valley, *Newry & Mourne* 106 B3
☎ 028 9074 1166
Silent Valley and Ben Crom reservoirs are set in the beautiful scenery of the Mourne Mountains with landscaped parkland, lakes and ponds in the grounds of the reservoirs. The damming of the Kilkeel river valley was completed in 1933 and today the reservoirs supply a large part of Belfast and most of County Down with water. An information centre explains the development of the Silent Valley and is a starting point for woodland walks.

Silent Valley   Photo © Northern Ireland Tourist Board

Skellig Experience, The, *Kerry* 128 A2
☎ 066 947 6306 www.skelligexperience.com
Skellig Michael has a remarkable series of 1000 year old steps cut into the cliff face rising to the remains of a 6th century monastery. The monks abandoned the island in the 12th century. The Skellig Experience offers information about the island's history and the abundant bird and marine life.

Skellig Michael Monastery, *Kerry* 128 A2
☎ 066 947 2589 www.skelligexperience.com
A World Heritage Site which was inhabited by Irish monks from the 6th to the 13th centuries. 600 steps lead to just below the summit of this 230m (755ft) high rock where six stone beehive huts and two oratories sit. They are extremely well-preserved, probably due to its remoteness.

Skibbereen Heritage Centre, *Cork* 130 A4
☎ 028 40900 www.skibbheritage.com
Comprises two main exhibitions: the Great Famine Commemoration Exhibition looks at the Great Famine of the 1840s as it was in this area that the worst effects of the famine were felt; Lough Hyne Visitor Centre has an aquarium containing many of the species that are found in this salt water marine lake, Ireland's first Marine Nature Reserve. There is also a trail highlighting the archaeology of the Skibbereen area and the history of the building in which the heritage centre is housed.

Slane Castle, *Meath* 114 B2
☎ 041 988 4400 www.slanecastle.ie
Dates from 1785 and designed by James Gandon, James Wyatt and Francis Johnston with the parklands being laid out by Capability Brown. The castle was reopened for guided tours in 2001 after a ten year restoration programme. The interior includes the King's Room and the Ballroom which were completed for the visit of King George IV in 1821. The Castle is also used for concerts and functions.

Slieve Bloom Display Centre, *Offaly* 124 B1
☎ 086 278 9147 www.slievebloom.ie
Located at Birr, this is an information centre for the Slieve Bloom Mountain area. Using illustrations, photographs and maps, the natural history, geology, archaeology and history of the mountains are explained.

Slieve Gullion Forest Park, *Newry & Mourne* 106 A4
☎ 028 4173 8284 www.forestserviceni.gov.uk
Covering over 6000ha (14,820 acres), the park is thickly wooded with the summit of Slieve Gullion rising above to a height of 577m (1894ft). A scenic 13km (8 miles) drive loops through the forest and from the road a trail leads to the mountain summit where there is a passage grave, cairn, volcanic lake and panoramic views of the surrounding mountains known as the Ring of Gullion. There are also woodland trails and a walk through an ornamental garden. The Slieve Gullion Courtyard at the centre of the park provides visitor information for the area as well as an educational facility.

Slieve Russell Hotel Golf & Country Club, *Cavan* 104 A4
☎ 049 952 6444 www.quinnhotels.com
Championship parkland course which has hosted the Irish PGA Championship and North West of Ireland Open in recent years.

Sligo Abbey, *Sligo* 102 B3
☎ 071 914 6406 www.heritageireland.ie
Founded originally as a Dominican Friary around 1252 by Maurice FitzGerald, Chief Justice of Ireland, the building was accidentally burned down in 1414 and further destroyed in 1641. The well preserved ruin has the cloisters, nave and choir arched tower remaining and contains the only surviving 15th century decorated high altar in any Irish monastic church as well as a wealth of Gothic and Renaissance tombs and monuments.

Sligo Folk Park, *Sligo* 102 B3
☎ 071 916 5001 www.sligofolkpark.com
Experience 19th century rural life through this fine collection of rural history and agricultural artefacts. The exhibition hall also houses an authentic village street with typical shops of the period including creamery, pub and grocers. Millview House has been restored to how it was when it was first built by George Reid in 1873 and is surrounded by workshops where the ongoing restoration takes place. There are also frequently changing displays, events and demonstrations including creel, butter and straw making, thatching, dried flower displays, lime plastering and wood turning. There is also an authentic forge in full working order, a collection of agricultural implements, henhouse, duck pond and a classroom of the period.

Sligo Racecourse, *Sligo* 102 B3
☎ 071 918 3342 www.air.ie
A right handed National Hunt and Flat racing course with six race days a year. Set in a scenic location to the south of Sligo overlooked by the distinctive Benbulben mountain.

Somme Heritage Centre, *Ards* 107 C1
☎ 028 9182 3202 www.irishsoldier.org
Presents a multimedia re-creation of the 1916 Battle of the Somme from a reconstructed trench system. The centre illustrates the contribution made by Irish troops to the First World War and the effects it had on their communities, with the voices of veterans recounting their experiences. Visitors are taken back in time to the recruitment and training of volunteers and in a hands-on activity area can try on uniforms and see trench rations.

Sonairte National Ecology Centre, *Meath* 115 C2
☎ 041 982 7572 / 7854 www.sonairte.ie
Sonairte is a registered charity which aims to promote awareness of environmental issues and sustainable living. On the 3ha (7 acre) site there are examples of renewable energy systems, nature conservation and organic growing with restored farm buildings providing shops and offices. There is also a nature trail alongside the River Nanny.

South Mayo Family Research Centre, *Mayo* 117 D1
☎ 094 954 1214
www.mayo.irishroots.net/centres.htm
The centre offers a full service to people wishing to trace their ancestors from the area and has a database of over one million records including church and civil records, lists of emigrants and migrants, the 1901 census, school registers, rent rolls, police indexes and gravestone inscriptions.

Spanish Arch, *Galway* 153 B3
☎ 091 567641
Situated in the medieval docks area of Galway, the Spanish Arch, built in 1584, was probably part of an extension to the city wall designed to protect the quays. An adjacent arch is known as Blind Arch and the site of two former inner arches is now occupied by the city museum. A map of 1610 shows a fort at this location, known as Ceann na Bhalla (end of the wall).

Spanish Arch   Photo © Ireland West

Sperrin Heritage Centre, *Strabane* 99 C4
☎ 028 8164 8142
The Sperrin Mountains, a range of mountains with five summits rising to over 610m (2000ft), is an area of outstanding natural beauty and steeped in history. The Heritage Centre, located in the Glenelly Valley, presents a 'Treasures of the Sperrins Exhibition' which illustrates the geological composition of the area, the wildlife and habitats, and gives an insight into local rural life and customs. Resident ghost Jimmy is the storyteller and visitors can pan for gold in a local stream.

Spiddal Craft Centre (Ceardlann an Spidéil), *Galway* 117 D3
☎ 091 553376 / 553478
A group of eight artisan workshops producing a variety of crafts including leatherwork, pottery, weaving, Celtic jewellery, woodturning, candle making and screen printing. The resident craftspeople draw their inspiration from the culture and landscape of the Irish speaking area of Connemara and there is also an art gallery exhibiting national and international artists.

Springhill, *Cookstown* 99 D4
☎ 028 8674 8210   www.ntni.org.uk
17th century Plantation House, home of the Conyngham family for 300 years and now in the care of the National Trust. Rooms of interest include a library, nursery and gun room and the house is filled with family portraits, furniture, papers and books. Irish costumes dating back to the 17th century are among the colourful collection in the old laundry. The walled gardens and estate paths are open to visitors.

Srahwee Megalithic Tomb, *Mayo* 117 C1
☎ 098 25711
Situated near to the roadside, the tomb is well preserved with double-walling, a fine large septal slab and traces of a cairn. The single large roof stone covering most of the main chamber of the gallery is over 4m (13ft) long. The site was formerly venerated as a holy well, known as 'The Altar Well' (Tobernahaltora).

Staigue Stone Fort, *Kerry* 129 C2
☎ 064 31633
Amid the beautiful scenery overlooking Kenmare Bay, Staigue is a stone 2500 year old ringfort made up of a 4m (13ft) thick rampart divided into terraces and linked by a system of stairways.

Stormont Castle, *Belfast* 106 B1
☎ 028 9024 6609
The Great Hall of the Northern Ireland Parliament buildings can be viewed by the public but tours can be arranged for parties in advance. Designed by Sir Anthony Thornley and constructed from Mourne granite and Portland Stone, it was officially opened in 1932 by the Prince of Wales, later to become King Edward VIII. The grounds are open to the public.

Stradbally Steam Museum & Narrow Gauge Railway, *Laois* 125 D2
☎ 057 864 1878   www.irishsteam.ie
This new attraction houses many steam, fire and farm engines including a Guinness loco Engine which was used in the streets around the Guinness Brewery over 50 years ago. There is a home-made steam tractor and a Land Rover Fire Engine which was stationed at Stradbally in the 1950s. The narrow gauge

Strokestown Park Walled Garden *(see page 84)*   Photo © Ireland West

railway runs in the grounds of Stradbally Hall and has a selection of steam and diesel locomotives which run on summer Bank Holiday weekends and on other special occasions.

Streamvale Open Farm, *Castlereagh* **107 C1**
☎ 028 9048 3244   www.streamvale.com
Family run dairy farm in the Gilnahirk hills on the edge of Belfast with a gallery to enable visitors to view the milking and opportunities to watch calves being born and to feed lambs; also a pets' corner and nature trail.

Strokestown Park House & Famine Museum, *Roscommon* **112 A1**
☎ 071 963 3013   www.strokestownpark.ie
Designed by Richard Cassells for the Mahon family, Strokestown Park House is a restored 18th century neo Palladian mansion and most of its original furnishings and family possessions have been retained. The grounds include the longest herbaceous border in Ireland, rose garden, large ornamental lily pond, Georgian peach house and vinery and a 17th century tower. The Famine Museum is housed in the former stable yards and has an extensive collection of estate documents including letters and pleas written by the tenants. Major Denis Mahon, landlord of Strokestown during that period, was assassinated after he had tried to clear two thirds of his destitute tenants from the estate.

Strokestown Park House   Photo © Ireland West

Suck Valley Visitor Centre, *Roscommon* **112 A3**
☎ 090 666 3602   www.suckvalley.com
Sitting on the banks of the River Suck, the visitor centre is housed in a former Church of Ireland dating from 1842. Details of excellent angling, walking and cycling in the area can be obtained from the centre which also has an extensive range of local arts & crafts for sale. There are two conference rooms, coffee shop and also frequent exhibitions of local artists.

Swiss Cottage, *South Tipperary* **132 B1**
☎ 052 41144   www.heritageireland.ie
Designed by Regency architect, John Nash, and built in the early part of the 19th century for the 1st Earl of Glengall, the Swiss Cottage is a large ornate cottage style building which was fashionable amongst the wealthy of Europe. The elegant interior has a graceful staircase and the salon is decorated with one of the first commercially produced Parisian wallpapers.

T.A.C.T Wildlife Centre, *Antrim* **106 A1**
☎ 028 9442 2900   www.tactwildlifecentre.org.uk
A sanctuary for sick, injured and abandoned birds and small mammals in a 200 year old walled garden. Run by volunteers of the T.A.C.T (Talnotry Avian Care Trust) who return as many to the wild as possible. Those for which this is not possible remain at the centre for the rest of their natural lives. Long term residents include owls, falcons, buzzards, gulls, gannets, foxes, rabbits and hedgehogs.

Tacumshane Windmill, *Wexford* **135 C3**
☎ 053 912 3111
Built in 1846, this is one of the last intact windmills in Ireland. It was last used in 1936 and was renovated in the 1950s. It is privately owned and the key is available on request.

Talbot Botanic Gardens, *Fingal* **115 D3**
☎ 01 890 5000
Covering 8ha (20 acres) and part of the Malahide Castle grounds, these gardens were created by Milo, the seventh Lord Talbot de Malahide, within the 101ha (250 acre) park now managed by Dublin County Council. Milo planted around 5000 plants largely of Australian and South American origin during the middle part of the 20th century. There is also a four acre walled garden.

Tannaghmore Animal Farm, *Craigavon* **106 A2**
☎ 028 3834 3244
Many domestic animal breeds which were traditionally kept on Irish farms at the end of the 19th century, but which are now rare, are to be seen on the farm. These include Irish Moiled, Kerry and Dexter cattle; Galway and Jacob sheep; also Tamworth, Saddleback and Gloucester Old Spot pigs. Formal rose gardens surround the Georgian farmhouse at Tannaghmore and old agricultural artefacts and farming practices are displayed in the barn museum.

Tarbert Bridewell Courthouse & Jail, *Kerry* **122 A2**
☎ 068 36500
Originally a courthouse and gaol built in 1831, now restored to include cells, exercise yard, courthouse and gaoler's quarters to show how 19th century justice was handed out. There is also a Famine Exhibition showing the effects of the famine both locally and nationally.

Tarbert House, *Kerry* **122 A2**
☎ 068 36198
A fine collection of Georgian furniture including a Chippendale mirror. The original trestles and gunracks still exist in the walls of the entrance hall. The Leslie ancestral home since 1690 and host to such visitors as Benjamin Franklin, Winston Churchill, Charlotte Brontë and Lord Kitchener.

Teach an Phiarsaigh (Patrick Pearse's Cottage), *Galway* **117 C3**
☎ 091 574292   www.heritageireland.ie
Patrick Pearse (1879–1916) was one of the leaders of the 1916 Easter Rising and he used this small cottage as a summer residence. Although the interior was burned during the War of Independence, the thatched cottage has been restored to how it would have been in Pearse's day.

Termonfeckin Castle, *Louth* 115 C1
☎ 041 983 7070

A three storey rectangular tower house dating from the 15th or 16th century. It has trefoil headed windows but its most striking architectural feature is the stone built vault with its corbelled roof, the same type of construction used at Newgrange Tomb. It is a National Monument.

Thoor Ballylee, *Galway* 119 C3
☎ 091 631436

The 13th century Norman tower house of Ballylee Castle is the Thoor Ballylee of W.B.Yeats' poems. A charming ivy clad tower on the banks of a river, Ballylee was the summer home of Yeats and his family in the 1920s and was where he wrote a volume of poems entitled 'The Tower'. After he left in 1929 the tower became a ruin once more until its restoration as a Yeats' Museum in 1965 which includes an audiovisual tour. The walls are 2m (7ft) thick with a single room on each of the four floors connected by a spiral stone staircase. There is a shop and tea room in the adjacent cottage and close by is the partially restored 17th century Ballylee Mill.

Thoor Ballylee   Photo © Ireland West

Thurles Cathedral, *North Tipperary* 124 B4
☎ 062 51457

Building of the cathedral was completed in 1872 and consecration took place in 1879 after completion of the interior. Major renovation work was carried out for the centenary celebrations. One of the features of the interior is a tabernacle that was created by Giacoma dello Porta who was a pupil of Michelangelo. It is ironic that the cathedral was designed to face a link road which has still not been built to alleviate the through traffic. This is why the first view is of the rear of the building.

Thurles Racecourse, *North Tipperary* 124 B4
☎ 0504 22253   www.thurlesraces.ie

A 2km (1.2 mile) National Hunt and Flat racing course located 1.6km (1 mile) from Thurles.

Timoleague Abbey, *Cork* 131 C3
☎ 023 33226

The origins of the abbey are unknown but probably date back to the 13th century. The remains are significant and include the church, infirmary, refectory, wine cellar and a walled courtyard. The abbey was sacked by the English in 1612 and remained in use until 1629.

Tintern Abbey, *Wexford* 134 A3
☎ 051 562650   www.heritageireland.ie

This fine 13th century Cistercian Abbey (named after its Welsh counterpart) was built here by William Marshall, Earl of Pembroke, after he was blown ashore during a storm; he vowed he would build an Abbey if he was saved. After 1541 it was partially converted into living quarters and the same family occupied it from the 16th century to the 1960s. The substantial remains include the nave, tower, chancel, cloister and chapel.

Tipperary County Museum, *South Tipperary* 133 C1
☎ 052 34550

The history of South Tipperary from prehistoric times to the present day is exhibited in this custom built museum.

Tipperary Racecourse, *South Tipperary* 132 A1
☎ 062 51357   www.tipperaryraces.ie

A left handed oval National Hunt and Flat racing course adjacent to Limerick Junction Railway.

Tollymore Forest Park, *Down* 106 B3
☎ 028 4372 2428   www.forestserviceni.gov.uk

Covering an area of almost 500ha (1235 acres), Tollymore is situated at the foot of the Mournes with panoramic views of the mountains and sea and with woodland rich in bird and wildlife. The park features an arboretum with a native strawberry tree and notable cork oak from Portugal; also several stone bridges and 19th century follies. Ample opportunities exist for walking and fishing while forestry and wildlife exhibits are displayed in the barn.

Torc Waterfall, *Kerry* 129 D1
☎ 064 31633

Situated in Killarney National Park, the Owengarriff River cascades over the Torc Waterfall into Muckross Lake. A pleasant walk leads though woodland to the top of this 18m (60ft) high waterfall. The foot of the waterfall is inaccessible.

Tower Museum, *Londonderry* 160 A2
☎ 028 7137 2411

Illustrates the history of the city from the earliest times with special exhibits on Celtic monasticism, the Plantation of Ulster, the siege of Derry and the Georgian period.

Tralee & Dingle Steam Railway, *Kerry* 121 D4
☎ 066 7121064   www.tdlr.org.uk

Europe's most westerly line and part of the Tralee-Dingle Light Railway which ran from 1891 to 1951. Trains run every hour during the summer on the 3km (1.9 mile) section between Tralee and Blennerville which takes about 20 minutes.

Tralee Aqua Dome, *Kerry* 121 D4
☎ 066 712 8899
www.discoverkerry.com/aquadome/
Leisure centre including a 75m (250ft) flume, gushers, waves, a castle with water cannon and also a sauna, steam room and cool pool.

Tralee Racecourse, *Kerry* 121 D4
☎ 066 712 6490   www.traleehorseracing.com
A round, left handed, National Hunt and Flat racing course with seven race days a year.

Tramore House Gardens, *Waterford* 133 D2
☎ 051 395555   www.gardensireland.com
A steep, sloping garden surrounding an elegant Victorian Town House dating from the late 1880s. The garden is undergoing restoration with both formal and informal planting. Box edged old rose beds front the house, there is a long herbaceous border, woodland and shrubbery. A stream cascades down the garden into a canal and thence to a pool. Other features include a rock garden, stone grotto and timber pavilion.

Tramore Racecourse, *Waterford* 133 D2
☎ 051 381425   www.tramore-racecourse.com
A right-handed undulating National Hunt and Flat racing course which hosts the four day summer festival meeting in August.

Trim Castle, *Meath* 114 B3
☎ 046 943 8619   www.heritageireland.ie
Located in the centre of Trim, this is the largest Anglo-Norman castle in Ireland. Hugh de Lacy first started construction in the 1170s, although the central keep – a three storey, 20 sided tower – was not completed until the 1220s. The massive curtain walls can still be seen today, largely intact. Trim was conquered three times, the most recent in 1649 by Cromwell's army. More recent fame was found in its use as a setting for the film 'Braveheart'.

Trinity College, *Dublin City* 147 B2
☎ 01 608 1000   www.tcd.ie
The original Elizabethan college was founded in 1592 but the present building was largely built between 1755–1759. The oldest surviving part of the college is the red brick apartment building from 1700 known as The Rubrics. The Library has over a million books and a magnificent collection of early illuminated manuscripts, including the famous Book of Kells. Edmund Burke, Oliver Goldsmith and Samuel Beckett are among famous former Trinity College students.

Trinity College

Tuam Cathedral & High Cross, *Galway* 119 C1
☎ 093 24141
Incorporating a 12th century chancel and 14th century cathedral, St Mary's Church of Ireland Cathedral at Tuam was re-built in Gothic revival style by Sir Thomas Dean in 1861. The 12th century decorated high cross in the cathedral commemorates the building of the first cathedral and the appointment of Tuam Hugh O'Hession as the first archbishop.

Tuam Mill Museum, *Galway* 119 C1
☎ 093 25486
Although closed for commercial operation in 1964, the cornmill has been restored and has an operating water wheel, the last remaining one in the Tuam area. Visitors can view the

Tuam Mill Museum   Photo © Ireland West

milling process and there is an exhibition of model mills in the adjacent miller's house.

Tullamore Dew Heritage Centre, *Offaly* 113 C4
☎ 057 932 5015   www.tullamoredew.com
This attraction is located in a canalside warehouse in the centre of the town. There are models, displays and many interactive activities explaining the history of the town and its links to the canal. There is also the story of Tullamore Dew Irish Whiskey and Liqueur, with a complimentary tasting after your visit.

Tully Castle & Gardens, *Fermanagh* 103 D2
☎ 028 9023 5000   www.ehsni.gov.uk
Overlooking Lower Lough Erne, Tully castle is the remains of a fortified house and bawn built for the Hume family in around 1613. It was captured and burnt out by the Maguires in 1641 and never re-occupied. In spite of this, the substantial ruin survives almost to its full height of two and a half storeys. In 1988 a formal garden was created with plants that would have been known in the 17th century and incorporating original cobbled paths.

Tullyarvan Mill, *Donegal* 98 A2
☎ 074 936 1613
As a cultural and exhibition centre, Tullyarvan Mill is the venue for traditional and folk concerts, visual arts and other cultural events throughout the year. Buncrana's 200 year old textile industry and the wildlife of Inishowen are also illustrated in permanent exhibitions in this restored 19th century corn mill. Also includes a 52 bed hostel.

Tullyboy Farm, *Roscommon* 112 A1
☎ 071 966 8031
A mixed family-run farm with dairy cows, deer, ostriches, horses and pigs and where displays of threshing and sheep-shearing are among the visitor attractions. Farm tours

include bottle feeding lambs and hand milking cows, and demonstrations of butter churning and breadmaking in the old farmhouse kitchen. The small farmhouse museum gives an insight into how the Irish famine of the 1840s affected people in this area.

Tullyhogue Fort, *Cookstown* 105 D1
☎ 028 8676 6727
Served as the ceremonial site for the inauguration of the kings of Ulster as O'Neills from 12th–16th centuries; Hugh O'Neill was the last to be crowned here in 1593. Reached by footpath, the earthwork has fine views over Tyrone.

Tullynally Castle, *Westmeath* 113 D2
☎ 044 966 1159   www.tullynallycastle.com
Originally a 17th century tower house, this structure was extensively remodelled in the early 1800s, by the second Earl of Longford, in the Gothic Revival style, to become one of Ireland's largest castles. Owned and lived in by the Packenhams since its construction, it contains fine portraits and Irish furniture. The grounds date from the 19th century and cover almost 12ha (30 acres). They include a walled garden, two ornamental lakes, a Chinese garden, Tibetan garden and an avenue of Irish Yews some 200 years old.

Turlough Round Tower, *Mayo* 110 B3
☎ 094 902 1207
A 9th century round tower standing 21m (70ft) high which was a fortified bell tower used by monks to protect themselves and their treasures in time of attack. It is one of the best preserved towers in the country. The adjacent church was built in the 18th century but incorporates a 16th century mullioned window.

Turoe Pet Farm, Leisure Park & Turoe Stone, *Galway* 119 D2
☎ 091 841580   www.turoepetfarm.com
Features rare animals and birds as well as more common farm animals and domestic fowl in a rural setting, with a nature trail around the farm. Old farm machinery is on display and there is a sheep wash in the river which runs through woodland. Other attractions include a pets' corner, two children's playgrounds and a football pitch. The Turoe Stone stands 1m (3ft) high and dates from around 200BC. It has curvilinear La Tène style Celtic decoration carved on the granite stone and may have been used for ritual purposes.

Tynan Cross, *Armagh* 105 C2
☎ 028 3752 1800
This high cross stands at the roadside in the village of Tynan but has been moved at least twice in its history. Dating back to the 10th century, it was restored in the 19th century and is made up of at least two crosses. The story of Adam and Eve are depicted on the central shaft and the head of the cross is decorated with circular bosses.

Tyrone Crystal, *Dungannon* 105 D1
☎ 028 8772 5335   www.tyronecrystal.com
Guided tours give visitors the opportunity to view this world famous lead crystal being blown by mouth and polished by hand. The original glasshouse was established in 1771 only two miles away.

Turlough Round Tower   Photo © Mayo Naturally

Tyrrellspass Castle, *Westmeath* 113 D4
☎ 044 922 3105
Dating from 1411, this restored defensive tower house castle still contains an original spiral staircase and a roof beam dating from 1280. The Tyrrells built many castles in Ireland but this was the only one left standing after the Cromwellian wars. During the 19th century, it was renovated and housed English troops for a time. More recently, a highly successful licensed restaurant has been established here.

Ulster American Folk Park, *Omagh* 104 B1
☎ 028 8224 3292   www.folkpark.com
An outdoor museum covering 20ha (50 acres) which depicts the story of Irish emigrants to North America in the 18th and 19th centuries.

Tullynally Castle   Photo © Fáilte Ireland

Life in both the Old and New Worlds is illustrated through a wide range of reconstructed period buildings. Visitors are transported via a typical Irish dockside through a full size replica emigrant ship to a typical colonial dockside street. Based at the park is the Centre for Migration Studies which includes a research library and Irish Emigration database.

Ulster Folk & Transport Museum, *North Down* 101 C4
☎ 028 9042 8428   www.uftm.org.uk
Buildings from various parts of Ulster have been re-erected here to recreate a village of days gone by with rural crafts, agriculture and industry illustrating how the way of life and traditions of people in Northern Ireland have changed and developed. Also features a typical Ulster town of around 1910 with terraced housing, shops and churches, a bank and school. Indoor galleries have a comprehensive collection of railway, road and aviation exhibits as well as a Titanic exhibition.

Ulster Hall, *Belfast* 139 B2
☎ 028 9032 3900   www.ulsterhall.co.uk
Historic venue for concerts and recitals, now owned by Belfast city council but first built in 1862 for the Ulster Hall Company. The classic English theatre organ was installed shortly after the hall was built and is still played today.

Ulster Wildlife Centre, *Down* 107 C2
☎ 028 4483 0282   www.ulsterwildlifetrust.org
Within a walled garden there is a variety of habitats including meadowland, native woodland, raised bogland and a pond, to illustrate the ecology and wildlife of Ulster. A Victorian conservatory has butterflies amongst the flowers and plants which include vines over a century old.

Vandeleur Walled Garden, *Clare* 122 A2
☎ 065 905 1760
This was once the walled garden of Kilrush House and has been restored using the original network of paths. A horizontal maze, arboretum and water features have been added and the old farmyard buildings have been developed into the Vandeleur Centre which includes meeting and conference rooms.

Vintage Cycle Museum, *Fermanagh* 104 A2
☎ 028 8953 1206
A collection of over 100 cycles, pedal cars and toys. Treasures include a Penny Farthing, an ice-cream tricycle and a folding army bike. Household memorabilia and farm machinery are also to be found in the museum.

Walls of Derry, *Londonderry* 160 A2
☎ 028 7126 7284
The only complete city walls in Ireland almost 2km (1 mile) in circumference. Views across the city are afforded from the cobbled walkway on top of the walls. In spite of withstanding many sieges the walls are well preserved and little changed since they were built in 1618.

Waterford County Museum, *Waterford* 133 C3
☎ 058 45960   www.dungarvanmuseum.org
Located in the Old Town Hall in Dungarvan, this local museum includes cameras, militia,

coin collections and trophies, amongst which is that presented to the winner of the very first bicycle race in Britain and Ireland in 1869. There are occasional lectures and articles and exhibits relating to the 1916 Easter Rising.

Waterford Crystal Visitor Centre, *Waterford* 133 D2
☎ 051 332500   www.waterfordvisitorcentre.com
The manufacture of crystal in Waterford has a history going back to 1783. Production stopped in 1851 due to excessive excise duties but restarted in the 1960s and by the 1980s was the largest producer of hand-crafted crystal in the world. Visitors are guided through the production areas to see the glass blowers, master cutters and engravers at work creating what is regarded by many as the world's finest crystal.

Waterford Crystal Visitor Centre   Photo © Fáilte Ireland

Waterford Treasures, *Waterford* 163 B1
☎ 051 304500   www.waterfordtreasures.com
Makes use of a sound guide which allows the visitor to make their way through the exhibition at their own pace. The collection of exhibits, artefacts and audiovisual presentations tells the 1000 year story of Ireland's oldest city. Amongst the exhibits are a Viking Kite Brooch from about AD1100 and a diamond encrusted Flint glass decanter from the 1790s.

Waterfront Hall, *Belfast* 139 C2
☎ 028 9033 4400   www.waterfront.co.uk
A conference and concert centre constructed as part of Belfast's riverfront regeneration.

Watertop Open Farm, *Monaghan* 100 A2
☎ 028 2076 2576
Extensive cattle and sheep farm with farm tours and many other family activities including pony trekking, boating, fishing, archery, mountain bike tours and walking. Sheep shearing demonstrations in summer.

Waterways Visitor Centre, *Dublin City* 147 C2
☎ 01 677 7510   www.waterwaysireland.org
Due to reopen July 2007. A modern centre built on piers over the Grand Canal, housing an exhibition about Ireland's inland waterways. Working models of various engineering features are displayed and there is an interactive multimedia presentation.

Wellbrook Beetling Mill, *Cookstown* 105 C1
☎ 028 8674 8210 / 8675 1735   www.ntni.org.uk
Set in a wooded glen on the banks of the Ballinderry River, Wellbrook is the last working beetling mill in Northern Ireland. Beetling was the last stage in manufacturing linen when the cloth was pounded with heavy wooden

hammers to give the distinctive sheen. Wellbrook operated as a mill for nearly 200 years, ceasing commercial production in 1961. There are hands-on demonstrations and an exhibition of how linen was produced. A National Trust property.

West Clare Railway Heritage Centre, *Clare* 121 D2
☎ 065 905 1284
The West Clare Railway opened in 1887 running between Ennis, Kilrush and Kilkee. It was a steam driven rail service which was converted to diesel in 1952 in an attempt to make it more commercially viable. By 1955 it was the only diesel run, narrow gauge railway in Britain and Ireland but by 1961 it had closed down. The old station buildings can still be seen at Ennis Station and the Heritage Centre is housed in the restored Moyasta Junction Station House.

West Cork Heritage Centre, *Cork* 131 C3
☎ 023 44193
Housed in Christchurch which was deconsecrated in 1973 and is reputedly the first building in Ireland to be built for the Church of Ireland. The exhibition includes a trip back in time with recreations of an old shop, schoolhouse and wheelwright and harness makers' workshops. There are also displays of archaeological interest, in fact some of the old town walls are incorporated into the fabric of the building.

West Cork Model Railway Village, *Cork* 130 B3
☎ 023 33224   www.modelvillage.ie
Including an exhibition of the pre-war cultural and industrial life of West Cork housed in a replica of the original station house at McCurtain Hill. When completed there will be 1:24 scale reconstructions of all of the towns on the route of the West Cork Railway, which closed in 1961 – Bandon, Bantry, Clonakilty, Dunmanway, Kinsale and Skibbereen. A road train, Tschu Tschu, takes visitors on a tour of Clonakilty and surrounding areas.

West Cork Regional Museum, *Cork* 130 B3
☎ 023 33115
Amongst the historical exhibits are displays about Clonkilty's own Michael Collins (1890–1922), his minor involvement in the 1916 Rising and his more central role in the War of Independence.

Westgate Tower, *Wexford* 135 C2
☎ 053 914 6506
Built in the early 1300s, this is the only surviving gate in Wexford's town wall, dating back to the Norman invasion. It houses the Westgate Heritage Centre which tells the story of the history of Wexford through displays and an impressive audiovisual display with special effects. The upper floors have fine Norman rooms and a walk along the battlements to Selskar Abbey.

Westport House, *Mayo* 109 C4
☎ 098 25430 / 27766   www.westporthouse.ie
The house, built around 1730, is by Dublin based architect Richard Cassells with additions by James Wyatt in 1778. Entered from the quay at Westport, the house is the home of the Marquess of Sligo and contains an ornate dual marble staircase, family paintings and other portraits, antique silver and furniture and Waterford glass. The park has an ornamental lake, a small theme park, miniature zoo and boating, fishing and golf facilities. A recent addition to this increasingly popular attraction is the Garden Retail Outlet situated in a large complex of farm buildings – the Old Farmyard. The memory of Grace O'Malley (Gráinne Uaile) is honoured by a new bronze statue by Michael Cooper. The current owners are direct descendants of the 16th century pirate queen of Connaught who was a thorn in the side of the English and also later the Spanish on both land and sea.

Wexford County Museum, *Wexford* 134 B2
☎ 053 923 5926
Located in a 13th century Norman castle in Enniscorthy, the history of County Wexford is dramatically told through artefacts and displays from agriculture, the military, the church, seafaring and industrial occupations.

Wexford Racecourse, *Wexford* 135 C2
☎ 051 421681   www.wexfordraces.ie
Just outside Wexford, this course hosts both flat and National Hunt racing.

Wexford Wildfowl Reserve, *Wexford* 135 C2
☎ 053 912 3129
The North Slobs mudflats are the overwintering home for between one third and half of the global population of Greenland White Fronted Geese. This reserve has a visitor centre with audiovisual information as well as hides and an observation tower for observing the geese and many other species.

Waterfront Hall   Photo © Northern Ireland Tourist Board

White Island, *Fermanagh* 103 D1
☎ 028 6862 1333
Situated on the island in Lower Lough Erne is a ruined 12th century church with a fine Romanesque doorway. Unusual stone figures set into the wall of the church are much older, perhaps dating back to the 6th century. White Island is reached by passenger ferry from Castle Archdale.

Wicklow Mountains National Park, *Wicklow* 127 C2
☎ 0404 45425   www.heritageireland.ie
Established in 1991, the total area managed is now 20,000ha (49,400 acres), with a core area based around the lakes at Glendalough. The Park includes Liffey Head Bog and the Glenealo Valley Heath and Bog as well as various wooded areas with old coppiced Sessile Oaks. The Wicklow Mountains themselves are granite and hold high concentrations of lead, tin, copper, iron and zinc, all of which have been mined in the past. Most of Ireland's mammals can be found here; various species of deer, foxes, badgers, brown and Irish hares, red squirrels, birds of prey, red grouse and many other birds and fish. The Park Information Office is near the Upper Glendalough lake.

Wicklow's Historic Gaol, *Wicklow* 127 D2
☎ 0404 61599   www.wicklowshistoricgaol.com
Wicklow's old county gaol has been here since 1702 and it was in service until 1924. Now it has been developed into a centre to tell the story of the thousands of people of all ages, both innocent and guilty, who passed through its doors. By using a combination of audiovisual material, displays and actor-interpreters, this history is brought to life through the eyes of the inmates. The fate of those who were transported abroad can be experienced by visiting a reconstruction of the prison ship Hercules.

Wilson Ancestral Home, *Strabane* 98 A4
☎ 028 7138 2204
This cottage with traditional hearth fire has remained virtually unchanged since James Wilson, grandfather of American President Woodrow Wilson, emigrated to America in 1807; authentic period artefacts on display.

Windsor Park, *Belfast* 106 B1
☎ 028 9024 4198   www.linfieldfc.com
The venue for Northern Ireland international football matches and also the home of Northern Ireland's most successful side, Linfield Football Club ever since it was opened in 1905. The current capacity is 20,400 although it used to hold as many as 60,000.

Woodstock Gardens, *Kilkenny* 134 A2
☎ 056 775 8797   www.woodstock.ie
The gardens were designed by Lady Louisa Tighe during the 19th century and were one of the finest examples of a Victorian garden. They gradually became overgrown but 20ha (50 acres) of formal gardens, arboretum and woodland are now being restored to their former glory. The Arboretum was planted between 1750 and 1900 and contains many rare, mature trees. There are many walks from which the terraced flower garden, bathhouse, walled garden, rose garden, dovecote, ice-house and several follies can be seen.

Woodville Farm, *Sligo* 102 B3
☎ 071 916 2741
Farm animals, including some rare breeds, live here in natural surroundings and there are guided walks round the historic farm buildings, across fields and through mature woodland. A farm museum is housed in 19th century horse stalls and visitors may collect free range eggs and feed pet lambs and donkeys.

Workhouse, The, *Donegal* 97 D2
☎ 074 913 6540
Presented as a series of tableaux, this 19th century Workhouse building depicts the harsh life endured by many at that time and the effects of the Great Famine of 1845–1847 after blight devastated the potato crop.

Workhouse Museum, *Londonderry* 161 C2
☎ 028 7131 8328
The Workhouse opened in 1840 and closed in 1948 but continued as a hospital until 1991. The Museum and Waterside Library is housed in two floors which were saved from demolition. Permanent displays include the part played by Derry in the Battle of the Atlantic during WWII in the Atlantic Memorial exhibition and the Great Famine, life in the Workhouse and poverty in general are all looked at in some detail. There are also frequently changing exhibitions.

Yeats Memorial Building, *Sligo* 102 B3
☎ 071 914 2693 / 914 7264   www.yeats-sligo.com
The Yeats Society provides information here about the Nobel poet William Butler Yeats (1865–1939) whose work was influenced by the culture and landscape of the county of Sligo. Among items on display are original manuscript drafts of some of Yeats' poems and landscape photographs of Sligo. Also housed within the building is the Sligo Art Gallery which presents up to 20 major exhibitions each year.

Yeats statue, Sligo   Photo © Fáilte Ireland

Yola Farmstead Folk Park, *Wexford* 135 C3
☎ 053 913 2610
This restored 18th century farmstead complex shows life as it was in the 1700s. It features a farmhouse, school, forge, working windmill, church, aviary, thatched cottages and rare and endangered species of birds and animals. Refreshments are available in 'Granny's Kitchen' with its authentic open fire. Yola Park is also a County Genealogy Centre.

Youghal Heritage Centre, *Cork* 132 B4
☎ 024 92447
The development of Youghal from the 6th century is outlined in the Heritage Centre which is located in the same building as the Tourist Office.

Key to map symbols 91

Motorway / Toll

Motorway junction with full / limited access

Primary / National primary route

'A' road / National secondary route

'B' road / Regional road

Minor road

Road under construction

Multi-level junction / roundabout

Road distance in miles (kilometres) between markers

Steep hill (arrows point downhill)

Car ferry route

Passenger ferry route

Railway line / station

International / domestic airport

Park and Ride

Youth Hostel / viewpoint

International boundary

BELFAST **District / County boundary**

National park

Forest park

Woodland

Summit height (in metres)

Canal

Beach

Town plans (pages 136-163)

Main road / Throughroute

Pedestrian street

Shopping street

Railway station

Car park

Garda/Pol **Police station**

Public toilet

Religious building

Tourist information
(NT) indicates property owned by the National Trust

Tourist information centre (open all year / seasonally)

Ancient monument

Battlefield

Castle

Cave

Country park

Ecclesiastical building

Garden

Golf course

Historic house

Major sports venue

Motor racing circuit

Museum / Art gallery

Nature reserve

Preserved railway

Racecourse

Theme park

Wildlife park or Zoo

Other interesting feature

water	0	100	200	300	400	500	700	1000	metres
	0	330	650	980	1310	1640	2295	3280	feet

SCALE

0   2   4   6   8   10 miles

0 2 4 6 8 10 12 14 16 km

1:411 840   6.5 miles to 1 inch / 4.1 km (2.6 miles) to 1 cm

Airport information

If dialling from the UK, replace the area code with the *italicised* number in brackets.

Belfast International Airport 100 A4
Aldergrove, Antrim
BT29 4AB
028 (028) 9448 4848
www.bial.co.uk

City of Derry Airport 98 B2
Airport Road, Eglinton
Londonderry
048 (028) 7181 0784
www.cityofderryairport.com

Connemara Airport 117 D3
Inverin, Galway
091 (00353 91) 593034
www.aerarannislands.ie

Cork Airport 131 D2
Cork
021 (00353 21) 431 3131
www.corkairport.com

Donegal Airport 96 B2
Carrickfinn, Donegal
074 (00353 74) 9548232
www.donegalairport.ie

Dublin Airport 115 C3
Fingal
01 (00353 1) 814 1111
www.dublinairport.com

Galway Airport 118 B2
Carnmore, Galway
091 (00353 91) 755569
www.galwayairport.com

George Best Belfast City Airport 106 B1
Belfast
BT3 9JH
048 (028) 9093 9093
www.belfastcityairport.com

Ireland West Airport Knock 111 C3
Charlestown, Mayo
094 (00353 94) 9367222
www.knockairport.com

Kerry Airport 121 D4
Farranfore, Killarney
Kerry
066 (00353 66) 976 4644
www.kerryairport.ie

Shannon Airport 122 B1
Shannon, Clare
061 (00353 61) 712000
www.shannonairport.com

Sligo Airport 102 B3
Strandhill, Sligo
071 (00353 71) 916 8396
www.sligoairport.com

South East Regional Airport Waterford 134 A3
Killowen, Waterford
051 (00353 51) 875589
www.flywaterford.com

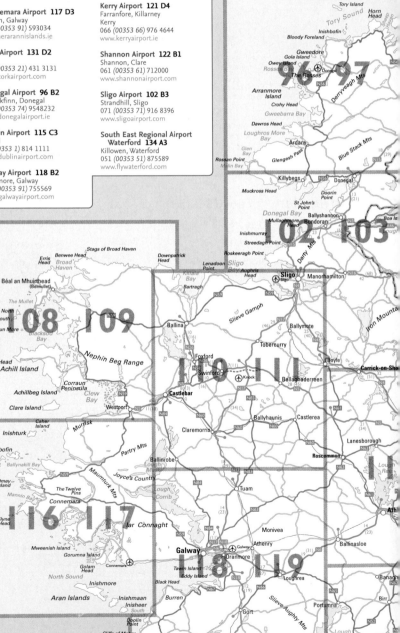

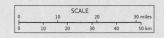

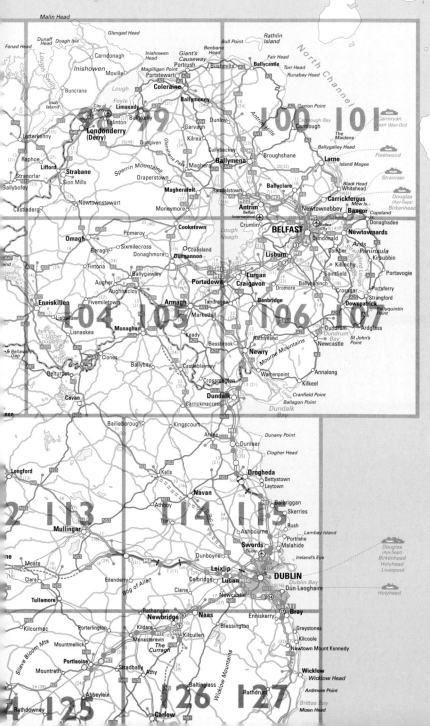

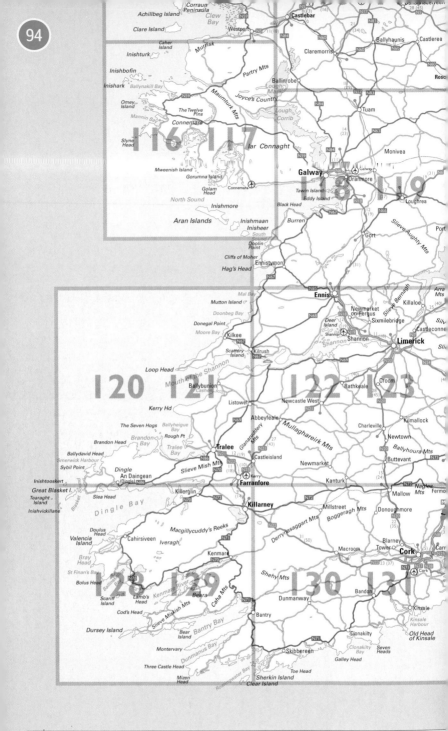

94

Ferry information

Use the first telephone number if phoning from the R of I, use the second *italicised* number if phoning from the UK.

Belfast to Birkenhead 106 B1
8 hrs
  All year
Norfolk Line
01 819 2999
0870 600 4321
www.norfolkline-ferries.co.uk

Belfast to Douglas 106 B1
2 hrs 45 mins
  April - September
Steam Packet Co
1800 80 50 55
08705 523 523
www.steam-packet.com

Belfast to Stranraer 106 B1
1 hr 45 mins - 3 hrs 15 mins
  All year
Stena Line
01 204 7777
08705 707070
www.stenaline.ie

Buncrana to Rathmullan 98 A2
30 mins May - September
Lough Foyle Ferry Company
074 938 1901
00 353 74 938 1901
www.loughfoyleferry.com

Burtonport to Arranmore 96 B3
30 mins
  All year
Arranmore Ferry Service
074 952 0532
00353 74 9520532
www.arranmoreferry.com

Carrigaloe to Glenbrook (Cork Harbour Ferry) 131 D2
5 mins
  All year
Cross River Ferries
021 481 1223
00353 21 481 1223

Cork to Roscoff 131 D2
13 hrs
  April - November
Brittany Ferries
021 427 7801
0870 366 5333
www.brittany-ferries.ie

Cork to Swansea 131 D2
10 hrs
  March - October
Swansea Cork Ferries
021 483 6000
01792 456116
www.swansea-cork.ie

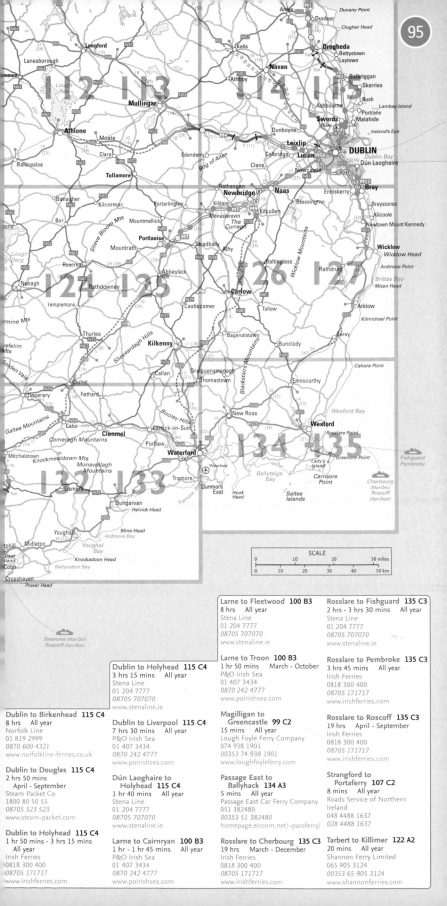

SCALE

0   10   20   30 miles

0   10   20   30   40   50 km

Dublin to Birkenhead 115 C4
8 hrs   All year
Norfolk Line
01 819 2999
0870 600 4321
www.norfolkline-ferries.co.uk

Dublin to Douglas 115 C4
2 hrs 50 mins
April - September
Steam Packet Co
1800 80 50 55
08705 523 523
www.steam-packet.com

Dublin to Holyhead 115 C4
1 hr 50 mins - 3 hrs 15 mins
All year
Irish Ferries
0818 300 400
08705 171717
www.irishferries.com

Dublin to Holyhead 115 C4
3 hrs 15 mins   All year
Stena Line
01 204 7777
08705 707070
www.stenaline.ie

Dublin to Liverpool 115 C4
7 hrs 30 mins   All year
P&O Irish Sea
01 407 3434
0870 242 4777
www.poirishsea.com

**Dún Laoghaire to
Holyhead** 115 C4
1 hr 40 mins   All year
Stena Line
01 204 7777
08705 707070
www.stenaline.ie

Larne to Cairnryan 100 B3
1 hr - 1 hr 45 mins   All year
P&O Irish Sea
01 407 3434
0870 242 4777
www.poirishsea.com

Larne to Fleetwood 100 B3
8 hrs   All year
Stena Line
01 204 7777
08705 707070
www.stenaline.ie

Larne to Troon 100 B3
1 hr 50 mins   March - October
P&O Irish Sea
01 407 3434
0870 242 4777
www.poirishsea.com

**Magilligan to
Greencastle** 99 C2
15 mins   All year
Lough Foyle Ferry Company
074 938 1901
00353 74 938 1901
www.loughfoyleferry.com

**Passage East to
Ballyhack** 134 A3
5 mins   All year
Passage East Car Ferry Company
051 382480
00353 51 382480
homepage.eircom.net/~passferry/

Rosslare to Cherbourg 135 C3
19 hrs   March - December
Irish Ferries
0818 300 400
08705 171717
www.irishferries.com

Rosslare to Fishguard 135 C3
2 hrs - 3 hrs 30 mins   All year
Stena Line
01 204 7777
08705 707070
www.stenaline.ie

Rosslare to Pembroke 135 C3
3 hrs 45 mins   All year
Irish Ferries
0818 300 400
08705 171717
www.irishferries.com

Rosslare to Roscoff 135 C3
19 hrs   April - September
Irish Ferries
0818 300 400
08705 171717
www.irishferries.com

**Strangford to
Portaferry** 107 C2
8 mins   All year
Roads Service of Northern
Ireland
048 4488 1637
028 4488 1637

Tarbert to Killimer 122 A2
20 mins   All year
Shannon Ferry Limited
065 905 3124
00353 65 905 3124
www.shannonferries.com

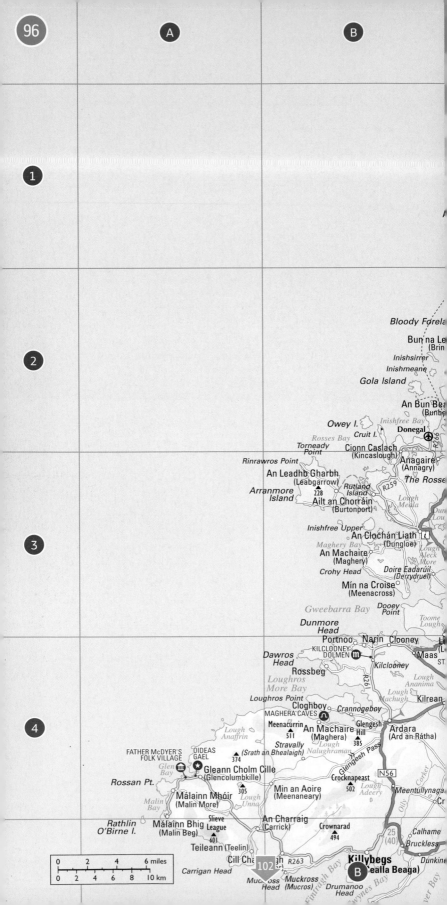

1

Tory Island

DIXON GALLERY

n Baile Thiar
(West Town)

Fair Head
Earra Thíre
(Arryheernabi

Melmore
Head

Machaire Dromann
(Magheradrumman)

Dumhaigh
(Doagh Beg

Tranarossan
Bay

Horn
Head

Dumhach
(Doagh)

Baile Uí Fhuaruisce
(Ballyhoorisky)

Fanad

Leel
Point

MILITAR
MUSEUM

Tory Sound

Sheep
Haven

Droaghnamaddy

Na Dúnaibh
(Downies)

Rosguill

Glinsk

Portsalon

Claggan 254

Inishbeg

207

Ballyheerin

Rosnakil

Tawny

R246

Inishbofin

THE WORKHOUSE

Knockduff

Carraig Airt
(Carrickart)

Knockalla
Mountain
363

Gleann
Bhairr
(Glenvar)

Inishdooey

THE GALLERY

Ranaghroe
Point

Inishbofin

Dooras
Point

Dunfanaghy

Ballymore

Ards
Forest Park

DOE
CASTLE

Cashel

R245

Cranford

Carrowkeel
Crockan

Lurga

Bloody
Foreland
314

R257

Mín Lárach
(Meenlaragh)

An Fál Carrach
(Falcarragh)

Creeslough

Glen

R246

FLIGHT OF THE EAR
HERITAGE CENTRE

2

Mín an Chladaigh
(Meenaclady)

Gort an Choirce
(Gortahork)

Muckish
Mountain
670

Lough
Salt
Mountain
471

Milford

Rathmull

Gweedore

Tievealehid

Cloghaneely

Crockawama

NATIONAL PARK
VISITOR CENTRE

Lough
Fern

R247

Ray
In

Doirí Beaga
(Derrybeg)
430

Aghla More
584

Lough
Aluirg

R25

Termon
(An Tearmann)

N56

Gaoth Dobhair
(Gweedore)

Altan
Lough

Dooish
654

GLENVEAGH
CASTLE

Lough
Beagh

ANCESTRY
CENTRE

R251

Errigal
752

Kilmacrenan

R249

98

Croithlí
(Crolly)

GLENVEAGH
NATIONAL PARK

GLEBE HOUSE
& GALLERY

15
(24)

(áltain)

IONAD COIS LOCHA

Dún Lúiche
(Dunlewy)

COLMCILLE
HERITAGE
CENTRE

Lough
Gartan

Treantagh

Ellistrin
260

Newtowncunni

Loch an Iúir
(Loughanure)

Crocknafarragh

Slieve
Snaght
683

Leahanmore

Church Hill

Letterkenny
(Leitir Ceanainn)

Ballylawn

Corderry

Moylenanav
540

Gleann Doimhin
(Glendowan)

R257

COUNTY
MUSEUM

i

Manorcu

Crovehy
316

Drumbologe

Rashedoge

R250

Old
Town

Pluck

14

An Dúchoraidh
(Doochary)

Breenagh
(Na Bruineacha)

New Mills

Knockbrack

3

R252

R254

Kingarrow
(An Cionn Garbh)

Lough
Deele

Glenmaquin

17
(27)

Baile na
Finne
(Fintown)

Tievedeevan Hill

Cark Mountain
367

NEWMILLS CORN
& FLAX MILLS

Raphoe
(Ráth Bhoth)

Croaghleheen
383

256

Béal an Átha Móir
(Bellanamore)

N13

R26

FINTOWN
RAILWAY

ISAAC BUTT
HERITAGE CENTRE

Aughagault

Convoy

CAV
CA

Ballynacarrick

R252

Drumnacross
Cloghroe

R236

Cloghfin

Liffor

ir Mhic an Bhaird
(termacaward)

Aghla
Mountain
598

An Clochán
(Cloghan)

Kilross

Carnowen

GRAY'S PRINTING
PRESS (NT)

CONNELL'S
USEUM

An Ghrafaidh
(Graffy)

R253

Mín an Arbhair
(Meenanarwa)

Welchtown

14 (23)

Liscooly

Castle

N1

Gaugin
Mountain
568

An Coimín
(Commeen)

Altnapaste

R252

Stranorlar
(Srath an
Urláir)

Killygordon

Cla

Glenties

Ballybofey
(Bealach Feich)

Gleneely

4

An tSeanga Mheáin
(Tangaveane)

Meenglass

Lismullyduff
Mountain
265

B50

Lough
Anna

Carnaween
522

Blue
Stack
676

Lough
Mourne

Meenreagh

Priestsessagh

Tullyhonwar

Blue Stack Mts

Croaghnageer
546

Dartans

Cas

Binbane
455

R262

19 (30)

Cross Hill
312

Corgary

Tullycar

Killen

Tamor
Lough

N15

KILLETER
FOREST

Letterbarra

Lough
Esk

Mullyfa
248

Killeter

Frosses

Drúmnalost

Croaghnameal
440

Ardmore Hill
329

Gargrim

Blacktown

Inver

Donegal
(Dún na nGall)

Drummenny

Mountcharles

i

RAILWAY
HERITAGE CENTRE

ST PATRICKS
PURGATORY

llymacavany

Carrick

SALTHILL
GARDENS

CRAFT
VILLAGE

C

103

D

Station
Island
363

Tullyvoos

Laghey

Doorin
Point

Mullancross

Bridgetown

Dunragh
Lough

A B

Inishtrahull

Inishtrahull Sound

Malin
Head

Garvin
Isles

Ballygorman

109

262

Glengad
Head

1

Glashedy
Island

Lag

R242

Portaleen

VISITOR
CENTRE

Doagh Isle

R243

Malin

Culdaff
Bay

Dunmore
Head

Tullagh
Point

Pollan
Bay

BALLYLIFFIN

Trawbreaga
Bay

Culdaff

Dunaff
Head

Ballyliffin

R238

Fanad Head

Earra Thíre na Binne
(Arryheernabin)

Dunaff

Raghtin
More
505

Straid

Clonmany

ST. PATRICK'S
CROSS

Carndonagh

Gleneely

Lec

Dumhaigh Bhig
(Doagh Beg)

Machaire Dromann
(Magheradrumman)

I n i s h o w e n

more
Head

Baile Uí Fhuaruisce
(Ballyhoorisky)

Fanad

Leel
Point

Lenan
Bay

Bulbin
497

Magherabane

R238

Glentogher

Crockavishane
322

Glinsk

Kinny
Lough

Urris Hills

R244

Slieve Snaght
615

Ballyheerin

Portsalon

Rosnakil

Tawny

MILITARY
MUSEUM

Drumfree

R240

LEISURELAND
Redcastle

Carraig Airt
(Carrickart)

Knockalla
Mountain
363

Gleann
Bhairr
(Glenvar)

Glebe

TULLYARVAN
MILL

Illies

Crocknacraddy
360

Whitecastle

Cranford

R245

R246

Crana

R247

Carrowkeel

Quigley's
Point

Glen

Carrowkeel

Crockanaffrin
346

Lurganboy

Buncrana
(Bun Cranncha)

i

Lough
Foyle

2

Lough
Saft
Mountain
471

R246

FLIGHT OF THE EARLS
HERITAGE CENTRE

Milford

Rathmullan

Scalp
Mountain
484

R238

Muff

Ba

Termon
(An Tearmann)

Lough
Fern

R247

Ray

Inch Top
222

Inch

Tooban

R239

Burnfoot

Culmore

A2

CITY OF
DERRY

17
(27)

R249

97

Inch Island

Baylet

Fahan

Coolkeeragh

Ba

ANCESTRY
CENTRE

GRIANAN-AILIGH
EXPERIENCE

Bridge
End

EARHART
CEN.

Campsey

Eglinton

Greys

HOUSE
RY

15
(24)

Ramelton
(Ráth Mealtain)

GRIANAN
AILIGH

244

ST. COLUMB'S
CATHEDRAL

22 (35)

Ellistrin
260

Newtowncunningham

LONDONDERRY
(DERRY)

HARBOUR MUS.

Lack

Letterkenny
(Leitir Ceanainn)

N13

Ballylawn

R237

WALLS OF DERRY

TOWER MUS.

i

WORKHOUSE
MUSEUM

LONDONDERRY
DERRY

Lettershendony
394

Loughen

COUNTY
MUSEUM

i

Church Town

Prehen

Drumahoe

Frvey Cross Road
WATERFALL

3

Old
Town

Pluck

Manorcunningham

Lismoghry

A40

Carrigans

New Buildings

NESS
WOOD

Killaloo

Knockbrack

St Johnstown

R236

Magheramason
Slievekirk
372

13
(21)

Bready

Claudy

B74

Cr

NEWMILLS CORN
& FLAX MILLS

N13

Glenmaquin

Raphoe
(Ráth Bhoth)

R264

Creaghadoos

R265

Cloghcor

Milltown

B48

B49

Lowertown

Liscloon

Donemana

B48

Tullintrain

Ballyneaner

Aughagault

Cloghfin

Convoy

Carnowen

CAVANACOR
GALLERY

Ballymagorry

Rossgeir

Artigarvan

B49

Crockdoorish

Carnanreagh

17
(27)

Kilross

Ballindrait

Lifford (Leifear)

i

Strabane

Altishane

Ballynamallaght

mnacross
loghroe

R236

Carnowen

GRAY'S PRINTING
PRESS (NT)

220

SEAT OF POWER
VISITOR CENTRE

Owenreagh
Hill
409

Craig

Mullaghcloga
636

HERIT
CEN

14 (23)

Liscooly

Castlefinn

B85

B72

Butterlope

fey
(ch)

Stranorlar
(Srath an
Urláir)

Killygordon

N15

Clady

WILSON
ANCESTRAL
HOME

Ligfordrum

S T R A B A N E

C

Meenglass

Glebe

Sion Mills

Plumbridge

Mullagholly
444

4

Ballyduff
ountain
265

R235

Gleneely

Victoria Bridge

Glashygolgan

B536

B48

Scotch Tow

Meenreagh

Priestsessagh

VISITOR
CENTRE

Iniscian

B164

B47

Gortin

Rousky

Corgary

Dartans

B50

B72

Ardstraw

B46

Curraghchosaly
418

B46

Tullycar
248

Mourne Beg

Spamount

Newtownstewart

Tircur

Mullaghcarn
542

Greencastl

ilyfa

Killen

Castlederg

Drumlegagh

Lough
Catherine

Bessy
Bell
423

Cashty

Mountfield

AN CREAGÁN
VISITOR CENTI

Corgary

Gargrim

B72

Killeter

Fairy Water

Blacktown

B84

ULSTER AMERICAN
FOLK PK.

Knockmoyle

Gortin Glen
Forest Park

Mountfield

Mountjoy

B505

Loughmacrory

gh
Nagealge
macavany

Dooish

Lough
Bradan

Drumquin

Gill

104

B50

Killyclogher

A5

Omagh

i

B4

Drumnakilly

B4

B

O M A G H

0   2   4   6 miles
0 2 4 6 8 10 km

Croaghdoo
Ballymagaraghy
rowmenagh
Kinnagoe Bay

Inishowen
Head

eemy · Stroove

reencastle
MARITIME MUSEUM
Magilligan Point
B241

Moville
(un an Phobail)
CASTLE & MUSSENDEN
TEMPLE
Downhill
B202

Magilligan

BINEVENAGH
Binevenagh
384

ymacran
Crindle
A2
Aghanloo
Bolea
A37

lykelly
A2
Limavady
ROE VALLEY

el
Dromore
B69

ih·
Glenhead
Drumsurn

gh
B192

Feeny
B44
BANAGHER
GLEN
Streeve
Mountain
385
Mullaghmore
556

rk
B40

Sawel
Mt.
883
Mullaghaneany
631

Sperrin Mountains
B47
Crockbrack
528

E
Mount Hamilton
Carnanelly
564

anagh
The Six
Towns

Glenhull
Broughderg
Davagh
Forest Park

Slievenagh
269
Oughtmore
382
WELLBROOK
BEETLING MILL

Crockbane
Dunnamore
A505

Creggan
Drum Manor
Forest Park
Gorteagh

Cregganconroe
302

Carrickmore
Pomeroy

ARTIKELLY

GIANT'S CAUSEWAY
Giants
Causeway
COUNTRYSIDE
CENTRE
PORTRUSH
PUFFER
Ramore
Head
FANTASY ISLAND
DUNLUCE CEN
Portstewart
Point
Portstewart
Castlerock
HEZLETT
HOUSE (NT)
Articlave
Ballinteer
Compaw
Macosquin
Crossgare
B186
Balnamore
Ringsend
B66
Boleran
Ballyrogan
B70
Garvagh
B192
Burnfoot
Gortnahey
Benbradagh
468
Foreglen
Derrychrier
Dungiven
Boviel
Carntogher
464
Upperlands
Glenshane Pass
Lisnamuck
Ranaghan
Moneyneany
Tobermore
Draperstown
Desertmartin
B40
Moneymore
Churchtown
A29
Lissan
Oritor
A53
Cookstown
Kildress
B73
TULLYHOGUE
FORT
1520
Tullyhogue
Donaghey

SCHOOL MUSEUM
Runkerry Point
Causeway Head
Portballintrae
B17
DUNLUCE
CAS.
Portrush
A29
Cloyfin
B17
Seneirl
Ballyrashane
COLERAINE
Damhead
MUS.
Castleroe
LESLIE HILL OPEN
FARM & GARDENS
B201
Aghadowey
B188
Moneydig
Craigavole
Bovedy
Swatragh
B75
O'Crilly
Inishrush
Culnady
Maghera
A42
Gulladuff
Knockcloghrim
B42
Curran
A6
CASTLE & MUSSENDEN

Benbane
Head
White
Park Bay
DUNSEVERICK
B146
A2
DISTILLERY
B17
Bushmills
Ballyloughbeg
B66
B67
Derrykeighan
B62
BENVARDEN
Ballybogy
Ballymoney
Milltown
B66
Bendooragh
B62
Finvoy
Vow
Ballymaconnelly
B64
Kilrea
B96
Lislea
Tamlaght
Clady
B96
PORTGLENONE
FOREST PARK
B52
Bellaghy
BELLAGHY
BAWN
B182

Ballintoy
Portbraddan
Lisnagunogue
Straid
Liscolman
Moss-side
B15
Stranocum
The Drones
Killyrammer
Dunaghy
15
A26
Caldanagh
Dunloy
Glarryford
B62
Crai
ARTHUR
ANCESTRAL HOME
Cullybackey
Portglenone
203
Ahoghill
New Ferry
Grange
Corner
Castledawson
Toome

CARRICK-
ROPE BRI
Lagavara
Carnc
Moyarget
B147
An
B15
2
Ar
100
Clough
Clo
A26
B182
Galg
Gracehill
A42
BALLYMENA MUS.
B93
Whitesides
Corner
Moneyglass
Roxhill
Randalstown
4
CASTLE
Staffordstown

KEBBL
Point
BOA

1

BALLYMONEY

COLERAINE

LIMAVADY

MAGHERAFELT
A31
Aughrim
A29
The Loup
Ballyronan
SPRINGHILL &
COSTUME MUSEUM (NT)
Derrychrin
Coagh
Moortown
Ardboe
COOKSTOWN
B160
The Diamond
ARDBOE CROSS
KINTURK
CULTURAL CENTRE
Stanierds Point
Ballinderry
Kil
Killycolpy

Antrim
ANT
BELFAST INT
Ardmo
Po
T.A.C.T. W
Rams Isla
THE BAL
Lough

Magherafelt
A54
Lough
Beg
Moyola

105

C

D

MAGHERAFELT

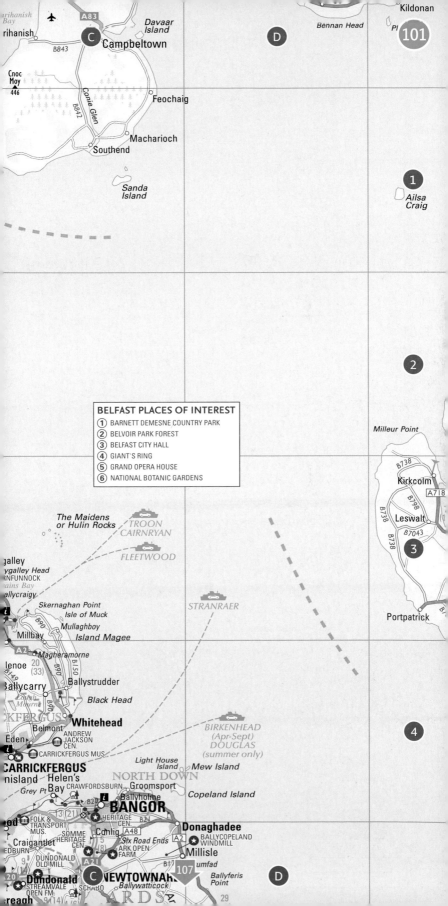

rihanish Bay

Campbeltown

Davaar Island

Kildonan
Bennan Head
Pl

Cnoc Moy 446

Feochaig

Macharioch

Southend

Sanda Island

Ailsa Craig

1

2

Milleur Point

BELFAST PLACES OF INTEREST
1. BARNETT DEMESNE COUNTRY PARK
2. BELVOIR PARK FOREST
3. BELFAST CITY HALL
4. GIANT'S RING
5. GRAND OPERA HOUSE
6. NATIONAL BOTANIC GARDENS

Kirkcolm

Leswalt

3

The Maidens or Hulin Rocks

TROON
CAIRNRYAN

FLEETWOOD

Portpatrick

galley
ygalley Head
RNFUNNOCK
rains Bay
allycraigy

STRANRAER

Skernaghan Point
Isle of Muck
Mullaghboy
Island Magee

Millbay

Magheramorne

lenoe
20
(33)

Ballycarry

Ballystrudder

Black Head

BIRKENHEAD
(Apr-Sept)
DOUGLAS
(summer only)

4

Belmont

Whitehead

ANDREW JACKSON CEN.

Eden

CARRICKFERGUS MUS.

CARRICKFERGUS

nisland

Helen's Bay

Grey Pt

Light House Island

Mew Island

NORTH DOWN

Copeland Island

CRAWFORDSBURN

Groomsport

FOLK & TRANSPORT MUS.

BANGOR

Ballyholme

HERITAGE CEN.

Conlig

SOMME HERITAGE CEN.

Craigantlet

EDBURN

DUNDONALD OLD MILL

Donaghadee

Six Road Ends

A48

BALLYCOPELAND WINDMILL

Millisle

ARK OPEN FARM

umfad

107

Ballyferis Point

STREAMVALE OPEN FM

Dundonald

NEWTOWNAR

SCHABO

Ballywatticock

reagh

RDS

29

D

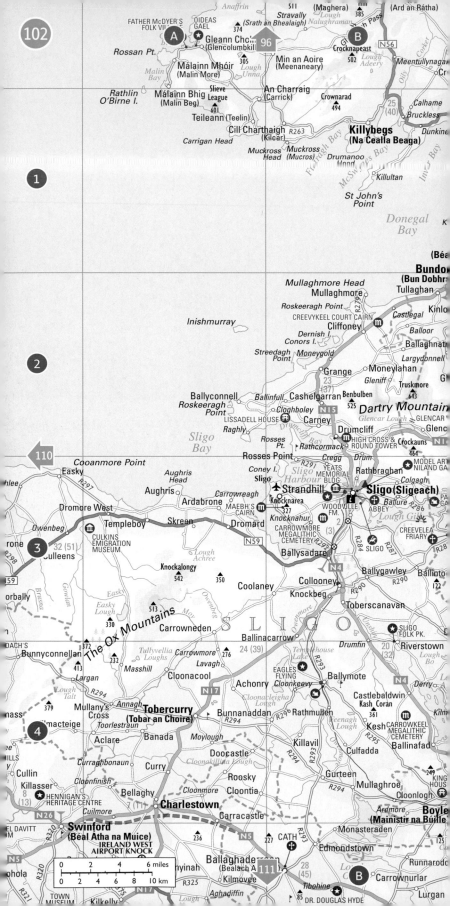

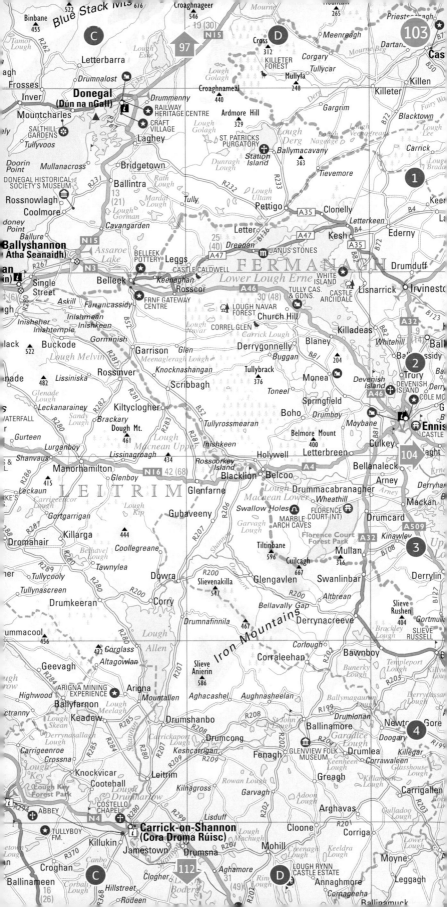

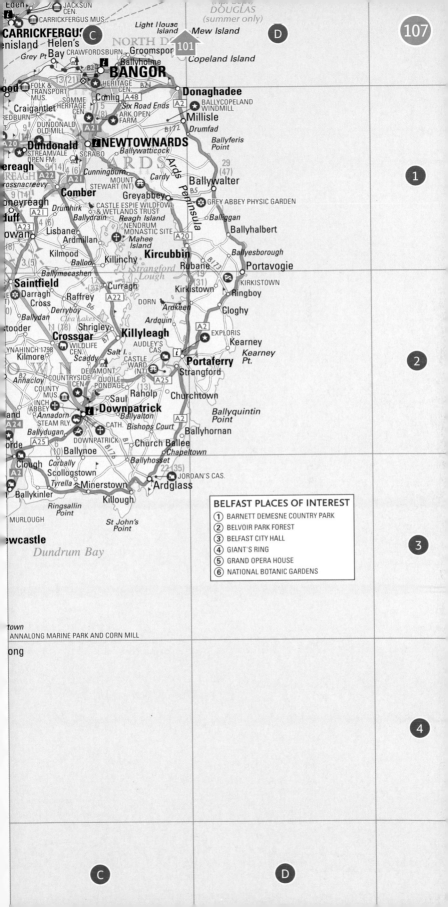

Eden
JACKSON CEN.
CARRICKFERGUS MUS.
CARRICKFERGUS
enisland   Helen's
Grey Pt Bay
CRAWFORDSBURN
Groomspor
Light House Island
Mew Island
DOUGLAS
(summer only)

NORTH DO
Ballyholme
BANGOR
101
Copeland Island
Copeland Island

C

D

FOLK &
TRANSPORT
MUS.
ood
HERITAGE
CEN.
Conlig
A48
Donaghadee
BALLYCOPELAND
WINDMILL
Craigantlet
SOMME
HERITAGE
CEN.
Six Road Ends
A2
Millisle
REDBURN
DUNDONALD
OLD MILL
ARK OPEN
FARM.
Drumfad
B172
Dundonald
NEWTOWNARDS
SCRABO
Ballywatticock
Ballyferis
Point
ereagh
STREAMVALE
OPEN FM.
ARDS
29
(47)

A22
Cunningburn
Cardy
Ballywalter
A21
MOUNT
STEWART (NT)
B5
Comber
Greyabbey
GREY ABBEY PHYSIC GARDEN
Drumhirk
CASTLE ESPIE WILDFOWL
& WETLANDS TRUST
Ballydrain
NENDRUM
MONASTIC SITE
Balliggan
Lisbane
Ardmillan
Reagh Island
Mahee
Island
A20
Ballyhalbert
Kilmood
Balloo
Killinchy
Kircubbin
Ballyesborough
Ballymacashen
Strangford
Lough
Rubane
B173
Portavogie
Saintfield
Darragh
Cross
Curragh
Kirkistown
KIRKISTOWN
Ringboy
Raffrey
DORN
Ardkeen
Derryboy
Ardquin
Cloghy
Clea Lakes
Shrigley
Crossgar
WILDLIFE
CEN.
Scaddy
Killyleagh
EXPLORIS
Kearney
Kearney
Pt.
Kilmore
COUNTRYSIDE
CEN.
Salt I.
AUDLEY'S
CAS.
CASTLE
WARD (NT)
Portaferry
Strangford
Annaclony
COUNTY
MUS.
QUOILE
PONDAGE
A25
INCH
ABBEY
STEAM RLY.
Raholp
Churchtown
Saul
Downpatrick
Ballyalton
Ballyquintin
Point
Annadorn
CATH.
A2
Bishops Court
Ballyhornan
Ballydugan
DOWNPATRICK
Ballynoe
Church Ballee
Chapeltown
Clough
Corbally
Scollogstown
Ballyhosset
22 (35)
JORDAN'S CAS.
Tyrella
Minerstown
Ardglass
Ballykinler
Killough
Ringsallin
Point
St John's
Point
ewcastle
Dundrum Bay

BELFAST PLACES OF INTEREST

1. BARNETT DEMESNE COUNTRY PARK
2. BELVOIR PARK FOREST
3. BELFAST CITY HALL
4. GIANT'S RING
5. GRAND OPERA HOUSE
6. NATIONAL BOTANIC GARDENS

town
ong
ANNALONG MARINE PARK AND CORN MILL

C

D

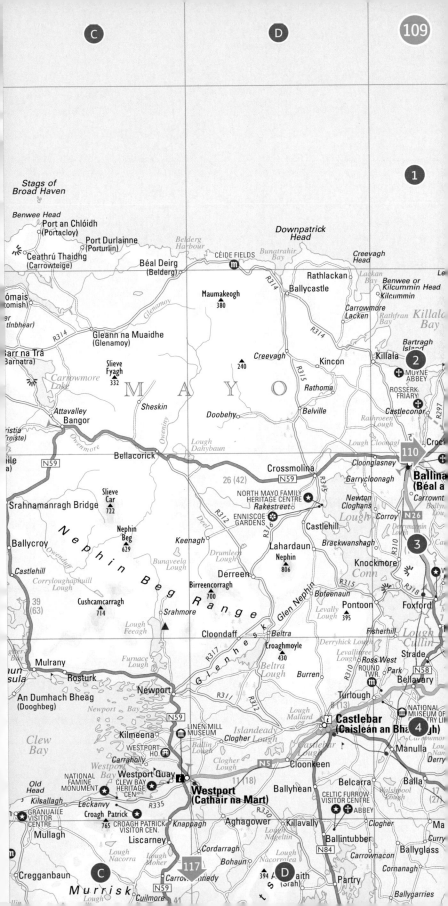

Stags of
Broad Haven

Benwee Head
Port an Chlóidh
(Portacloy)
            Port Durlainne
            (Porturlin)
Ceathrú Thaidhg
(Carrowteige)   Belderg
            Harbour   CÉIDE FIELDS   Bunatrahir   Creevagh
                                              Bay   Head
Ómais   Downpatrick
tomish)   Head
tlnbhear)   Rathlackan   Benwee or
                              Ballycastle   Kilcummin Head
er   Maumakeogh   Kilcummin
Barr na Trá   R314   380   Carrowmore   Rathfran   Killala
Barnatra)   Lacken   Bay   Bay
            Gleann na Muaidhe   R314
            (Glenamoy)   Creevagh   Kincon   Bartragh
Carrowmore   240   Killala   Island
Lake   Slieve   Rathoma   MUYNE
            Fyagh   Belville   ABBEY
            332   M   A   Y   O   ROSSERK
            Sheskin   Rahroeen   FRIARY
Attavalley   Doobehy   Lough   Castleconor
Bangor   Lough Cloonagh   Crocl
ristía   Lough   110
Troiste)   Owenmore   Dahybaun   Crossmolina   Ballina
ile   N59   Bellacorick   R315   Cloonglasney   (Béal a
a)   26 (42)   N59   Garrycloonagh   Carrownt
Srahnamanragh Bridge   Slieve   NORTH MAYO FAMILY   Newton   N26
            Car   HERITAGE CENTRE   Cloghans   Corroy
            722   Rakestreet   ENNISCOE   Derr
Ballycroy   Nephin   GARDENS   Castlehill   Lough   3
            Beg   Keenagh   R310
Castlehill   629   Drumlee   Lahardaun   Brackwanshagh
Corryloughaphuill   Lough   Nephin   Knockmore
Lough   Cushcamcarragh   Derreen   806   Conn   R318   W
            714   Birreencorragh   Bofeenaun   R315   Foxford
            700   Srahmore   Pontoon   R315
            Lough   Cloondaff   Beltra   Levally   395
            Feeagh   Croaghmoyle   Lough   Fisherhill   Lough
Mulrany   Furnace   Beltra   430   Derryhick Lough   Cullin
sula   Lough   Lough   Burren   Levallinree   Strade
            Rosturk   Newport   Beltra   Lough   ROSS WEST   N58
An Dumhach Bheag   Lough   Park   ROUND   Bellavary
(Dooghbeg)   Newport Bay   N59   Turlough   TWR.
Clew   LINEN MILL   Islandeady   NATIONAL
Bay   Kilmeena   MUSEUM   Clogher Lough   Castlebar   MUSEUM OF
            Carraholly   WESTPORT   Ballin   (Caisleán an Bha   TRY LIF
Westport   HO.   Lough   Clogher   Manulla
Bay   NATIONAL   CLEW BAY   Lough   N5   Lou
Old   FAMINE   HERITAGE   Clogher   Cloonkeen   Nan
Head   MONUMENT   CEN.   Lough   Ballyhean   Belcarra   Balla   Derry
            Westport Quay   CELTIC FURROW   17
Kilsallagh   Leckanvy   Westport   Ballyglass   VISITOR CENTRE   (27
GRANUAILE   Croagh Patrick   (Cathair na Mart)   ABBEY   Clogher   Ma
VISITOR   765   CROAGH PATRICK   Knappagh   Aghagower   Killavally   Curry
CENTRE   VISITOR CEN.   Cordarragh   Bohaun   Lough   Ballintubber   Ballyglass
Mullagh   Liscarney   394   Nageltin   Carrownacon   Cornanagh
Cregganbaun   Lough   Lough   Nacorra   N84
            Nacorra   Moher   Carrowkennedy   aith   Partry
            C   N59   (Srah)   Ballygarries
Murrisk   Cuilmore   D

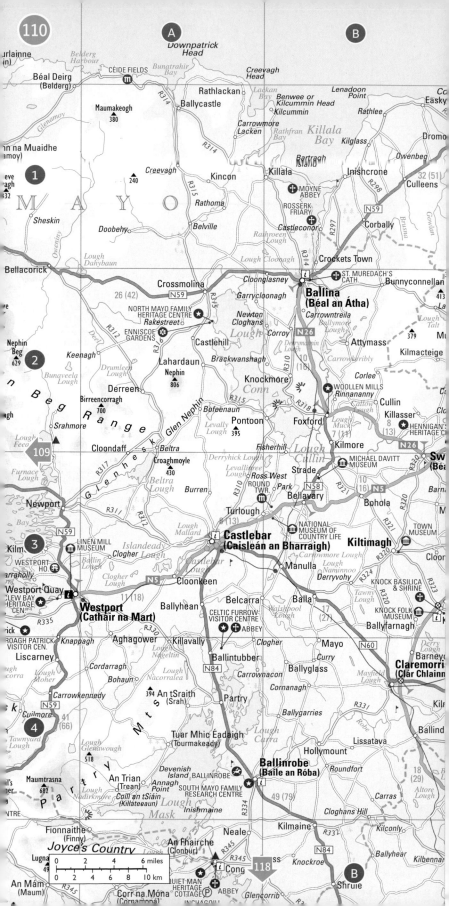

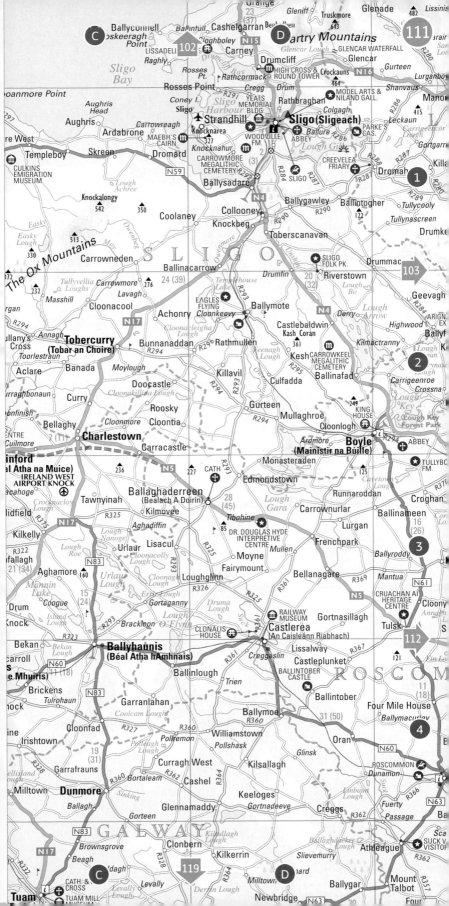

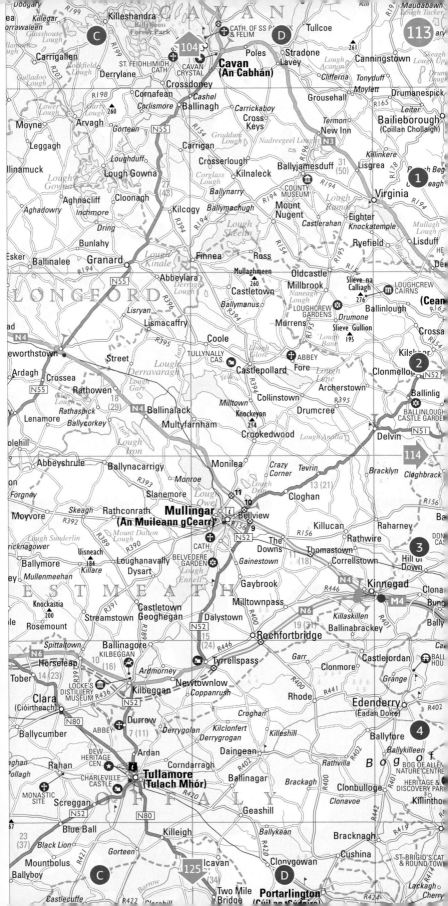

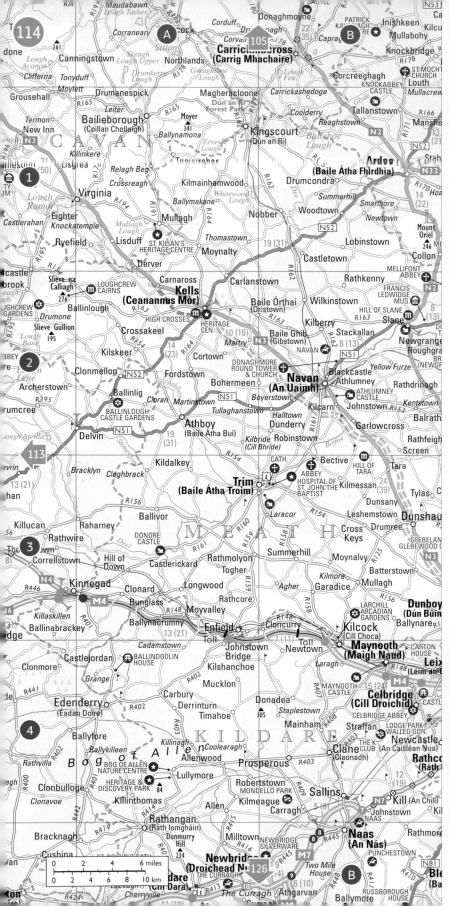

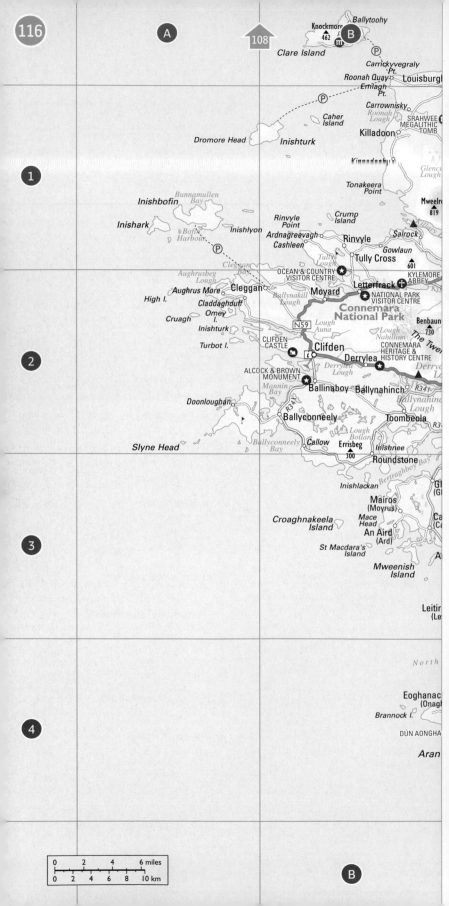

A

108

Ballytoohy
Knockmore
462
B
Clare Island

Carrickyvegraly
Pt.
Roonah Quay
Emlagh
Pt.
Louisburgh

Carrownisky
Roonah
Lough
SRAHWEE
MEGALITHIC
TOMB
Caher
Island
Killadoon

Dromore Head
Inishturk

Kinnadoohy

Glenc
Lough

1

Tonakeera
Point

Mweelre
819

Bunnamullen
Bay
Inishbofin

Rinvyle
Point
Crump
Island

Inishshark
Inishlyon
Ardnagreevagh
Cashleen
Rinvyle
Salrock

Gowlaun
Tully Cross
601

Bofin
Harbour

Tully
Lough
OCEAN & COUNTRY
VISITOR CENTRE
KYLEMORE
ABBEY

Aughrusbeg
Lough
Cleggan
Bay

Letterfrack
NATIONAL PARK
VISITOR CENTRE

Aughrus More
Cleggan
Moyard
Connemara
National Park

High I.
Claddaghduff
Ballynakill
Lough
Benbaun
730

Cruagh
Omey
I.
Inishturk
N59
Lough
Auna
Lough
Nahillion
The Twe

2
Turbot I.
CLIFDEN
CASTLE
Clifden
CONNEMARA
HERITAGE &
HISTORY CENTRE

Derrylea
Derrylea
Lough
Derry
L

ALCOCK & BROWN
MONUMENT
Ballinaboy
Ballynahinch
R341

Doonloughan
Mannin
Bay
Ballynahinch
Lough

Ballyconneely
Toombeola
R3

Slyne Head
Ballyconneely
Bay
Callow
Lough
Bollard
Errisbeg
300
Inishnee

Roundstone
Bertraghboy
Bay

Inishlackan
Gl
(Gl

3
Croaghnakeela
Island
Máiros
(Moyrus)

Mace
Head
Ca
(Ca
An Aird
(Ard)
St Macdara's
Island

Mweenish
Island

Leitir
(Le

North

4
Eoghanac
(Onag
Brannock I.

DÚN AONGHA

Aran

0   2   4   6 miles
0   2 4 6 8 10 km

B

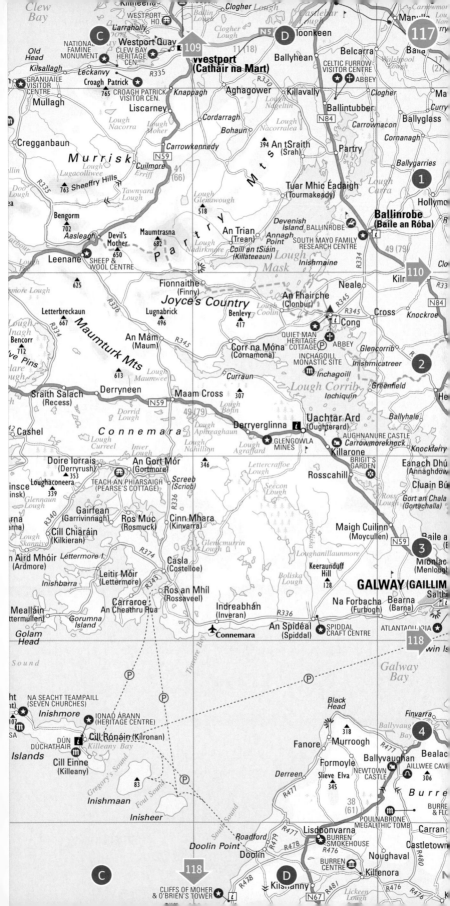

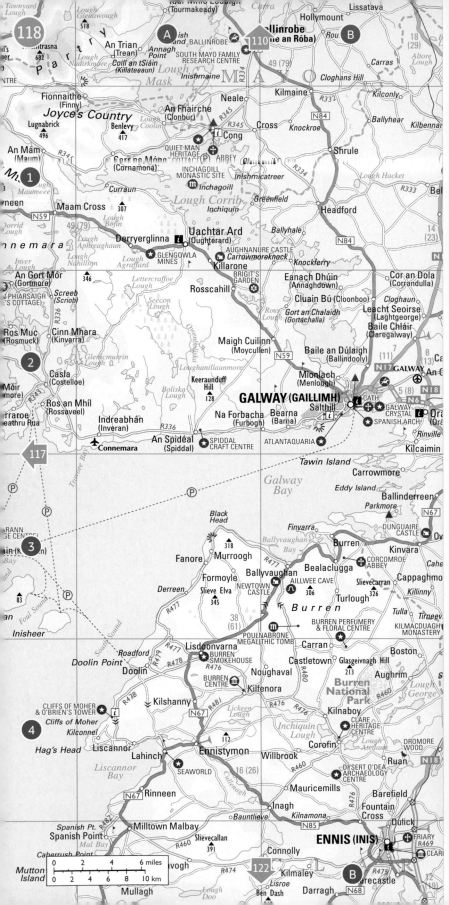

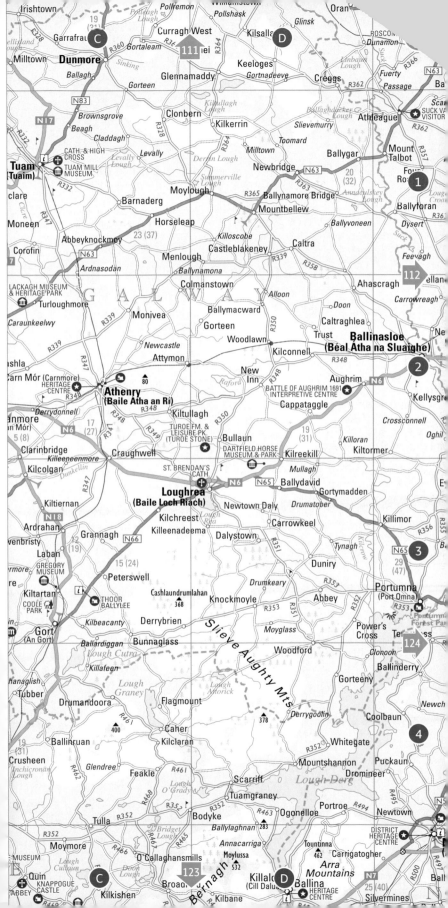

A   B

ATLANTIC

OCEAN

1

2

3

4

Brandon Pt.   Fahamor
Brandon Head   *Brandon Bay*
Cé Bhréanainn   Caher Pt.   Lou Gil
(Brandon)
Stradbally
Ballydavid Hd.   Kilcummi
An Fheothanach   Brandon Mountain   An Clochán
(Feohanagh)   ▲ 953   (Cloghane)
Beenoskee
Sybil Hd.   *Smerwick Harbour*   Baile an Lochaigh   ▲ 827
Ard na Caithne   (Ballinloghig)   *Dingle*
(Smerwick)   An Mhuiríoch   Ballysitteragh
Sybil Pt.   (Murreagh)   ▲ 624   Knockmulanane
GALLARUS   Cill Maoilchéadair   Conor Pass   ▲ 594
ORATORY   (Kilmalkedar)
Baile an Fheirtéaraigh
(Ballyferriter)   OCEANWORLD   Anascaul
Baile an Mhuilinn
Inishtooskert   (Milltown)
THE BLASKET   Dún Chaoin   An Daingean   Lios Póil
CENTRE   (Dunquin)   (Dingle)   (Lispole)
Great   Mt. Eagle
Blasket I.   ▲ 516   Ceann Trá   Minard
Tearaght   (Ventry)   Parkmore   Bull's   Head
Croaghmore   R559   Pt.   Head
0   2   4   6 miles   Slea   *Bay*
0   2   4   6   8   10 km   Head   128   B   *g le*
Inishnabro

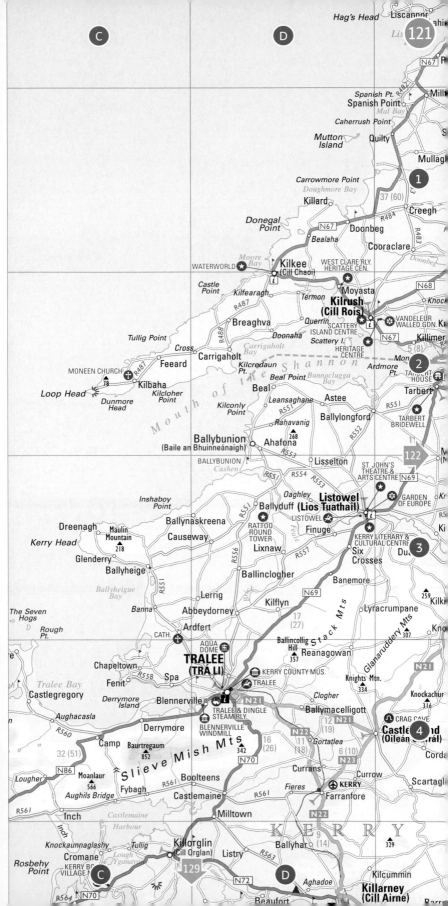

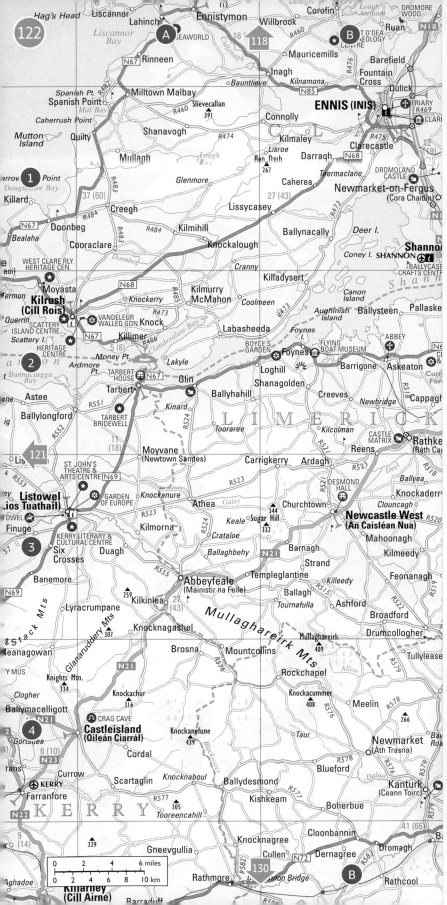

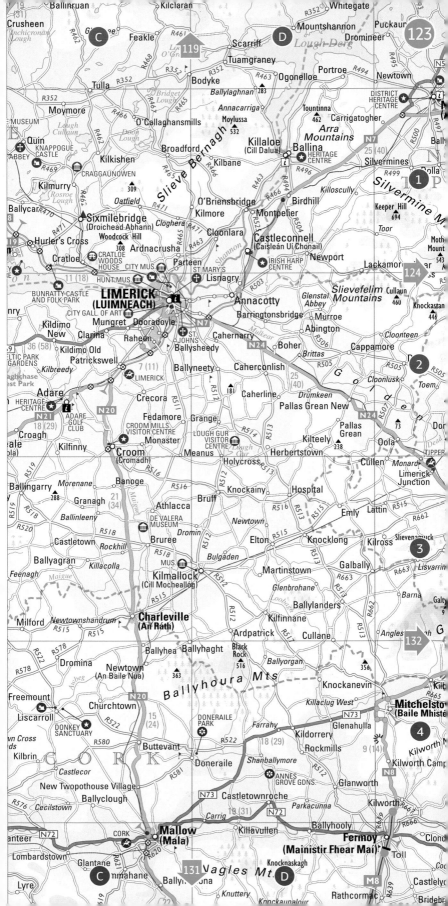

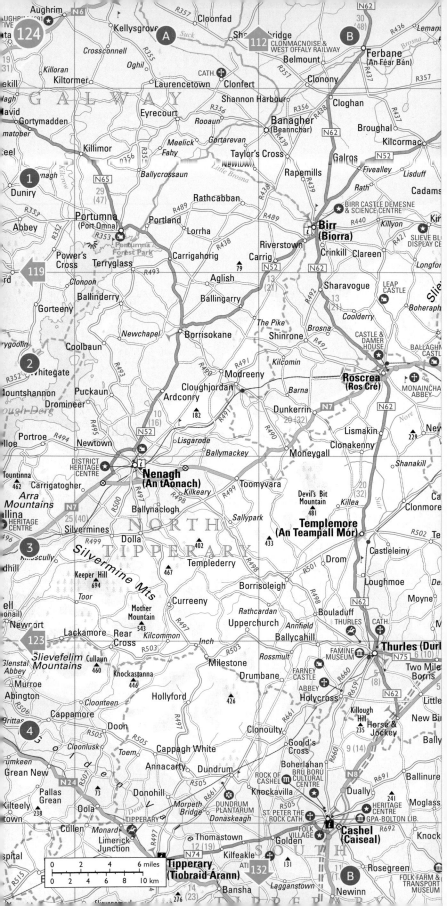

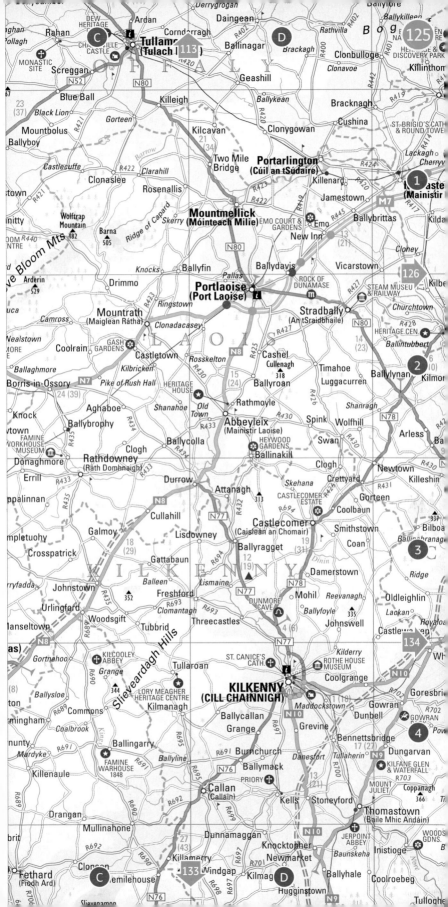

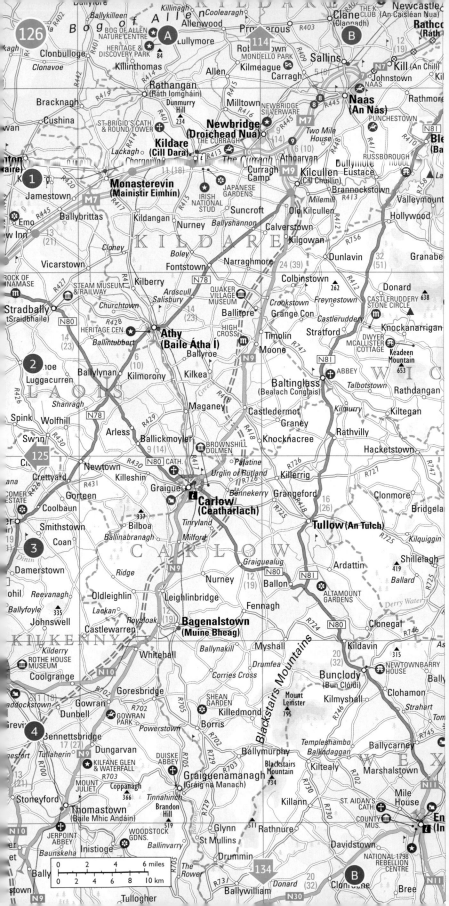

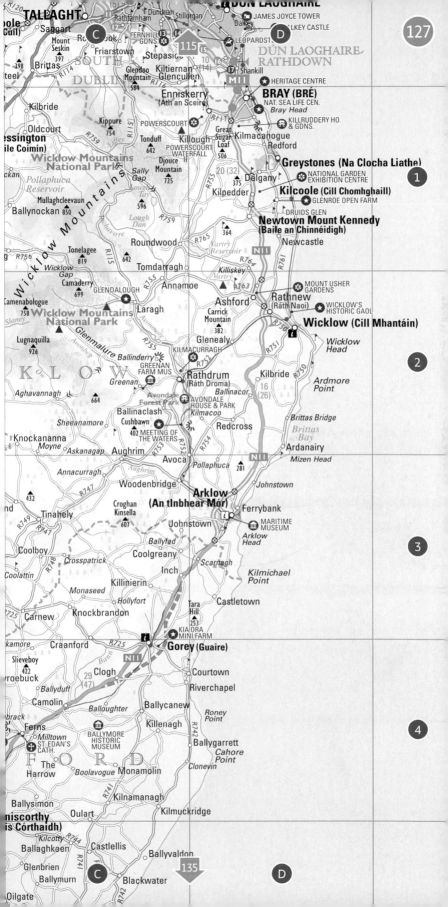

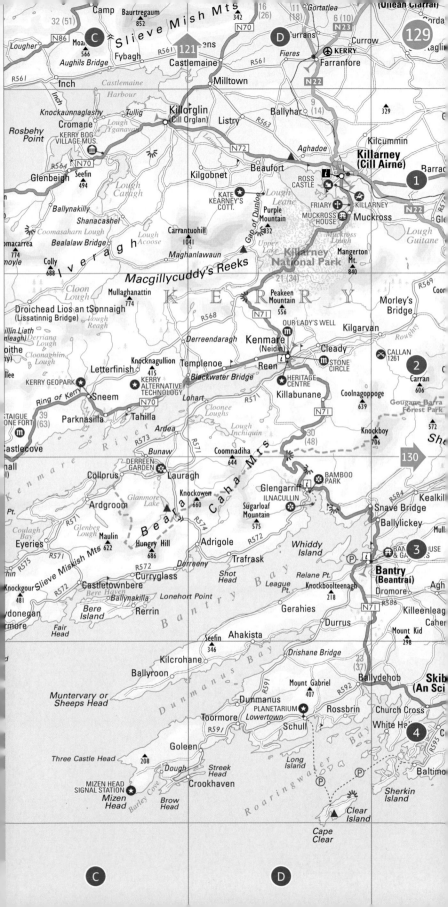

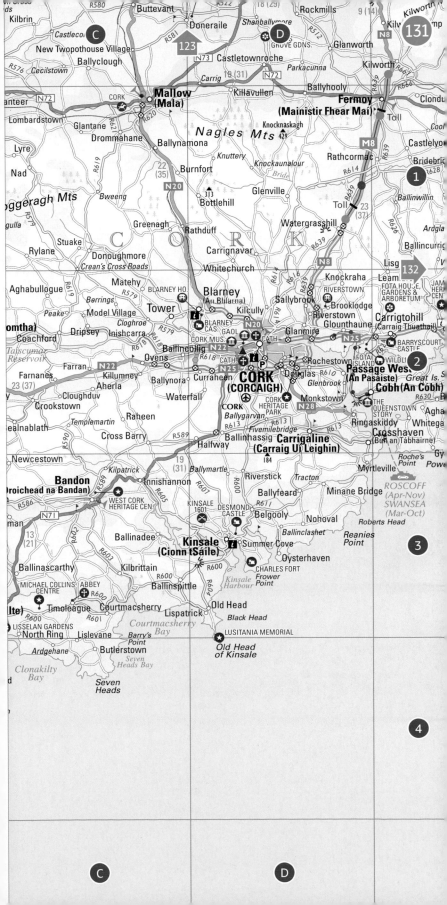

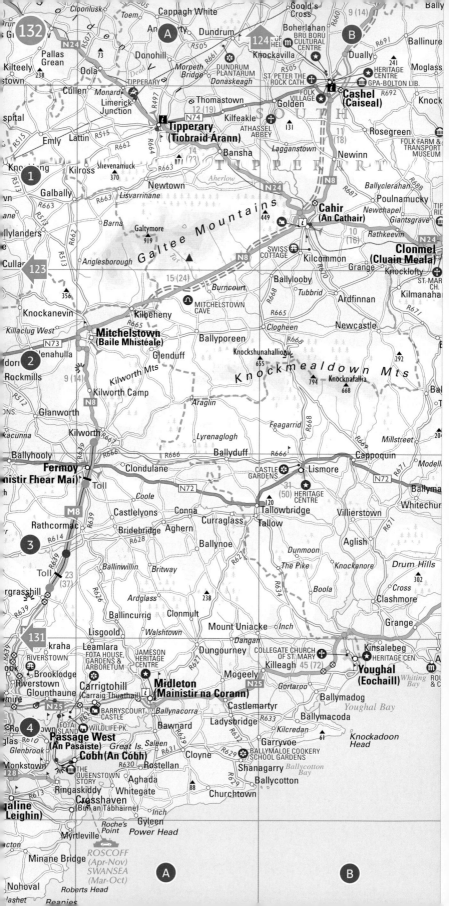

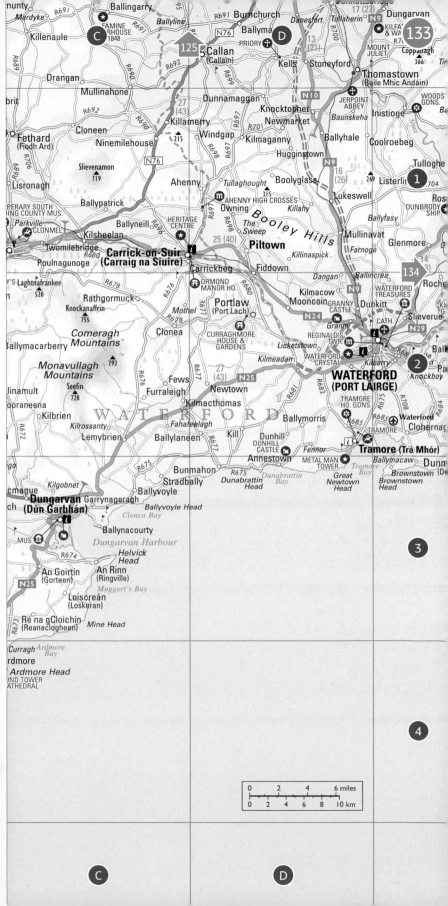

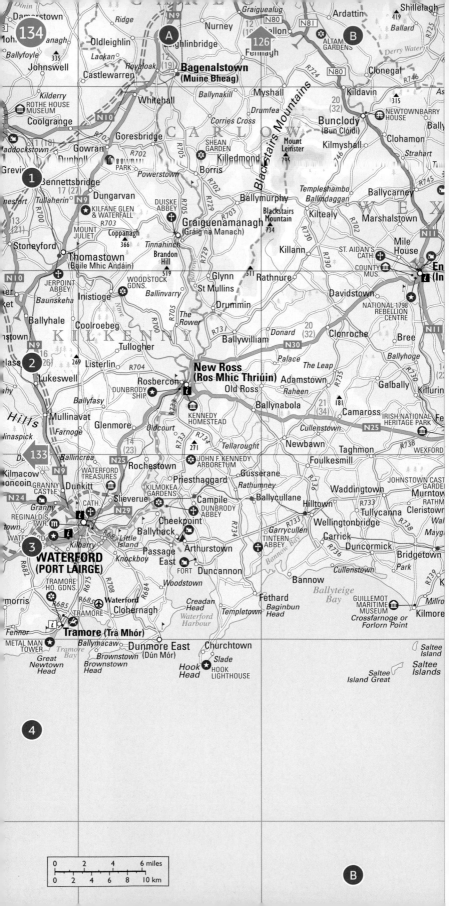

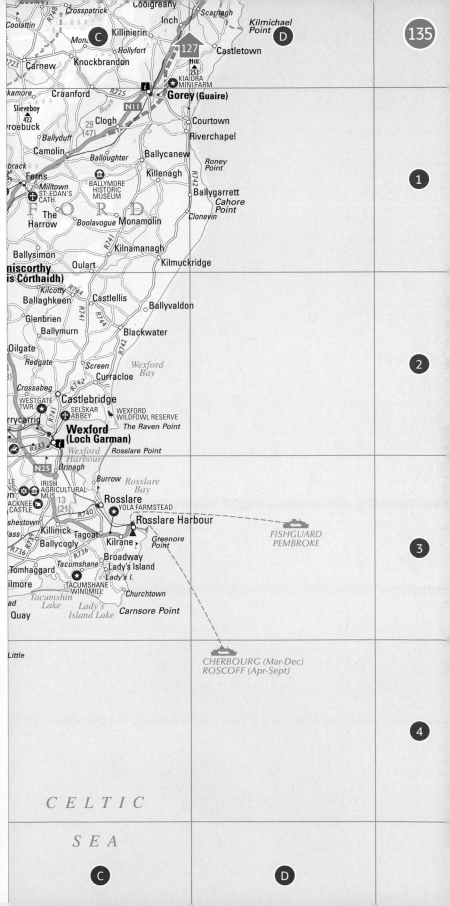

Population: 58,388
Tourist Information Centre: Quay St
☎ 028 912 0069
www.discovernorthernireland.com

INDEX TO PLACES OF INTEREST

INDEX TO STREET NAMES

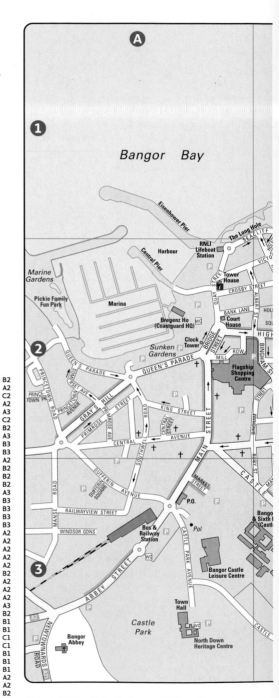

Situated 19km (12 miles) east of Belfast, Bangor is the third largest town in Northern Ireland and historically one of Northern Ireland's main holiday destinations. Sitting on the southern shore of Belfast Lough, it is a maritime resort with one of the largest marinas in Ireland and is home of the Royal Ulster Yacht Club.

Tower House, which is now home to the Tourist Information Centre, dates from around 1605 when King James I gave the land on which Bangor now sits to the Scot Sir James Hamilton. The harbour was

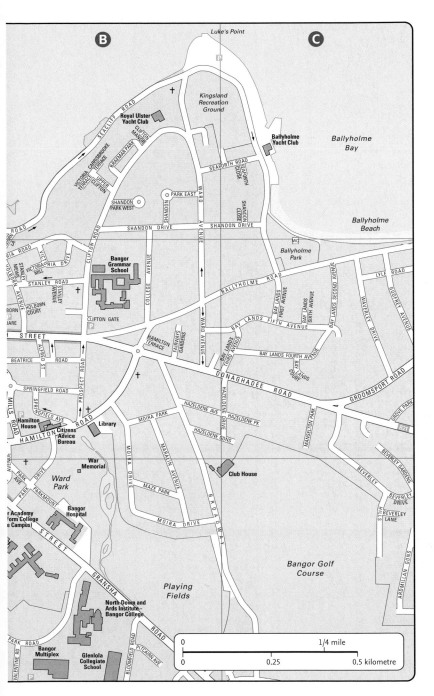

improved in the late 18th century which helped to forge the roots of the town as it is today and the introduction of the railway network in the 1860s brought the town within easy reach of Belfast. Many of the old houses surrounding the harbour that have survived the recent development, date from this period of expansion.

There is a pleasant coastal walk from the sea front at Bangor westwards past several headlands, to the beach at Crawfordsburn and on to Helen's Bay or even Holywood for the more energetic. Crawfordsburn Country Park lies adjacent to the coastline and encompasses Stricklands Glen, at the head of which is an impressive waterfall. There is also a visitor centre and wartime remnants including Grey Point Fort, a coastal battery and gun emplacement dating from the early 20th century.

INDEX TO PLACES OF INTEREST

INDEX TO STREET NAMES

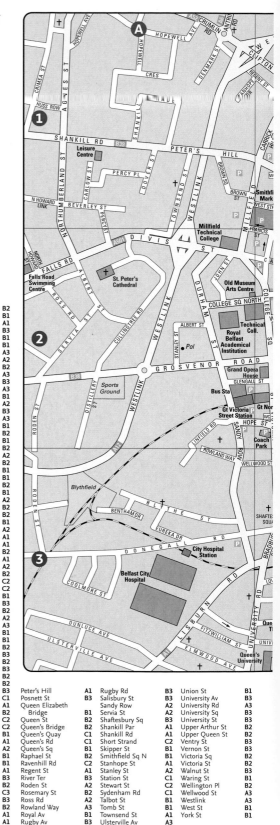

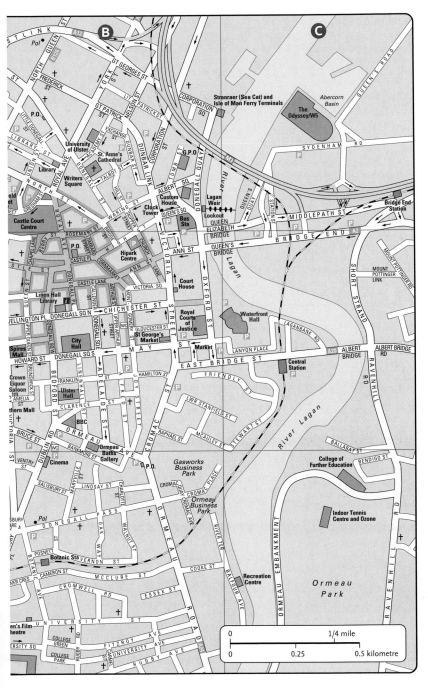

The capital of Northern Ireland whose development as a major port started in 1613 continuing in the 1840s with the elimination of bends in the River Lagan creating Victoria Channel. The Industrial Revolution and the Great Famine led to a population explosion in the 19th century leading to increased tension between the Catholic and Protestant communities, which continued through the partition of Ireland in 1920. The British Army entered Belfast in 1969 to aid the RUC in maintaining calm after continual rioting, resulting in the construction of the 'peace lines' – the early ones being grim concrete and iron walls separating Catholic and Protestant communities such as the Falls Road and Shankill Road areas of West Belfast. The 1996 Good Friday Agreement started the process which has hopefully brought a lasting peace to Northern Ireland.

General information

Population 276,459. The capital of Northern Ireland. Sited on the River Lagan at the mouth of Belfast Lough, the city grew from a small village during the industrial revolution with industries such as linen, rope making and shipbuilding.

Tourist information

The **Belfast Welcome Centre** at 47 Donegall Place, Belfast BT1 5AD provides an information and accommodation booking service ☎ 028 9024 6609 www.gotobelfast.com

Opening times:

Oct – May	Mon to Sat 9.00am – 5.30pm
Jun – Sept	Mon to Sat 9.00am – 7.00pm
	Sun 12.00pm – 5.00pm

Closed Christmas Day and Boxing Day

The Northern Ireland Tourist Board website is available at www.discovernorthernireland.com

Getting around

Two bus services run in and around Belfast city. Ulsterbus transports people in and out of the city and serves all major towns and villages. Metro runs around the city, departing and terminating in the city centre. For information on Metro, Ulsterbus and Northern Ireland Railways contact **Translink** ☎ 028 9066 6630 www.translink.co.uk

The main railway station in Belfast is Central Station, East Bridge Street. For rail enquiries contact **Translink** ☎ 028 9066 6630 www.translink.co.uk

Places of interest

The places of interest section (pages 20-90) includes many places to visit within Belfast city centre. Buildings of architectural interest include **Belfast City Hall** which dominates Donegall Square. It is a striking classical Renaissance style building completed in 1906 and its great copper dome is a landmark throughout the city. Nearby, the **Linen Hall Library** is Belfast's oldest library and is the leading centre for Irish and local studies in Northern Ireland. Specialising in Irish culture and politics, it also has a unique collection of early printed books from Belfast and Ulster. At Queen's University the **Queen's Visitor Centre** provides information about the university and presents a varied programme of exhibitions. Located at the heart of the campus in the Lanyon Room, the centre is named after Charles Lanyon who was the architect of the main Queen's building and many other public buildings in Ireland. Another visitor centre is the **Lagan Lookout Centre** on Donegall Quay which has a multimedia and audiovisual display explaining the history of the Lagan Weir and the industrial and cultural history of Belfast.

City Hall

Photo © Northern Ireland Tourist Board

The extravagant **Crown Liquor Saloon** on Great Victoria Street is of historic interest. It dates from Victorian times and is one of the most famous public houses in Belfast. More recent attractions include **The Odyssey,** a multi-functional entertainment centre which includes an 10,000 seat arena, the W5 interactive discovery centre, cinema and leisure complex. Another well known city centre attraction are the colourful hand painted political murals of West Belfast. They adorn the walls and gable ends of many houses expressing the political viewpoints of the Protestant Shankill Road and the Catholic Falls Road and have become just as much a part of the tourist industry as the more traditional sites of the city. Black cab tours, with commentaries and photo stops, are available to view them.

To the north is **Belfast Castle** which overlooks the city from 122m (400ft) above sea level. Completed in 1870 by the 3rd Marquis of Donegall, this magnificent sandstone castle was refurbished over a 10 year period by Belfast City Council at a cost of more than £2m and was reopened to the public in 1988. East of the city is **Stormont Castle,** the home of the Northern Ireland Parliament. The Main Hall is open to the public and tours for groups can be arranged in advance.

Theatres, concert halls & festivals

Belfast Waterfront Hall ☎ 028 9033 4400 is Northern Ireland's premier concert and conference centre which covers a wide variety of entertainment in its flagship building. The **Grand Opera House** on Great Victoria Street ☎ 028 9024 1919 stages opera, drama, musicals, concerts and pantomime. The declining opulence of the building was restored in 1980 to transform it into a modern theatre whilst still retaining its lavish Victorian interior. **Ulster Hall,** first built in 1862 on Bedford Street ☎ 028 9032 3900, with its interior dominated by a massive English theatre organ, has been a favourite venue for concerts for over 140 years. The **King's Hall** ☎ 028 9066 5225 is another venue for concerts and gala shows. Many international and national events such as the Belfast Telegraph Ideal Home Exhibition and the Ulster Motor Show are held there. The main city centre theatre is the **Lyric Theatre** ☎ 028 9038 1081 which presents both classic and contemporary plays with an emphasis on Irish productions.

Annual events and festivals held in Belfast include the **Belfast Festival** which is held in late autumn at the campus of Queen's University and other city venues. Hosting international theatre, dance, music and comedy, it is Ireland's largest arts festival. The **Cathedral Quarter Arts Festival** is held in May to celebrate the best of the local talent as well as new international work.

Belfast Festival

Photo © Northern Ireland Tourist Board

Shopping

The main city centre shopping area is Donegall Place, most of which is pedestrianised. Belfast is also renowned for its selection of malls and shopping centres. **Castle Court Shopping Centre** in Royal Avenue is Northern Ireland's largest shopping centre, with over 70 shops extending over 3.4ha (8.5 acres). Opposite Castle Court is the modern **Smithfield Market** which replaced the old Victorian market destroyed by fire in 1974. The **Spires Centre and Mall** was refurbished in 1992 to become one of Belfast's most attractive buildings and is the place to shop for designer fashion and giftware.

Castle Court

Photo © Northern Ireland Tourist Board

Parks & gardens

Ormeau Park opened in 1871 and is the largest park in the centre of the city. South of the city the **National Botanic Gardens** are one of Belfast's most popular parks. The restored Palm House was built in 1840 and is one of the earliest examples of a curved glass and wrought iron glasshouse. North of the city **Belfast Zoo** is set in landscaped parkland on the slopes of Cave Hill. Over 160 species are housed there and the zoo increasingly focuses on wildlife facing extinction so has specialised collections with breeding programmes for endangered species.

Banks

The unit of currency is sterling and banks are usually open from Monday to Friday 9.30am until 4.30pm with the larger branches also open on Saturday mornings. There are numerous ATMs (Automatic Teller Machines) located at banks, shopping centres and petrol stations. For visitors from the Republic of Ireland there are also branches of Bank of Ireland throughout Northern Ireland.

Internet Cafes

Belfast Welcome Centre, 47 Donegal Place ☎ 028 9024 6609
Friends Café, 109-113 Royal Avenue ☎ 028 9024 1096
ITXP, 175-177 Ormeau Road ☎ 028 9022 8111
ITXP, The Kennedy Centre, Falls Road ☎ 028 9096 2222
Revelations, 27 Shaftesbury Square ☎ 028 9032 0337

Telephoning

If telephoning from Great Britain or Northern Ireland use the area code and telephone number. If telephoning from the Republic of Ireland replace 028 with 048 and follow with the required telephone number.

Population: 186,239
Tourist Information Centre: Grand Parade
☎ 021 425 5100
www.corkkerry.ie

INDEX TO PLACES OF INTEREST

INDEX TO STREET NAMES

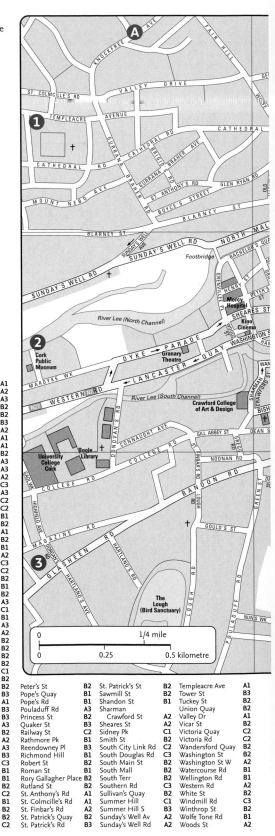

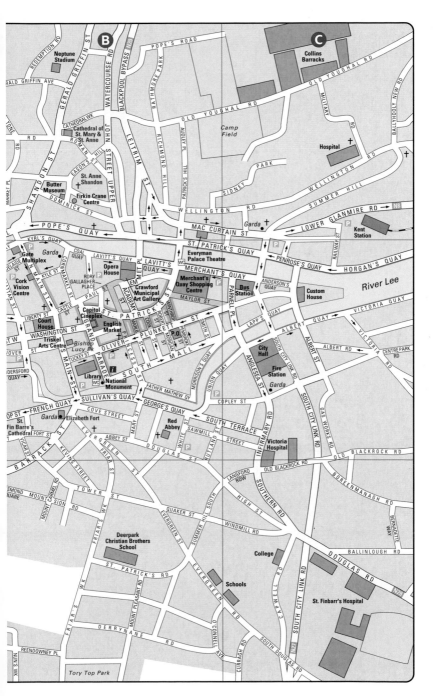

Cork is Ireland's third largest city behind Dublin and Belfast. The Irish form is Corcaigh, meaning marshy place, though the marshes are no longer in evidence. The city developed on the estuary of the River Lee and is now the cultural capital of the south west as well as a major commercial centre. Its origins date back to the 6th century when St Finbar set up a monastic settlement. Subsequently the Vikings established the trading centre and developed in the 12th century by the Normans, starting the growth into the city as it is known today. This growth was interrupted in 1349 when bubonic plague took the lives of almost half of the city's population. The Great Famine of the 1840s led to a huge increase in population as people left the country in search for food and work which had the effect of increasing poverty and reducing the overall standard of living in the city. Parts of the city walls that once surrounded the city still survive.

Population: 31,020
Tourist Information Centre: Mayoralty St
☎ 041 983 7070
www.eastcoastmidlands.ie

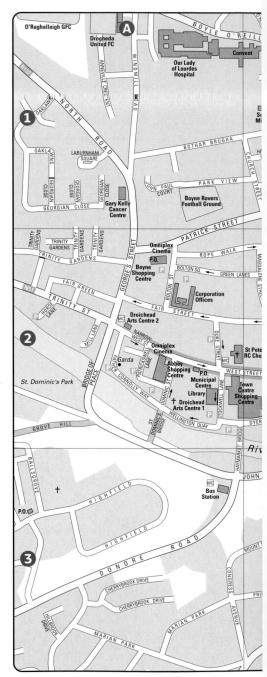

Drogheda is known as the 'Gateway to the Boyne Valley' is situated 51 km (32 miles) north of Dublin. The recent construction of the M1 motorway from Dundalk to Dublin has brought the town to within easy reach of Dublin and Dublin Airport. The nearby Irish Sea coast has beautiful sandy beaches stretching from Clogherhead in the north past Laytown to just north of Balbriggan. Most are accessible by car and are popular for a wide variety of sports including swimming, horse riding, power kites, land yachts and kite surfing and fishing. Laytown Strand is unique in having an annual three

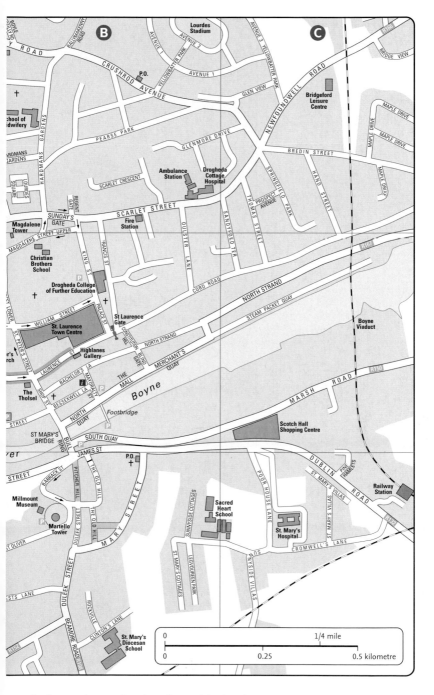

day horse racing meeting, the only remaining beach meeting run to Jockey Club rules. The tradition started in 1876 and features a grandstand cut into the sand dunes.

It is thought that St. Patrick founded a monastery on the site of Drogheda in the 5th century. The modern town dates back to the Norman invasion when two separate towns were established, linked by a bridge over the River Boyne which gives the town its name Droichead Atha, 'the bridge of the ford'. After much fighting between the two settlements they were united into a single borough in 1412. The head of Oliver Plunkett, the Archbishop of Armagh, is on display in St Peter's Church. He was arrested for conspiring to organise a rebellion against the crown, found guilty of treason and hung, drawn and quartered at Tyburn in London in 1681. He was canonised in 1975.

INDEX TO PLACES OF INTEREST

INDEX TO STREET NAMES

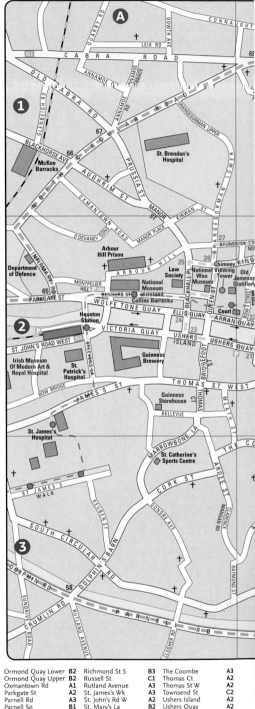

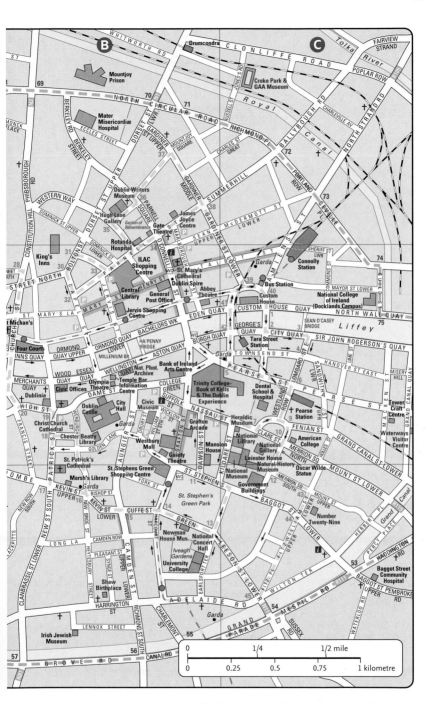

B WHITWORTH RD · Drumcondra · CLONLIFFE ROAD · Tolka · FAIRVIEW STRAND
C · POPLAR ROW · River

Mountjoy Prison

Croke Park & GAA Museum · JONES'S RD · Royal · CHARLEVILLE AV

NORTH CIRCULAR ROAD · RICHMOND PL · BALLYBOUGH · NORTH STRAND RD
69 · 70 · 71 · 72 · 73 · 74

Mater Misericordiæ Hospital · ECCLES STREET · MOUNTJOY SQUARE · CHARLES ST GREAT · PORTLAND ROW · SEVILLE PL

BERKELEY RD · BERKELEY STREET · DORSET ST UPPER · GARDINER ST UPPER · SUMMERHILL · McDERMOTT ST LOWER

PHIBSBOROUGH RD · WESTERN WAY · 37

Dublin Writers Museum · 36 · James Joyce Centre · GARDINER MIDDLE · SEAN McDERMOTT ST LOWER

CONSTITUTION HILL · DOMINICK ST UPPER · 35 · Garden of Remembrance · Gate Theatre · GARDINER ST LOWER · AMIENS ST

King's Inns · 31 · Rotunda Hospital · PARNELL SQUARE · SHERIFF ST LWR

28 · 30 · DOMINICK ST LOWER · 33 · ILAC Shopping Centre · O'CONNELL ST UPPER · Garda · Connolly Station · COMMONS ST · MAYOR ST LOWER · 74

Central Library · St. Mary's Cathedral · Dublin Spire · General Post Office · Custom House · Bus Station · National College of Ireland (Docklands Campus) · 40 · 75

STREET NORTH · 32 · CAPEL STREET · JERVIS ST · HENRY ST · Jervis Shopping Centre · Abbey Theatre · 39 · CUSTOM HOUSE QUAY · NORTH WALL QUAY

St Michan's · Four Courts · BACHELORS WK · EDEN QUAY · GEORGE'S QUAY · CITY QUAY · SEAN O'CASEY BRIDGE · Liffey

INNS QUAY · ORMOND QUAY UPPER · ORMOND QUAY LOWER · Ha'penny Bridge · BURGH QUAY · Tara Street Station · SIR JOHN ROGERSON'S QUAY · 42 · TOWNSEND ST · Garda

MERCHANTS QUAY · WOOD QUAY · ESSEX QUAY · MILLENIUM BR · ASTON QUAY · Bank of Ireland Arts Centre · PEARSE ST · LOMBARD ST · HANOVER ST EAST · MISERY HILL

Dublinia · Civic Offices · WELLINGTON QUAY · Nat. Phot. Archive · COLLEGE GREEN · Trinity College- Book of Kells & The Dublin Experience · Dental School & Hospital · Tower Craft Centre

HIGH ST · 19 · Olympia Theatre · Temple Bar Information Centre · DAME ST · SUFFOLK ST · NASSAU ST · Heraldic Museum · Pearse Station · 10 · GRAND CANAL ST LOWER · Waterways Visitor Centre

Christ Church Cathedral · 20 · Dublin Castle · City Hall · Civic Museum · WICKLOW ST · Grafton Arcade · National Library · American College · FENIAN ST · MOUNT ST LOWER

18 · Chester Beatty Library · GOLDEN LANE · Westbury Mall · Mansion House · National Gallery · Natural History Museum · Oscar Wilde Statue · MERRION SQ

FRANCIS ST · St Patrick's Cathedral · Gaiety Theatre · DAWSON ST · KILDARE ST · Leinster House · National Museum · Government Buildings · 43 · MOUNT ST UPPER

Marsh's Library · Garda · St Stephens Green Shopping Centre · ST. STEPHEN'S GREEN · 12 · 44 · Number Twenty-Nine · Grand · HERBERT PL

KEVIN ST UPPER · 16 · BISHOP ST · YORK ST · St. Stephen's Green Park · LEESON ST LOWER · FITZWILLIAM ST LWR · PERCY PL

17 · KEVIN ST LOWER · 15 · CUFFE ST · 14 · GREEN · 13 · Newman House Mus. · National Concert Hall · i · 53 · HADDINGTON RD

NEW ST SOUTH · NEW BRIDE ST · CAMDEN ST UPPER · CAMDEN ROW · PLEASANT ST · Iveagh Gardens · University College · EARLSFORT TER · WILTON TER · Baggot Street Community Hospital

BLACKPITTS · LONG LA · SYNGE ST · HEYTESBURY STREET · Shaw Birthplace · HARRINGTON ST · BAGGOT ST UPPER · PEMBROKE RD

CLANBRASSIL ST LOWER · LENNOX STREET · RICHMOND ST SOUTH · CHARLEMONT · ADELAIDE · Garda · MESPIL RD · WATERLOO RD · 54

Irish Jewish Museum · 55 · GRAND PARADE · SUSSEX RD

57 · GROVE RD · CANAL RD · 56

0 · 1/4 · 1/2 mile
0 · 0.25 · 0.5 · 0.75 · 1 kilometre

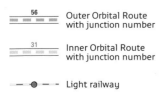

— 56 — Outer Orbital Route with junction number

— 31 — Inner Orbital Route with junction number

●— Light railway

The historic heart of the city is south of the River Liffey which is where the city originated, with the main shopping areas centred around O'Connell and Grafton Streets. The Cultural Quarter of the Temple Bar area was first developed in the 19th century and is a lively, rejuvenated collection of pubs, restaurants, music venues and the more alternative shops. There are numerous festivals including the Theatre Festival held in late September to mid October, the Film Festival in March, the Writers Festival in June and Art Ireland Exhibition in November.

General information

Population 1,004,614. The capital of the Republic of Ireland. The name is derived from the Irish 'Dubh Linn' meaning Black Pool. It originated south of the River Liffey and this is still the historic heart of the city.

Tourist information

Information lines   ☎ 1850 230 330 (Republic of Ireland)
                              ☎ 08000 397000 (G.B & N. Ireland)

Accommodation reservations ☎ 1800 668 668 (Republic of Ireland)
                              ☎ 00800 668 668 66 (G.B & N. Ireland)

The main **Dublin Tourism Centre** is on Suffolk Street, Dublin 2 ☎ 01 605 7700.

Formerly St Andrew's Church, the centre provides details of visitor attractions and events in the city as well as acting as a ticket and accommodation bureau.

Opening times:

Oct – Jun   Mon to Sat 9.00am – 5.30pm
July – Aug   Mon to Sat 9.00am – 8.00pm
Sept   Mon to Sat 9.00am – 7.00pm
Sun & Bank Holidays: 10.30am – 3.00pm

There are also Tourism Centres open all year at:
O'Connell Street (Mon to Sat 9.00am-5.00pm; closed Bank Holidays)
Dublin Airport (8.00am – 10.00pm)
Dún Laoghaire (Mon to Sat 10.00 – 1.00pm, 2.00pm – 6.00pm)

The official tourist information website for Dublin is www.visitdublin.com

There is an **Irish Tourist Board (Bord Fáilte)** office at Baggot Street Bridge, Dublin 2.
☎ 01 602 4000 (Mon to Fri 9.30am – 12.00pm, 12.30pm – 5.00pm. Closed Bank Holidays).

The **Dublin Pass** allows fast-track entry to many visitor attractions for a 1, 2, 3 or 6 day period. It can also be used on public transport and to obtain discount in some shops and restaurants. www.dublinpass.ie

Getting around

Dublin is linked with the cities and towns of Ireland by a network of rail and bus services overseen by **Córas Iompair Éireann (CIÉ),** which is Ireland's National Transport Authority www.cie.ie

National bus services between Dublin, Dublin Airport and other major cities and towns are provided by **Irish Bus (Bus Éireann)** ☎ 01 836 6111 www.buseireann.ie

Dublin Bus (Bus Átha Cliath) operates the public bus services in Dublin and the surrounding area with its head office at 59 O'Connell Street Upper. ☎ 01 873 4222 www.dublinbus.ie

The two mainline railway stations, Dublin Connolly and Dublin Heuston, are operated by **Irish Rail (Iarnód Éireann)** ☎ 1850 366222 www.irishrail.ie. Irish rail also operates the suburban rail network in Dublin and DART (Dublin Area Rapid Transit) with stations between Howth on the north of Dublin Bay to Bray in the south.

Luas (the Irish for speed), the Dublin light railway system runs from Tallaght to Connolly station and from Sandyford to St Stephen's Green ☎ 1800 300 604 www.luas.ie

Taxis are available at taxi ranks, including ones on O'Connell Street, Dame Street and St. Stephen's Green West.

Places of interest

The places of interest section (pages 20-90) includes many places to visit within Dublin city centre - **Christ Church Cathedral, Dublin Castle,** the **National Museum of Ireland** and **St Patrick's Cathedral.** There are of course many more.

Landmark buildings include the fine **City Hall** building which was completed in 1779 as the Royal Exchange. Subsequent use included a prison and corn exchange before being taken over by the city in 1852. Another building of architectural interest is the **Custom House,** with its magnificent long river frontage. The **Four Courts** building with its shallow dome is one of the most distinctive landmarks in Dublin. The name derives from the traditional four judicial divisions of Ireland: - Chancery, King's Bench, Exchequer and Common Pleas. It was extensively damaged during the Irish Civil War of 1921-22 but was, externally, restored to the original plans with only minor modifications. The interior was substantially changed. The **General Post Office** in O'Connell Street was the headquarters of the 1916 Rising and further down O'Connell Street stands the Millennium Spire on the site of Nelsons Pillar that was partially blown up by the IRA in 1966 to celebrate the anniversary of the Rising. Museums include the **Dublin Writers Museum** which traces the history of Irish literature from its earliest times to the 20th century. Another literary attraction is the **James Joyce Centre,** devoted to the great novelist and run by members of his family in a restored Georgian town house. **Number 29** is an elegant four-storey house, restored and finished in detail for the period 1790-1820. The **Trinity College** complex of cobbled quadrangles and peaceful gardens has a library of over a million books, including the famous Book of Kells. Galleries include the **National Gallery of Ireland** with its Old Masters, illustrious 20th century European artists and the National Collection of Irish Art and the **Hugh Lane Municipal Art Gallery** which has an extensive collection of 19th and 20th century paintings, sculpture and stained glass.

There are many bridges crossing the River Liffey including the recent **Millennium Bridge** & **Sean O'Casey Bridge** and the famous **Ha'penny Bridge** which was opened in 1816. It is officially the **Wellington Bridge** but is better known as the Ha'Penny after the toll that used to be levied to cross the bridge. A major restoration programme was completed in 2001 when it was restored to its original paintwork. It was the only footbridge across the Liffey until the Millennium Bridge was opened in 2000.

Ha'penny Bridge

Theatres, concert halls & festivals

The **Abbey Theatre** ☎ 01 878 7222 is Ireland's National Theatre. Classic Irish plays are staged in the main theatre whilst the **Peacock Theatre** downstairs presents new and experimental drama. Other Dublin theatres include the **Crypt** at Dublin Castle ☎ 01 671 3387, the **Gaiety Theatre** ☎ 01 677 1717 and the **Project Arts Centre** ☎ 01 881 9613. The **National Concert Hall,** Earlsfort Terrace ☎ 01 417 0000, is the home of the National Symphony Orchestra of Ireland and is also a venue for international artists and orchestras, jazz, contemporary and traditional Irish music.

Throughout the year Dublin hosts numerous festivals – the Theatre Festival held in late September to mid October, the Film Festival in March, the Writers Festival in June and the Art Ireland Exhibition in November.

Shopping

The main city centre shopping areas are around Grafton Street and Nassau Street to the south of the Liffey and around Henry Street (off O'Connell Street) to the north of the river. Both Grafton Street and Henry Street are pedestrianised. Many up-market and international designer stores can be found in Grafton Street as well as the department stores of Arnotts and Brown Thomas. Shops in Henry Street include the department stores of Dunnes and Roches. The rejuvenated cultural quarter of **Temple Bar** is the area to go for craft and specialist stores, as well as more alternative shops. Shopping centres include the **St Stephen's Green Centre,** the **ILAC Centre** in Henry Street, the **Irish Life Shopping Mall** in Abbey Street, the **Jervis Shopping Centre** in Jervis Street and the **Powerscourt Centre** in South William Street.

Parks, gardens & monuments

In the heart of the city **St Stephen's Green** was originally an open common but was enclosed in 1663. Opened to the general public in 1877, it is laid out as a public park with flowerbeds, an ornamental pond and several sculptures.

Northwest of the city centre **Phoenix Park** covers over 712 ha (1760 acres) and is Europe's largest enclosed city park. It was laid out in the mid 18th century and was the scene of the Phoenix Park murders in 1882, when the Chief Secretary and Under-Secretary for Ireland were assassinated. The park contains several buildings, including Áras an Uachtaráin, the official residence of the President of Ireland. In the southeast corner, by the main entrance, is **Dublin Zoo** and also the Victorian style ornamental planting of **The People's Garden.**

Many statues and monuments are to be found around Dublin, many of which have colourful nicknames – the statue of **Molly Malone** on Grafton Street has been known as the Tart with the Cart, Fish with the Dish and Dolley with the Trolley amongst others. In O'Connell Street stands a statue of the 19th century nationalist leader **Daniel O'Connell** in which bullet holes from the 1916 Rising can still be seen.

Molly Malone Statue, Grafton Street

Telephoning

If telephoning from the Republic of Ireland use the area code and telephone number. If telephoning from Great Britain or within Northern Ireland use the code 00353, delete the 0 from the area code and follow with the required telephone number.

Population: 24,447
Tourist Information Centre: Ferry Terminal
☎ 1850 230330 (08000 397000 from UK)
www.visitdublin.com

Situated on the coast about 11km (7 miles) south of Dublin, Dún Laoghaire derives from the Irish 'Fort of Laoghaire', after an ancient king of Ireland. In 1821 it was renamed Kingstown to commemorate the visit of King George IV and remained so until 1921 when it reverted to its Irish name. It hosts the annual three day 'Festival of World Cultures' at the end of August celebrating arts and entertainment throughout the world in over 40 venues across the town www.festivalofworldcultures.com. It is one of the main ferry ports for the Republic of Ireland and is within easy reach of Dublin by both private and public transport by DART (Dublin Area Rapid Transport).

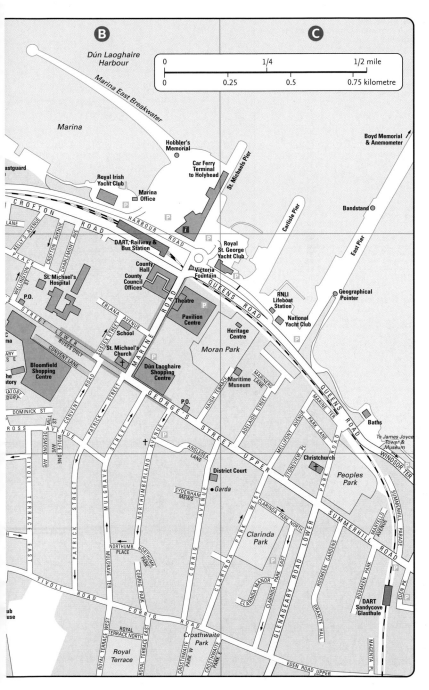

Dún Laoghaire Harbour

Marina East Breakwater

Marina

| 0 | | 1/4 | | 1/2 mile |
| 0 | 0.25 | 0.5 | 0.75 kilometre |

astguard

Hobbler's Memorial

Boyd Memorial & Anemometer

Car Ferry Terminal to Holyhead

Royal Irish Yacht Club

St. Michaels Pier

Marina Office

Carlisle Pier

Bandstand

CROFTON ROAD

HARBOUR ROAD

LANE

ELLI's AVENUE

PLACE

CROFTON AVENUE

CHARLEMONT AVE

WELLINGTON

DART, Railway & Bus Station

East Pier

Royal St. George Yacht Club

County Hall

Victoria Fountain

Geographical Pointer

St. Michael's Hospital

County Council Offices

EBLANA AVENUE

P.O.

STREET

MARINE ROAD

QUEENS ROAD

RNLI Lifeboat Station

Theatre

SUSSEX STREET

LOWER

BUSES ONLY

Pavilion Centre

National Yacht Club

CONVENT LANE

School

Heritage Centre

ma

St. Michael's Church

Moran Park

Bloomfield Shopping Centre

itory

Dún Laoghaire Shopping Centre

DOMINICK ST

GEORGE'S

P.O.

HAIGH TERRACE

Maritime Museum

MARINERS LANE

MARINE TER

ROSS

AVENUE

WOLFE TONE

PATRICK

STREET

STREET

MULGRAVE

ADELAIDE STREET

MELLIFONT AVENUE

PARK LANE

Baths

To James Joyce Tower & Museum

DESMOND AVE

STREET UPPER

ANGLESEA LANE

STONEVIEW PL

Christchurch

WINDSOR TER

TIVOLI

NORTHUMBERLAND AVENUE

CORRIG AVENUE

SYDENHAM MEWS

District Court

Garda

PARK WEST

Peoples Park

SUMMERHILL ROAD

MARTELLO AVENUE

SUMMERHILL PARADE

TERRACE

CLARINDA PARK NORTH

Clarinda Park

CLARINDA PARK EAST

GLENAGEARY ROAD LOWER

ROSMEEN GARDENS

ROSMEEN PARK

EAST

NORTHUMB PLACE

NORTHUMB PARK

CLARINDA PARK

CLARINDA MANOR

GRANITE HALL

DART Sandycove/ Glasthule

PATRICK STREET

MULGRAVE TER

CORRIG PARK

TIVOLI ROAD

CORRIG ROAD

ROYAL TERRACE NORTH

ROYAL TERRACE EAST

Crosthwaite Park

EDEN ROAD UPPER

MAGENTA PL

ub use

ROYAL TERRACE WEST

ROYAL TERRACE

ROYAL TERRACE W

Royal Terrace

CROSTHWAITE PARK W

CROSTHWAITE PARK E

The beautiful Wicklow Mountains are easily accessible to the south and the completion of the M50 Dublin orbital motorway has meant much easier access to the central and western parts of Ireland giving Dún Laoghaire even greater value as the point of entry for visitors to Ireland.

19 km (12 miles) outside the harbour at Dún Laoghaire was the scene of the greatest disaster in Irish naval history when the RMS Leinster was torpedoed by a German U-Boat in 1918 with the loss of 501 of the 771 on board. Many of those who died were soldiers returning from or going on leave as the Great War was coming to an end. A plaque commemorating the dead was unveiled on the seafront in 2005 where there is also a restored anchor that was recovered from the wreck in 1996. After the war was over it emerged that the U-Boat that sank the Leinster was lost in the North Sea on the way home after striking a mine.

Population: 66,163
Tourist Information Centre: Forster St
☎ 091 537700
www.irelandwest.ie

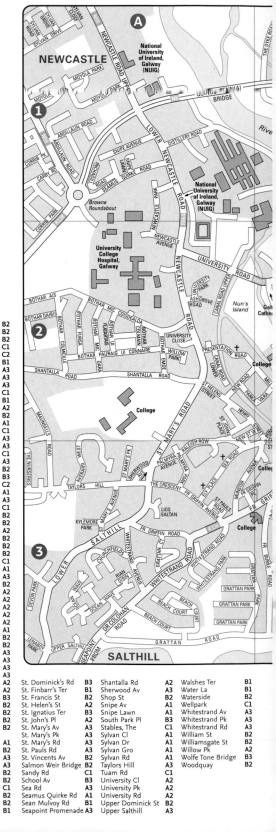

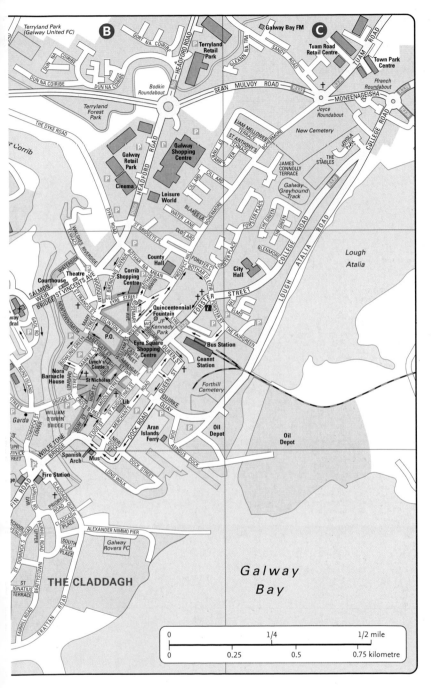

Originated as a small fishing village centred on the River Corrib and by the 17th century, Galway city was ruled by fourteen wealthy merchant families loyal to the king to whom the term "The Tribes of Galway" was attributed during the time of Cromwell. Galway city is now known and "City of The Tribes" and the names of these fourteen tribes are now represented on roundabouts in running across the north side of the city. It is in the gateway to the Gaeltacht region in Connemara and as such is has a large Irish influence on day-to-day life with both An Taibhdhearc (the National Irish Language Theatre www.antaibhdhearc.com) and TG4 (the Irish National Television Station www.tg4.ie) headquarters in the city. The recent expansion of flights into Galway Airport and the increasing motorway network have made the west more accessible than it has ever been before.

Population: 13,137
Tourist Information Centre: Beech Rd
☎ 064 31633
www.corkkerry.ie

INDEX TO PLACES OF INTEREST

INDEX TO STREET NAMES

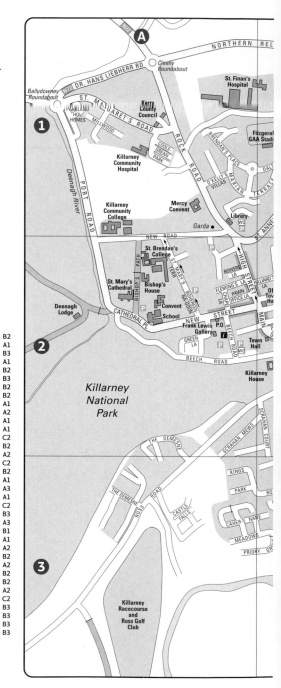

More important as a centre for exploring the surrounding countryside of the Kerry and Dingle Peninsulas and the Killarney National Park than as a place of particular interest in its own right. The Killarney National Park runs to the outskirts of the town and has a variety of landscapes to enjoy. From pleasant parkland, the beautiful Lakes of Killarney - where a particularly fine walk can be taken by circumnavigating Muckross Lake - to the foothills of the rugged Macgillycully's Reeks which includes the highest mountain Ireland, Carrantuohill, and also the wild Gap of Dunloe. The Derrynasaggart Mountains

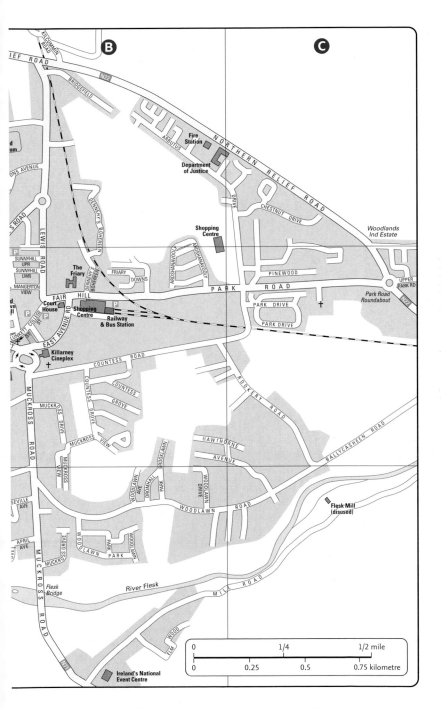

are to the east which, while not as spectacular as the Macgillycuddy's Reeks, offer fine views from the peaks of Stoompa, Crohane and The Paps.

The main early influence on Killarney were the gaelic clans of O'Donoghue and MacCarthy, who repelled Norman invaders in the 13th century. Although most of their lands were confiscated by Cromwell in the 17th century during his invasion of Ireland, the MacCarthy's managed to hold onto some land which was at first leased to, and in 1770 owned by, the Herbert family. In 1843 Henry Arthur Herbert built Muckross House which houses the Killarney National Park Visitor Centre. The town was given some prominence and its popularity as a tourist centre boosted by the visit of Queen Victoria to Muckross House in 1861.

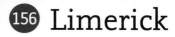

Population: 86,998
Tourist Information Centre: Arthurs Quay
☎ 061 317522
www.shannonregiontourism.ie

INDEX TO PLACES OF INTEREST

INDEX TO STREET NAMES

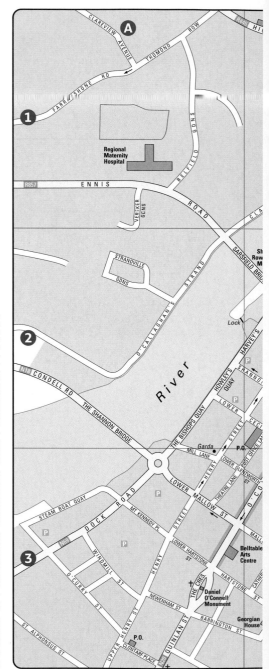

Limerick is historically of strategic significance by being both a port accessible to sea-going vessels and also by its situation at the head of the Shannon Estuary where it controlled the first major crossing point of the Shannon. The city has a great deal to offer but is also an ideal base to explore the west of Ireland from the rugged coastal landscapes and the Burren in County Clare down to the peninsulas of Kerry and Dingle. The proximity to Shannon Airport makes it easily accessible and a first port of call for many American tourists.

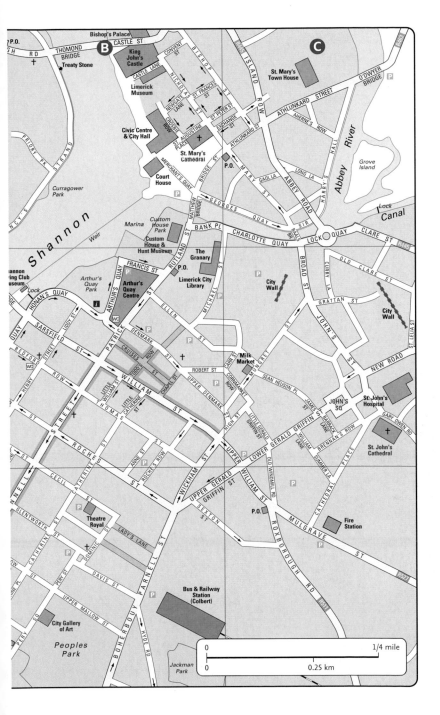

After being routed at Boyne by William of Orange, the forces of James II retreated to Limerick and came under attack for the first time in 1690 but managed to repel Williams onslaught. After the Irish had suffered a defeat and the loss of their French leader St Ruth at Aughrim in 1691, the second siege took place later the same year and ended after a request for a truce by the Irish forces. The subsequent Treaty of Limerick allowed around 12,000 members of the Irish garrison free passage to France but the agreements made with regard civil issues, in particular the tolerance of the Catholic faith, were not carried out with the same success. Limerick is still known in some quarters as 'the City of the Broken Treaty'.

Population: 71,403
Tourist Information Centre: Lisburn Sq
☎ 028 9266 0038
www.discovernorthernireland.com

INDEX TO PLACES OF INTEREST

INDEX TO STREET NAMES

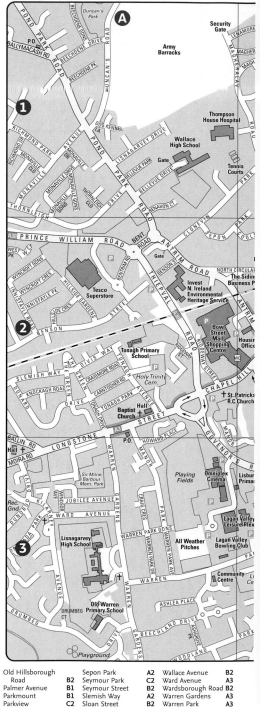

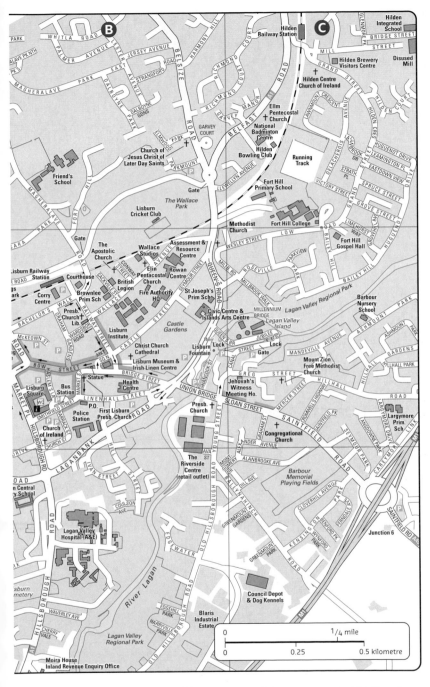

Eight miles south west of Belfast, Lisburn was granted city status as part of the Queen's golden jubilee celebrations in 2002. It has its origins with the Irish chieftain of Killultagh who formed a fortress against the English at Lisnagarvoch in the 1600s. During the rebellion of 1642 the town stayed loyal to the crown but the rebels burnt it to the ground - the name was subsequently changed to Lisburn. A fire again destroyed much of the city in 1707 including Conway Castle, which was never rebuilt although the castle gardens remain to this day. It grew to be an important centre for linen production until the 1920s when the industry went into terminal decline. The Irish Linen Centre and Lisburn Museum tells the story of the industry.

Population: 83,699
Tourist Information Centre: Foyle St
☎ 028 7126 7284
www.derryvisitor.com

INDEX TO PLACES OF INTEREST

INDEX TO STREET NAMES

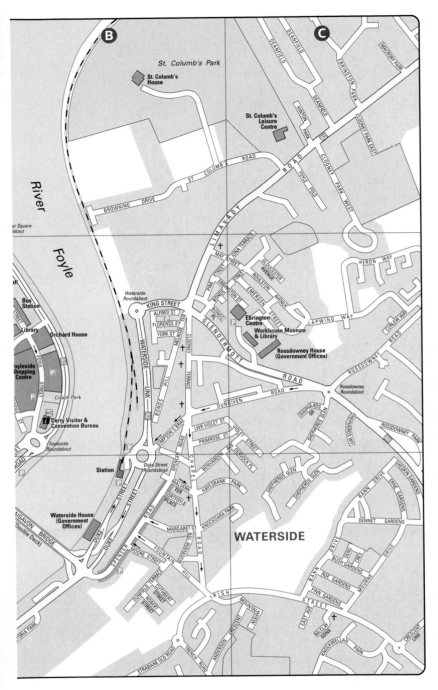

The origins of Derry, from the Irish 'Doire' meaning a 'grove of oak trees', are in the 5th century when St Columb founded a monastery on the site of the present day city. The city as it is known today dates from the 17th century when the ruined medieval city was rebuilt by English colonists financed by the City of London, hence the name Londonderry. The construction of the Foyle River Bridge in 1790 allowed expansion to take place across the Foyle to what is now Waterside. The still intact city walls were completed in 1618 and are 5.5m (18ft) thick and 1 mile round giving wonderful views across the city and beyond. The original layout of the four streets radiating from The Diamond has been preserved as have the four gateways though the walls. Amelia Earhart landed here in 1932 becoming the first woman to fly solo across the Atlantic. The Amelia Earhart Centre at Ballyarnett to the north of the city tells her story.

Population: 44,594
Tourist Information Centre: The Granary,
The Quay ☎ 051 875 823
www.southeastireland.com

INDEX TO PLACES OF INTEREST

INDEX TO STREET NAMES

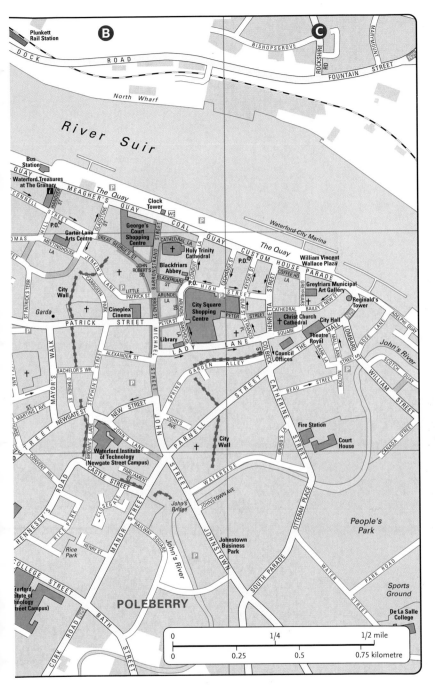

Waterford was founded by the Vikings at Port Láirge in the 10th century who changed the name to Vadrafjord meaning 'wether inlet' - it is from here that wethers (castrated rams) were loaded onto boats for transportation to other ports. It originated around the area of Reginald's Tower, which had been built by 1088 making it the oldest civic building in Ireland. Waterford grew to be an important European port by the 17th century and although it was the only city in Ireland to withstand the onslaught of Cromwell in 1649, it fell to his deputy, General Ireton, a year later. A period of prosperity came to the city in the 18th century during which much of the fine architecture seen today was built. In 1783 George and William Penrose founded a glass factory that was to grow into the world famous Waterford Crystal. The original business ceased in 1851 but was revived in 1947 and the site is now 20 times larger than the original factory established by the Penroses.

Places of interest are shown in purple type. The **bold** number after some entries, e.g. Belfast City Hall **3**, refers to the reference numbers appearing in Belfast and Dublin.

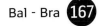

Meenglass 97 D4
Meenlaragh (Min Larach) 97 C2
Meenreagh 97 D4
Meentullynagarn 96 B4
Meeting of the Waters *Wicklow* 127 C2
Meigh 106 A3
Mellifont Abbey *Louth* 115 C2
Menlough *Galway* 119 D1
Menlough (Mionlach) *Galway* 118 B2
Metal Man Tower *Waterford* 133 D3
Michael Collins Centre *Cork* 131 C3
Michael Davitt Museum *Mayo* 110 B3
Middletown 105 C3
Midfield 110 B3
Midleton (Mainistir na Corann) 132 A4
Mile House 126 B4
Milemill 126 B1
Milestone 124 A4
Milford *Carlow* 126 A3
Milford *Cork* 123 C3
Milford *Donegal* 97 D2
Mill Town 100 A4
Millbay 101 C4
Millbrook *Larne* 100 B3
Millbrook *Meath* 113 D2
Millford 105 D2
Millisle 107 C1
Millmount Museum *Louth* 115 C2
Millroad 134 B3
Millstreet (Sráid an Mhuilinn) *Cork* 130 B1
Millstreet *Waterford* 132 B2
Millstreet Country Park *Cork* 130 B1
Milltown *Ballymoney* 99 D2
Milltown *Banbridge* 106 A3
Milltown *Cavan* 104 A4
Milltown *Craigavon* 105 D1
Milltown *Galway* 119 D1
Milltown *Galway* 111 C4
Milltown *Kerry* 121 D4
Milltown (Baile an Mhuilinn) *Kerry* 120 B4
Milltown *Kildare* 126 A1
Milltown *South Dublin* 115 C4
Milltown *Strabane* 98 A3
Milltown *Westmeath* 113 D2
Milltown *Wexford* 127 C4
Milltown Malbay 122 A1
Milltownpass 113 D3
Min an Aoire (Meenaneary) 96 B4
Mín an Arbhair (Meenanarwa) 97 C4
Mín an Chladaigh (Meenaclady) 97 C2
Min Larach (Meenlaragh) 97 C2
Mín na Croise (Meenacross) 96 B3
Minane Bridge 131 D3
Minerstown 107 C1
Mionlach (Menlough) 118 B2
Mitchelstown (Baile Mhistéale) 132 A2
Mitchelstown Cave *South Tipperary* 132 A2
Mizen Head Signal Station *Cork* 129 C4
Moate (An Móta) 112 B4
Model Arts & Niland Gallery *Sligo* 102 B3
Model Village 131 C2
Modelligo 132 B3
Modreeny 124 A2
Mogeely 132 A4
Moglass 124 B4
Mohil 125 D3
Mohill 112 B1
Móinteach Milie (Mountmellick) 125 D1
Moira 106 A1
Monaghan (Muineachán) 105 C3

Monaghan County Museum *Monaghan* 105 C3
Monaincha Abbey *North Tipperary* 124 B2
Monamolin 127 C4
Monanclogh 100 A2
Monard 132 A1
Monaseed 127 C3
Monaster 123 C2
Monasteraden 111 D3
Monasterboice *Louth* 115 C1
Monasterevin (Mainistir Eimhín) 126 A1
Mondello Park Race Circuit *Kildare* 114 B4
Monea 103 D2
Monea Castle *Fermanagh* 103 D2
Moneen *Galway* 118 B1
Moneen *Roscommon* 112 A2
Moneen Church *Clare* 121 C2
Moneycarragh 106 B3
Moneydig 99 D3
Moneygall 124 B2
Moneyglass 100 A4
Moneygold 102 B2
Moneylahan 102 B2
Moneymore *Cookstown* 99 D4
Moneymore *Louth* 115 C2
Moneyneany 99 C4
Moneyreagh 107 C1
Moneyslane 106 B3
Monilea 113 D3
Monivea 119 C2
Monkstown 131 D2
Monroe 113 C3
Monteith 106 A2
Montpelier 123 D1
Mooncoin 133 D2
Moone 126 A2
Moone High Cross *Kildare* 126 A2
Moorfields 100 A4
Moortown 105 D1
Morenane 123 C3
Morley's Bridge 130 A2
Mornington 115 C2
Morpeth Bridge 124 A4
Mosney 115 C2
Mossley 100 B4
Moss-side 100 A2
Mothel 133 C2
Mount Hamilton 99 C4
Mount Juliet Golf Club *Kilkenny* 125 D4
Mount Norris 105 D3
Mount Nugent 113 D1
Mount Stewart *Ards* 107 C1
Mount Talbot 112 A3
Mount Temple 112 B3
Mount Uniacke 132 A3
Mount Usher Gardens *Wicklow* 127 D2
Mountallen 103 C4
Mountbellew 119 D1
Mountbolus 125 C1
Mountcharles 103 C1
Mountcollins 122 A4
Mountfield 104 B1
Mountjoy *Dungannon* 105 D1
Mountjoy *Omagh* 104 B1
Mountmellick (Móinteach Milie) 125 D1
Mountrath (Maiglean Rátha) 125 C2
Mountshannon 119 D4
Moville (Bun an Phobail) 99 C2
Mowhan 105 D3
Moy 105 D2
Moyallon 106 A2
Moyard 116 B2
Moyarget 100 A2
Moyasta 121 D2
Moybane 103 D2
Moycullen (Maigh Cuilinn) 118 B2
Moydow 112 B2
Moygashel 105 D1

Moyglass 119 D3
Moylett 113 D1
Moylough *Galway* 119 D1
Moylough *Sligo* 111 C2
Moymore 123 C1
Moynalty 114 A1
Moynalvy 114 B3
Moyne *Longford* 113 C1
Moyne *North Tipperary* 124 B3
Moyne *Roscommon* 111 D3
Moyne *Wicklow* 127 C2
Moyne Abbey *Mayo* 110 B1
Moyrus (Maíros) 116 B3
Moyvalley 114 A3
Moyvane (Newtown Sandes) 122 A3
Moyvore 113 C3
Moyvoughly 113 C3
Mucklon 114 A4
Muckross (Mucros) *Donegal* 102 B1
Muckross *Kerry* 129 D1
Muckross Friary *Kerry* 129 D1
Muckross House *Kerry* 129 D1
Mucros (Muckross) 102 B1
Muff 98 B2
Muine Bheag (Bagenalstown) 126 A3
Muineachán (Monaghan) 105 C3
Mulhuddart 115 C3
Mullabohy 105 D4
Mullabrack 106 A2
Mullach Íde (Malahide) 115 D3
Mullacrew 114 B1
Mullagh *Cavan* 114 A1
Mullagh *Clare* 122 A1
Mullagh *Galway* 119 D3
Mullagh *Mayo* 117 C1
Mullagh *Meath* 114 B3
Mullaghbane 105 D4
Mullaghboy 101 C4
Mullaghmassa 104 B1
Mullaghmore 102 B2
Mullaghroe 102 B4
Mullan 103 D3
Mullanacross 103 C1
Mullans Town 105 C1
Mullany's Cross 111 C2
Mullartown 106 B3
Mullen 111 D3
Mullenmeehan 113 C3
Mullinahone 125 C4
Mullinavat 133 D1
Mullingar (An Muileann gCearr) 113 D3
Mullingar Cathedral *Westmeath* 113 D3
Mulrany (An Mhala Raithní) 109 C4
Multyfarnham 113 D2
Mungret 123 C2
Murley 104 B2
Murlough National Nature Reserve *Down* 106 B3
Murntown 135 C3
Murreagh (An Mhuiríoch) 120 A4
Murrens 113 D2
Murroe 123 D2
Murroogh 117 D4
Myrtleville 131 D3
Myshall 126 B3

N

Na Bruíneacha (Breenagh) 97 D3
Na Cealla Beaga (Killybegs) 102 B1
Na Clocha Liathe (Greystones) 127 D1
Na Dúnaibh (Downies) 97 D2
Na Forbacha (Furbogh) 118 B2
Na Gleannta (Glenties) 97 C4
Na Sceirí (Skerries) 115 D2
Na Seacht Teampaill (Seven Churches) *Galway* 117 C4
Naas (An Nás) 126 B1
Naas Racecourse *Kildare* 126 B1

Port Láirge (Waterford) 134 A3
Port Laoise (Portlaoise) 125 D2
Port Mearnóg (Portmarnock)
115 D3
Port Omna (Portumna) 124 A1
Port Reachrann (Portrane)
115 D3
Portacloy (Port an Chlóidh)
109 C1
Portadown 106 A2
Portaferry 107 C2
Portaleen 98 B1
Portarlington (Cúil an tSúdaire)
125 D1
Portavogie 107 D2
Portballintrae 99 D1
Portbraddan 100 A1
Portglenone 99 D3
Portglenone Forest Park
Ballymena 99 D3
Portland 124 A1
Portlaoise (Port Laoise) 125 D2
Portlaw (Port Lach) 133 D2
Portmagee 128 A2
Portmarnock (Port Mearnóg)
115 D3
Portmarnock Golf Club Fingal
115 D3
Portnoo 96 B4
Portrane (Port Reachrann)
115 D3
Portroe 119 D4
Portrunny 112 A3
Portrush 99 D1
Portrush Countryside Centre
Coleraine 99 D1
Portrush Puffer Coleraine 99 D1
Portsalon 98 A1
Portstewart 99 D2
Portumna (Port Omna) 124 A1
Portumna Castle & Gardens
Galway 124 A1
Portumna Forest Park Galway
124 A1
Porturlin (Port Durlainne) 109 C1
Poulanargid 130 B2
Poulgorm Bridge 130 A1
Poulnabrone Megalithic Tomb
Clare 118 B3
Poulnagunoge 133 C1
Poulnamucky 132 B1
Power's Cross 119 D3
Powerscourt Wicklow 127 D1
Powerstown 126 A4
Poyntz Pass 106 A3
Prehen 98 B3
Priesthaggard 134 A3
Priestsessagh 98 A4
Prince August Toy Soldier Factory
& Visitor Centre Cork 130 B2
Proleek Dolmen Louth 106 A4
Prosperous 114 B4
Puckaun 124 A2
Punchestown Racecourse Kildare
126 B1

Q

Queenstown Story, The Cork
131 D2
Querrin 121 D2
Quiet Man Heritage Cottage
Mayo 117 D2
Quilty 122 A1
Quin 123 C1
Quin Abbey Clare 123 C1
Quoile Countryside Centre Down
107 C2
Quoile Pondage Down 107 C2

R

Raffrey 107 C2
Raghly 102 A2
Rahan 113 C4
Rahan Monastic Site Offaly
113 C4
Rahara 112 A3
Raharney 114 A3
Rahavanig 121 D2

Raheen Cork 131 C2
Raheen Limerick 123 C2
Raheen Wexford 134 B2
Raheny 115 D4
Raholp 107 C2
Rakestreet 109 D3
Raloo 100 B4
Ramelton (Ráth Mealtain) 98 A2
Ranaghan 99 C4
Randalstown 100 A4
Rapemills 124 B1
Raphoe (Ráth Bhoth) 98 A3
Rashedoge 97 D3
Rath 124 B1
Ráth Bhoth (Raphoe) 98 A3
Ráth Caola (Rathkeale) 122 B2
Ráth Cúil (Rathcoole) 115 C4
Ráth Domhnaigh (Rathdowney)
125 C3
Ráth Droma (Rathdrum) 127 C2
Ráth Iomgháin (Rathangan)
126 A1
Ráth Mealtain (Ramelton) 98 A2
Ráth Naoi (Rathnew) 127 D2
Rathangan (Ráth Iomgháin)
126 A1
Rathaspick 113 C2
Rathbraghan 102 B3
Rathcabban 124 A1
Rathcardan 124 B3
Rathconrath 113 C3
Rathcool 130 B1
Rathcoole (Ráth Cúil) 115 C4
Rathcor 106 A4
Rathcore 114 A3
Rathcormac 132 A3
Rathcormack 102 B2
Rathdangan 126 B2
Rathdowney (Ráth Domhnaigh)
125 C3
Rathdrinagh 114 B2
Rathdrum (Ráth Droma) 127 C2
Rathduff 131 C1
Rathfarnham 115 C4
Rathfarnham Castle South Dublin
115 C4
Rathfeigh 115 C2
Rathfriland 106 A3
Rathgormuck 133 C2
Rathkeale (Ráth Caola) 122 B2
Rathkeevin 132 B1
Rathkenny 114 B2
Rathlackan 109 D2
Rathlee 110 B1
Rathleek 114 B4
Rathmacknee Castle Wexford
135 C3
Rathmolyon 114 A3
Rathmore Kerry 130 A1
Rathmore Kildare 126 B1
Rathmoyle 125 D2
Rathmullan 98 A2
Rathmullen 102 B4
Rathnew (Ráth Naoi) 127 D2
Rathnure 134 B2
Rathoma 109 D2
Rathowen 113 C2
Rathumney 134 A3
Rathvilla 113 D4
Rathvilly 126 B2
Rathwire 113 D3
Ratoath 115 C3
Rattoo Round Tower Kerry
121 D3
Ravensdale 106 A4
Ravernet 106 B1
Ray 98 A2
Ré na gCloichín (Reanaclogheen)
133 C3
Ré na nDoirí (Reananeree)
130 B2
Readypenny 115 C1
Reaghstown 114 B1
Reanaclogheen (Ré na gCloichín)
133 C3
Reanagowan 121 D4
Reananeree (Ré na nDoirí) 130 B2
Reanascreena 130 B3

Rear Cross 124 A4
Recess (Sraith Salach) 117 C2
Redburn Country Park Belfast
106 B1
Redcastle 98 B2
Redcross 127 D2
Redford 127 D1
Redgate 135 C2
Redhills 104 B4
Reen 129 D2
Reens 122 B2
Reevanagh 125 D3
Reginald's Tower Waterford
134 A3
Relagh Beg 114 A1
Rerrin 129 C3
Rhode 113 D4
Richhill 105 D2
Ridge 126 A3
Rineen 130 A4
Ring of Kerry Kerry 129 C2
Ringaskiddy 131 D2
Ringboy 107 D2
Ringsend 99 D2
Ringstown 125 C2
Ringville (An Rinn) 133 C3
Rinnananny 110 B2
Rinneen 118 A4
Rinville 118 B2
Rinvyle 116 B1
River 108 B3
Riverchapel 127 C4
Riverside 106 B4
Riverstick 131 D3
Riverstown Cork 131 D2
Riverstown North Tipperary
124 B1
Riverstown Sligo 102 B4
Riverstown House Cork 131 D2
Roadford 118 A4
Robertstown 114 A4
Robinstown 114 B2
Rochestown Cork 131 D2
Rochestown Kilkenny 134 A3
Rochfortbridge 113 D3
Rock of Cashel South Tipperary
124 B4
Rock of Dunamase Laois
125 D2
Rockbrook 115 C4
Rockchapel 122 B4
Rockcorry 105 C4
Rockhill 123 C3
Rockmills 123 D4
Rodeen 112 A1
Roe Valley Country Park Limavady
99 C2
Rogerstown Estuary Nature
Reserve Fingal 115 D3
Rooaun 124 A1
Roonah Quay 108 B4
Roosky Mayo 111 C2
Roosky Roscommon 112 B1
Ros an Mhíl (Rossaveel) 117 C3
Ros Cathail (Rosscahill) 117 D3
Ros Comáin (Roscommon)
112 A2
Ros Cré (Roscrea) 124 B2
Ros Mhic Thriúin (New Ross)
134 A2
Ros Muc (Rosmuck) 117 C3
Rosbercon 134 A2
Roscommon (Ros Comáin)
112 A2
Roscommon Castle Roscommon
112 A2
Roscommon Heritage & Genealogy
Centre Roscommon 112 A1
Roscommon Racecourse
Roscommon 112 A2
Roscrea (Ros Cré) 124 B2
Roscrea Castle & Damer House
North Tipperary 124 B2
Rosegreen 132 B1
Rosemount 113 C3
Rosenallis 125 C1
Rosmuck (Ros Muc) 117 C3
Rosnakil 98 A2

✳ Summer opening only. All tourist information centres provide a room reservation service.

Northern Ireland

Local telephone numbers are shown. To telephone Northern Ireland from the Republic of Ireland, replace 028 with 048.

Antrim, *Antrim*	☎ 028 9442 8331	**100 A4**
Armagh, *Armagh*.	☎ 028 3752 1800	**105 D2**
Ballycastle, *Moyle*	☎ 028 2076 2024	**100 A1**
Ballymena, *Ballymena*	☎ 028 2563 8494	**100 A3**
Banbridge, *Banbridge*	☎ 028 4062 3322	**106 A2**
Bangor, *North Down*	☎ 028 9127 0069	**101 C4**
Belfast, *Belfast*	☎ 028 9024 6609	**101 B1**
Belfast Int'l Airport, *Antrim*	☎ 028 9448 4677	**100 A4**
Carrickfergus, *Carrickfergus*	☎ 028 9335 8049	**101 C4**
Coleraine, *Coleraine*	☎ 028 7034 4723	**99 D2**
Cookstown, *Cookstown*	☎ 028 8676 6727	**105 D1**
Downpatrick, *Down*	☎ 028 4461 2233	**107 C2**
Enniskillen, *Fermanagh*	☎ 028 6632 3110	**104 A2**
Giant's Causeway, *Moyle*	☎ 028 2073 1855	**99 D1**
Hillsborough, *Lisburn*	☎ 028 9268 9717	**106 B2**
Kilkeel, *Newry & Mourne*	☎ 028 4176 2525	**106 B4**
Killymaddy, *Dungannon*	☎ 028 8776 7259	**105 C1**
Larne, *Larne*	☎ 028 2826 0088	**100 B3**
Limavady, *Limavady*	☎ 028 7776 0307	**99 C2**
Lisburn, *Lisburn*	☎ 028 9266 0038	**106 B1**
Londonderry, *Londonderry*	☎ 028 7126 7284	**98 B3**
Magherafelt, *Magherafelt*	☎ 028 7963 1510	**99 D4**
Newcastle, *Down*	☎ 028 4372 2222	**106 B3**
Newry, *Newry & Mourne*	☎ 028 3026 8877	**106 A3**
Newtownards, *Ards*	☎ 028 9182 6846	**107 C1**
Omagh, *Omagh*	☎ 028 8224 7831	**104 B1**
✳ Portaferry, *Ards*	☎ 028 4272 9882	**107 C2**
✳ Portrush, *Coleraine*	☎ 028 7082 3333	**99 D1**
✳ Strabane, *Strabane*	☎ 028 7188 3735	**98 A4**

Republic of Ireland

Local telephone numbers are shown. If telephoning from Great Britain or within Northern Ireland replace the initial 0 with 00 353.

✳ Achill, *Mayo*	☎ 098 45384	**108 B2**
Adare, *Limerick*	☎ 061 396255	**123 C2**
Aran Islands, *Galway*	☎ 099 61263	**117 C4**
✳ Arklow, *Wicklow*	☎ 0402 32484	**127 D3**
✳ Athlone, *Westmeath*	☎ 090 649 4630	**112 B3**
✳ Ballina, *Mayo*	☎ 096 70848	**110 B2**
✳ Ballinasloe, *Galway*	☎ 090 964 2604	**112 A4**
✳ Ballinrobe, *Mayo*	☎ 094 954 2150	**117 D1**
✳ Bantry, *Cork*	☎ 027 50229	**130 A3**
✳ Birr, *Offaly*	☎ 057 912 0110	**124 B1**
Blarney, *Cork*	☎ 021 438 1624	**131 D2**
✳ Boyle, *Roscommon*	☎ 071 966 2145	**102 D4**
Brú na Bóinne, *Meath*	☎ 041 988 0305	**115 C2**
✳ Buncrana, *Donegal*	☎ 074 936 2600	**98 A2**
Bundoran, *Donegal*	☎ 071 984 1350	**103 C2**
✳ Cahirsiveen, *Kerry*	☎ 066 947 2589	**128 B2**
✳ Cahir, *South Tipperary*	☎ 052 41453	**132 B1**
Carlow, *Carlow*	☎ 059 913 1554	**126 A3**
✳ Carrick-on-Shannon, *Leitrim*	☎ 071 962 0170	**112 A1**
Carrick-on-Suir, *South Tipperary*	☎ 051 640200	**133 C1**
Cashel, *South Tipperary*	☎ 062 62511	**132 B1**
✳ Castlebar, *Mayo*	☎ 094 902 1207	**109 D4**
Cavan, *Cavan*	☎ 049 433 1942	**104 B4**
✳ Clifden, *Galway*	☎ 095 21163	**116 B2**
✳ Cliffs of Moher, *Clare*	☎ 065 708 1171	**118 A4**
Clonakilty, *Cork*	☎ 023 33226	**130 B3**
✳ Clonmacnoise, *Offaly*	☎ 090 647 4134	**112 B4**
✳ Cong, *Mayo*	☎ 094 954 6542	**117 D2**
Cork, *Cork*	☎ 021 425 5100	**131 D2**
Dingle, *Kerry*	☎ 066 915 1188	**120 B4**
Donegal, *Donegal*	☎ 074 972 1148	**102 C1**
Drogheda, *Louth*	☎ 041 983 7070	**115 C2**
Dublin Airport, *Fingal* (R O I)	☎ 1850 230 330	**115 C3**
(U K)	☎ 020 7493 3201	**115 C3**
Dublin, O'Connell Street, *Dublin City* (R O I)	☎ 1850 230 330	**115 C4**
(U K)	☎ 020 7493 3201	**115 C4**
Dublin Tourism Centre, Suffolk Street, *Dublin City*	☎ 01 605 7700	**115 C4**
Dublin, Irish Tourist Board	☎ 01 602 4000	**115 C4**
Dundalk, *Louth*	☎ 042 933 5484	**106 A4**
Dungarvan, *Waterford*	☎ 058 41741	**133 C3**
✳ Dungloe, *Donegal*	☎ 074 952 1297	**96 B3**
Dún Laoghaire, *Dún Laoghaire-Rathdown* (R O I)	☎ 1850 230 330	**115 D4**
(U K)	☎ 020 7493 3201	**115 D4**
Ennis, *Clare*	☎ 065 682 8306	**122 B1**
✳ Enniscorthy, *Wexford*	☎ 053 923 4699	**134 B2**
Galway, *Galway*	☎ 091 537 700	**118 B2**
✳ Glengarriff, *Cork*	☎ 027 63084	**129 D3**
Gorey, *Wexford*	☎ 055 21248	**135 C1**
✳ Kenmare, *Kerry*	☎ 064 41233	**129 D2**
✳ Kildare, *Kildare*	☎ 045 521240	**126 A1**
✳ Kilkee, *Clare*	☎ 065 905 6112	**121 D2**
Kilkenny, *Kilkenny*	☎ 056 775 1500	**125 D4**
✳ Killaloe, *Clare*	☎ 061 376866	**123 D1**
Killarney, *Kerry*	☎ 064 31633	**129 D1**
✳ Kilrush, *Clare*	☎ 065 905 1577	**121 D2**
Kinsale, *Cork*	☎ 021 477 2234	**131 D3**
✳ Knock, *Mayo*	☎ 094 938 8193	**110 B3**
Letterkenny, *Donegal*	☎ 074 912 1160	**97 D3**
Limerick, *Limerick*	☎ 061 317522	**123 C2**
✳ Listowel, *Kerry*	☎ 068 22590	**121 D3**
✳ Longford, *Longford*	☎ 043 46566	**112 B2**
✳ Macroom, *Cork*	☎ 026 43280	**130 B2**
✳ Midleton, *Cork*	☎ 021 461 3702	**132 A4**
✳ Monaghan, *Monaghan*	☎ 047 81122	**105 C3**
Mullingar, *Westmeath*	☎ 044 934 8650	**113 D3**
✳ Nenagh, *North Tipperary*	☎ 067 31610	**124 A3**
New Ross, *Wexford*	☎ 051 421857	**134 A2**
Oranmore, *Galway*	☎ 091 790811	**118 B2**
Oughterard, *Galway*	☎ 091 552808	**117 D2**
Portlaoise, *Laois*	☎ 057 862 1178	**125 D2**
✳ Roscommon, *Roscommon*	☎ 090 662 6342	**112 A2**
Roundwood, *Wicklow*	☎ 012 816557	**127 C1**
✳ Salthill, *Galway*	☎ 091 520500	**118 B2**
Shannon Airport, *Clare*	☎ 061 471664	**122 B1**
Skibbereen, *Cork*	☎ 028 21766	**130 A4**
Sligo, *Sligo*	☎ 071 916 1201	**110 D1**
✳ Thoor Ballylee, *Galway*	☎ 091 631436	**119 C3**
Tipperary, *South Tipperary*	☎ 062 51457	**132 A1**
Tralee, *Kerry*	☎ 066 712 1288	**121 D4**
✳ Tramore, *Waterford*	☎ 051 381572	**133 D2**
✳ Trim, *Meath*	☎ 046 943 7111	**114 B3**
✳ Tuam, *Galway*	☎ 093 25486	**119 C1**
Tullamore, *Offaly*	☎ 057 935 2617	**113 C4**
Waterford, *Waterford*	☎ 051 875823	**134 A3**
Waterford, *Waterford* (Crystal Visitor Centre)	☎ 051 358397	**134 A3**
✳ Waterville, *Kerry*	☎ 066 947 4646	**128 B2**
Westport, *Mayo*	☎ 098 25711	**109 C4**
Wexford, *Wexford*	☎ 053 912 3111	**135 C2**
Wicklow, *Wicklow*	☎ 0404 69117	**127 D2**

Distance chart

DISTANCE IN KILOMETRES

City order along the diagonal:
ARKLOW, ARMAGH, ATHLONE, BALLINA, BALLYMENA, BANTRY, BELFAST, CASTLEBAR, CAVAN, CLIFDEN, CLONMEL, COLERAINE, CORK, DONEGAL, DOWNPATRICK, DROGHEDA, DUBLIN, DUNDALK, DÚN LAOGHAIRE, ENNIS, ENNISKILLEN, GALWAY, KILKEE, KILKENNY, KILLARNEY, LARNE, LIMERICK, LONDONDERRY, NEWRY, OMAGH, PORTLAOISE, ROSCOMMON, ROS…

Kilometres (upper triangle) — distances from each town to those following it:

- ARKLOW: 208 201 364 270 320 238 327 187 367 153 314 229 301 229 121 74 156 60 262 238 288 298 121 298 272 225 306 179 251 137
- ARMAGH: 153 217 97 446 60 249 72 309 299 106 360 146 76 87 134 51 148 282 84 230 338 254 391 93 264 116 31 61 203
- ATHLONE: 163 246 293 212 126 80 166 134 249 203 177 217 130 127 146 142 129 132 87 185 117 220 246 111 230 167 175 71
- BALLINA: 266 401 267 40 169 124 296 256 323 134 293 237 245 235 259 182 134 117 233 264 328 299 219 208 243 177 217
- BALLYMENA: 526 43 295 153 378 364 43 441 172 79 148 196 113 211 362 132 311 418 312 454 34 344 84 92 89 283
- BANTRY: 494 360 373 362 183 542 92 483 483 389 343 412 328 219 425 283 180 227 72 528 182 523 433 468 257
- BELFAST: 307 132 385 333 87 402 200 35 117 164 82 179 341 142 290 397 282 433 34 323 119 61 116 245
- CASTLEBAR: 177 84 256 285 283 163 309 251 253 238 267 142 163 77 193 243 288 328 179 237 259 206 196
- CAVAN: 237 219 169 283 114 148 93 113 92 127 209 51 158 266 182 301 166 192 150 98 95 130
- CLIFDEN: 257 369 257 246 373 296 293 303 307 143 246 79 195 188 290 412 180 320 323 290 103
- CLONMEL: 388 92 311 323 216 169 243 154 114 266 179 171 51 138 367 77 369 272 314 103
- COLERAINE: 452 122 122 193 240 158 254 378 146 322 462 351 499 77 389 48 135 103 299
- CORK: 406 391 298 251 320 237 142 335 206 198 135 90 436 105 433 341 383 166
- DONEGAL: 219 190 227 166 241 264 63 200 311 295 410 206 301 74 172 84 245
- DOWNPATRICK: 106 154 71 169 332 159 295 388 270 422 69 312 154 50 135 132
- DROGHEDA: 47 35 61 240 127 217 296 164 330 151 220 190 56 135 85
- DUBLIN: 82 14 232 164 214 288 117 298 198 195 232 105 177 85
- DUNDALK: 97 261 103 224 317 200 351 116 241 156 21 101 142
- DÚN LAOGHAIRE: 246 179 229 303 103 312 212 209 246 119 192 146
- ENNIS: 245 64 56 142 146 375 37 339 282 298 146
- ENNISKILLEN: 190 306 233 352 166 243 98 109 43 182
- GALWAY: 116 171 211 323 101 274 254 233 148
- KILKEE: 198 98 431 93 389 352 349 203
- KILKENNY: 182 315 105 332 220 277 51
- KILLARNEY: 467 109 451 372 396 211
- LARNE: 357 117 95 122 183
- LIMERICK: 341 262 286 109
- LONDONDERRY: 146 55 280
- NEWRY: 92 183
- OMAGH: 225

Miles (lower triangle):

- 129
- 125 95
- 226 135 101
- 168 60 153 165
- 199 277 182 249 327
- 148 37 132 166 27 307
- 203 155 78 25 183 224 191
- 116 45 50 105 95 232 82 110
- 228 192 103 77 235 225 239 52 147
- 95 186 83 184 226 114 207 159 136 160
- 195 66 155 159 27 337 54 177 105 229 241
- 142 224 126 201 274 57 250 176 176 160 57 281
- 187 91 110 83 107 300 124 101 71 153 193 76 252
- 142 47 135 182 49 300 22 192 92 232 201 76 243 136
- 75 54 81 147 92 242 73 156 58 184 134 120 185 118 66
- 46 83 79 152 122 213 102 157 70 182 105 149 156 141 96 29
- 97 32 91 146 70 256 51 148 57 188 151 98 199 103 44 22 51
- 37 92 88 161 131 204 111 166 79 191 96 158 147 150 105 38 9 60
- 163 175 80 113 225 136 212 88 130 89 71 235 88 164 206 149 144 162 153
- 148 52 82 83 82 264 88 101 32 153 165 91 208 39 99 79 102 64 111 152
- 179 143 54 73 193 176 180 48 98 49 111 200 128 124 183 135 133 139 142 40 118
- 185 210 115 145 260 112 247 120 165 121 106 281 123 193 241 184 179 197 188 35 190 72
- 75 158 73 164 194 141 175 151 113 117 32 218 84 183 168 102 73 124 64 88 145 106 123
- 185 243 137 204 282 45 269 179 187 180 86 310 56 255 262 205 185 218 194 91 219 131 61 113
- 169 58 153 186 21 328 21 204 103 256 228 48 271 128 43 94 123 72 132 233 103 201 268 196 290
- 140 164 69 136 214 113 201 111 119 112 48 242 65 187 194 137 121 150 130 23 151 63 58 65 68 222
- 190 72 143 129 52 325 74 147 93 199 229 30 269 46 96 118 144 97 153 210 61 170 242 206 280 73 212
- 111 19 104 151 57 269 38 161 61 201 169 84 212 107 31 35 65 13 74 175 68 158 219 137 231 59 163 91
- 156 38 109 110 55 291 57 128 59 180 195 64 238 52 84 84 110 63 119 185 27 145 217 172 246 76 178 34 57
- 85 126 44 135 176 160 152 122 81 141 64 186 103 152 145 82 53 101 62 91 113 92 126 32 131 173 68 174 114 140
- 142 94 20 71 144 202 141 58 49 98 103 186 146 90 134 98 96 90 105 89 69 49 121 93 157 152 89 130 103 96 64
- 109 133 35 126 183 148 159 113 85 117 48 190 91 145 152 95 77 108 86 67 117 68 102 38 112 180 44 178 121 144 24 55
- 55 179 124 215 218 182 198 202 161 217 78 245 125 232 196 125 96 147 87 149 193 168 184 62 168 219 126 254 161 220 80 144 100
- 143 93 69 42 123 259 129 60 73 112 152 117 211 41 140 120 132 105 141 123 41 83 152 142 214 144 146 87 109 68 113 49 104 204
- 119 178 80 160 228 112 204 135 130 136 24 235 55 190 197 139 110 153 119 47 162 87 82 45 83 225 24 223 166 189 57 100 45 102
- 201 228 133 200 278 65 265 175 183 176 106 288 76 251 258 201 185 214 194 87 215 128 41 129 20 286 64 276 166 242 119 153 121 225
- 66 188 103 194 219 133 200 181 143 185 29 254 76 214 194 127 98 149 89 100 175 136 135 30 119 227 77 236 168 202 62 123 68 49
- 44 168 113 214 207 171 187 191 150 206 67 234 114 221 185 114 85 136 76 138 182 157 173 51 157 208 115 243 150 209 69 133 89 11
- 16 114 110 183 153 215 133 188 101 213 111 180 158 172 127 60 31 82 22 175 133 164 201 79 201 154 156 175 96 141 84 127 108 71

DISTANCE IN MILES

Road distances

The distance between two selected towns will be found at the intersection of the respective vertical and horizontal rows, e.g. the distance between Belfast & Dublin is 102 miles / 164 km.

In general, distances are based on the shortest routes by classified roads. Where a route includes a ferry journey, the mileage is shown in *italics*.